THE AIRLINE THAT PRIDE ALMOST BOUGHT

MICHAEL E.
MURPHY

THE
AIRLINE
THAT
PRIDE
ALMOST
BOUGHT

THE STRUGGLE
TO TAKE OVER
CONTINENTAL
AIRLINES

A GROLIER COMPANY

Franklin Watts
New York   1986   Toronto

For Mary Catherine

Library of Congress Cataloging-in-Publication Data

Murphy, Michael E., 1942–
The airline that pride almost bought.

Bibliography: p.
Includes index.
1. Continental Airlines.   I. Title.
HE9803.C65M87   1986   387.7′065′73   86-1520
ISBN 0-531-15018-6

CONTENTS

AUTHOR'S
NOTE

In June of 1981, my eye caught a column by Kevin Starr in the *San Francisco Examiner*. "Does anyone really understand the profound implications of the effort of the employees at Continental Airlines, led by Capt. Paul Eckel, to acquire 51% of the stock in their company?" Starr asked. Before abandoning the legal profession, I had worked for seven years as a corporate attorney, specializing in employee benefit programs, and had gained some strong convictions about the need for a form of corporate democracy that includes representation of employees. At Continental Airlines, an authentic employee movement, in response to a takeover bid by Texas International Airlines, was attempting to put this ideal into practice. When the plan failed and Texas International acquired control of the airline, I hoped that someone would at least tell the employees' story. Two years later, I took on the task. I have talked to one hundred and forty people over a period of a year and a half and researched voluminous records on file with the state and federal courts, the Civil Aeronautics Board (CAB), the Securities Exchange Commission (SEC), the California Department of Corporations, and the California legislature. Everywhere I have found that doors were open to me. People on both sides of the struggle have wanted to tell me what happened.

The story of the takeover struggle has turned out to be a better and a different story than I originally imagined. I was interested in the employee struggle, but in many ways the hero was Continental Airlines' president, Al Feldman, a remarkable but flawed man. Though a highly competent executive, he was poorly prepared by background and temperament for this kind of contest. The surge of emotion that enveloped the company during the long takeover struggle finally consumed him. On August 9, 1981, he took his own life. When I began my research, I could never have foreseen the sequel of the employee struggle: a Chapter 11 bankruptcy filing that promises to be the most successful bankruptcy in history, and one carried out uniquely at the expense of employees rather than creditors. By use of the bankruptcy laws, the new management of Continental has broken the airline's three major unions, reduced average compensation almost in half, and emerged in only six months as a strong competitive force in the airline industry.

This book is not a reconstruction of events in the mode of recent popular accounts of corporate dramas but a history of what actually took place. The story stays strictly within the limits of what I have learned from credible sources. There has been no embroidery of known facts. Every word can be documented.

THE AIRLINE THAT
PRIDE
ALMOST BOUGHT

CHAPTER ONE

TALE OF TWO AIRLINES

"It was the most hopeful year of my life and the most devastating," says Houston mechanic Doug Schoen as he recalls the effort of Continental Airlines employees in 1981 to acquire control of their own airline. His words reflect the memories of many other Continental employees. When Texas International made a successful tender offer for 48.5 percent of Continental's stock, the employees organized to thwart the apparently inevitable takeover and proposed a plan for employee purchase of newly issued stock that was designed to be an experiment in corporate democracy. It sparked a unique employee movement, buoyed by a dream of community and self-determination, and it came very close to success. At 7:00 A.M. on June 23, 1981, a group of about twenty-five lawyers and bankers sat around a large conference table in downtown Los Angeles behind piles of executed documents, awaiting a telephone call. To close the employee stock purchase, they needed only telephonic notification of an anticipated New York Stock Exchange decision. But the telephone call did not come, and the takeover struggle continued for another five months to become one of the longest and most bitterly fought in the history of American business. In the end, Continental was acquired by Texas International with consequences that fulfilled many of the employees' worst apprehensions.

The drama of the Continental employees' struggle is rooted in the distinct corporate cultures of Continental and Texas International. The story of Continental Airlines begins with

Robert F. Six who in 1936 took control of a three-plane mail service between El Paso and Denver and led it into the ranks of the major passenger carriers. The son of a plastic surgeon in Stockton, California, Six dropped out of high school after two years and spent his youth in an assortment of odd jobs. He invested his mother's inheritance in a small plane, but a series of crash landings and other mishaps blocked his career in commercial aviation. At the age of twenty-nine opportunity knocked. Six borrowed $90,000 from his father-in-law to purchase a 40 percent interest in the small mail carrier, Varney Air Transport. The young Six was brash, volatile, profane, and completely lacking in formal credentials, but he possessed an ability to instill confidence and loyalty. An early business associate at Varney Air Transport recalls, "I saw a lot of potential in Six. He was very aggressive and ambitious, with a great desire to learn."[1] Six devoted himself with singular energy to the small carrier, and after becoming president, changed its name to Continental Airlines.

The airline soon entered scheduled passenger service with a fleet of two-engine planes. In the years before and after the war, Six repeatedly modernized the fleet and expanded its routes in Texas and the mountain states. By 1953, Continental served thirty-six cities with a fleet of twenty-one planes and was known as a progressive carrier that kept up with the latest advances in aviation technology. It joined the ranks of the major carriers after securing a CAB award of the important Los Angeles–Denver–Chicago route and became one of the first airlines to fly turboprops and jets. After moving its corporate headquarters to Los Angeles, Continental participated in the rapid expansion of the industry during the sixties and seventies. Its revenues roughly quadrupled in each decade— rising from $46 million in 1958 to $775 million in 1978—but it remained in ninth or tenth place among U.S. air carriers throughout the period.

In a cyclical industry Continental achieved a remarkable record of consistent profitability. Before the advent of deregulation in 1979, it suffered a net loss only twice in the postwar era (in 1958 and 1975), and it usually maintained one of the highest margins of profit in the industry, generally excelled only by Northwest and Delta. Continental maintained this strong market position by competing successfully against larger rivals. It seized about 25 percent of the Los Angeles–Denver–Chicago market from United Airlines and American Airlines by offering the first jet service. A decade later, it entered the Hawaii market with an array of promotional gimmicks—special economy fares, movies for all three classes, five-abreast seating for coach class, and a special snack cart featuring sandwiches, champagne, and fruit—and again gained over 20 percent of the highly competitive Los Angeles-Honolulu route, besting five other carriers and trailing only United Airlines.

Over the years, Continental's principal business strategy consisted of marketing a superior quality of service. Six was determined to have the best of new equipment. Once he paid options for the purchase of the supersonic Concorde. During the early jet era, the airline achieved a genuine preeminence in the field of passenger service. It served the first hot meals in the industry, feted first class passengers with French pastries, champagne, and brandy, and offered to all passengers the full allowance of wine and cocktails permitted by agreed industry standards. The stylish flight attendant uniforms adopted in 1963, a simple but elegant black dress with loosely fitting jacket, was the first to depart from the military cut then prevalent in the industry. To supplement the attentions of flight attendants, Continental was the first airline to assign a director of passenger service to its flights. Equipped with a special radio telephone, his job was to write tickets, make advance reservations for hotels and cars, and inform relatives or business associates if a flight was delayed. Gold, a symbol of opulence, was a recurring element in the Continental image. Its planes could be identified by a golden tail with the airline's logo in black. In the seventies, Continental continued to enjoy a reserve of goodwill among the category of traveler that counted most on its routes —the business traveler, sensitive to comfort and amenities. Continental employees are fond of telling about passengers who would go out of their way to fly on their jets.

The quality service of Continental reflected—and engendered—a remarkable esprit de corps. The director of personnel, John Bidlake, recalls, "Continental viewed itself as a real class organization. There was tremendous commitment to delivering the product better than the competitor. It was a very spirited, upbeat, fast-moving organization." Another employee, John Clayton, uses a military analogy: "I believe that Continental Airlines was like the U.S. Marines Corps. We thought there is nothing we can't do. We were a band of people to whom the spirit of the corps was everything. If somebody had said, 'John charge up that hill for Continental, but you may get killed,' I'd charge!"

The advertising of Continental stressed the theme of pride: "The Proud Bird with the Golden Tail" and "The Airline Pride Built." Perhaps absorbed subliminally, the term "pride" reflected an authentic feeling among employees. Pat Simpson, a San Jose ticket agent, says, "Continental was a premier carrier. If you were working for Continental, you were working for a carrier that was first class. Everything was first class from the meals on down." Another ticket agent, Donna Shaffer, asserts, "Continental was very special. There was a camaraderie and a caring atmosphere. At times we would fight among ourselves, but if anyone from outside tried to attack us, that's when we would really stick together."

One cannot talk to many Continental employees without hearing another affirmation: there was a "family feeling" in the company. Craig Adcox, a Portland employee, typically says, "In Portland, we were a family. People would help each other out when they needed it. The ramp person would help checking bags or the ticket agent would help loading bags. Our important concern was to see how good a job we could do and how fast we could do it. People were always eager to help. They cared about passengers, and they cared about each other." An employee's circle of closest friends often consisted of other Continental employees. In Denver, ticket agents would have social gatherings after work two or three times a month and would periodically organize potluck dinners for slack periods in the daily schedule.

A little less than half the work force belonged to three major unions. Fleet and passenger service employees, who are represented by unions at most other airlines, never opted for union representation at Continental. Among union employees, one also found pride and camaraderie, but it was mediated by loyalty to the union and sometimes tempered by a history of adversary relations with management. Of the major unions, the International Association of Machinists (IAM)—representing mechanics, cabin cleaners, and flight kitchen employees—had the most amicable relations with the company. The president of the local, Hal Alexander, recalls that it was "almost like a marriage." There were disputes, but the company was willing to grant the standard industry wage and live with the restrictive work rules found at other carriers. The parties had a good history of working problems out.

A would-be aviator himself, Six long stood as a favorite of the pilots; he was fond of visiting the cockpit, and in 1962 he was the second company president to be invited to speak to the annual convention of the Air Line Pilots' Association (ALPA). The day-to-day management of flight operations was handled to the pilots' general approval by a crusty pilot, Red Stubben, who possessed bad grammar but a sharp mind. The good feelings between pilots and management were unfortunately interrupted in 1976 by a strike—the first strike in the airline's history.

Government wage controls had had the effect of holding the pilots' level of compensation below that of other major carriers, and the pilot leadership was determined to regain parity with the most generous contracts in the industry. Opinions differ as to why the strike occurred; some pilots charge that the union leadership simply overplayed its hand. Six shut the airline down for twenty-five days before yielding to most of the pilots' demands.

The management's emphasis on quality service had a distinct impact on flight attendants: their own personal appearance was regarded as an aspect of the quality of cabin service. It was no different at other airlines. Management hired young women (usually age twenty-one) of a similar height, weight, and personal attractiveness. They were expected to maintain

5

their hairstyle, eyebrows, and facial makeup according to certain guidelines. Putting on weight was ground for dismissal. All flight attendants were subject to mandatory retirement upon marriage or reaching the age of thirty-two. While this policy may have enhanced the airline's public image, it had the effect of treating flight attendants as part of the decor. The Civil Rights Act of 1964, as amended and interpreted a decade later, signaled a new era. Throughout the seventies, the flight attendants' union struggled successfully to establish their occupation as a dignified career. The Continental flight attendants were fortunate to have a leader of unusual ability, Darenda Hardy. An art major from East Texas, Darenda joined the airline when flight attendants were represented by the Association of Flight Attendants, a division of ALPA. Five feet ten inches tall and blond haired, she possessed striking physical beauty, enhanced by personal charm and self-composure. As a union leader she displayed a quick wit and an easy grasp of complex issues. Darenda led the flight attendants out of ALPA and formed an autonomous union, the Union of Flight attendants (UFA), organized along democratic lines. During the seventies, the union contested every indignity in arbitration and litigation. One case of a disputed hairstyle was arbitrated for thirteen days. The flight attendants knew that conditions were no better elsewhere, but the struggle for equal rights took its toll. Many flight attendants became resentful of what they perceived to be the sexist attitudes of the Six management team.

Despite the flight attendant problems, the Continental employees generally enjoyed a sense of community that demands an explanation. Mike Conway, the corporate controller, attributes it to the personal influence of Six. Certainly Six made his presence felt throughout the system. He traveled widely on Continental jets, always alert for small discrepancies. In later years, he acquired a somewhat legendary persona: with his big frame, craggy face, and inimitable voice, he seemed bigger than life. Most employees agree that Six displayed good judgment in the choice of managers, many of whom rose from the ranks. Six remarked paternally that the greatest pleasure of his job was "seeing my young employees come up and get ahead. Since Audrey and I have no children, I get a great feeling from watching our young people develop."[2]

The employee esprit de corps was fortified by two other factors: generous compensation and long job tenure. With a few exceptions such as Northwest Airlines and National Airlines, air carriers tended to find it most economic to avoid labor strife by passing increased payroll costs on to the consumer in the form of higher fares. The CAB would approve fare increases, applicable to all carriers on a route, that reflected increased labor costs. Continental followed the inflated industry wage levels generated by this process. The pilots were the greatest beneficiaries. In 1981, the average annual pay of a pilot (excluding benefits) was $65,000 and the median wage for a captain approached $100,000. Mechanics earned more than $30,000; flight attendants averaged a more modest $23,000. To lessen the threat of union organization, nonunion employees were paid at the same levels as those of competing carriers represented by the International Brotherhood of Teamsters and other unions. Baggage handlers could earn as much as $30,000. Ticket agents with seniority earned $26,000, and clerical workers tended to receive about 30 percent more than in comparable positions outside the airline industry.

It is not surprising that most employees hoped to continue to work for Continental. Employee tenure rivaled that of a Japanese corporation. In the corporate headquarters, the typical employee, below the executive level, was not likely to do better elsewhere and considered his job a career. Mechanics could more easily find comparable work in the southern California aerospace industry, but an electrician observed that all his fellow workers intended to work at Continental until retirement. The flight attendants' struggle with management reflected a basic satisfaction with their job; the annual attrition rate was, incredibly enough, between 2 percent and 3 percent. In the case of pilots, long job tenure was dictated by the seniority system. Throughout the industry, pilots advance strictly on the basis of years of service; if a pilot should take a job with another carrier, he would have to start again at the bottom rank. In April 1981, the most junior second officers at Continental earned about $38,000 while the most senior captains earned no less than $115,000 under comparable schedules. It was worth waiting to rise to that level.

The last year of full CAB regulation of the industry, 1978, was a good year for Continental: it had the fourth strongest balance sheet of any major carrier and earned $53 million on revenues of $775 million. But the airline was peculiarly ill-prepared for the new era of competition. Continental operated a complex network of long-haul routes, reflecting an accumulation of CAB route awards, that received traffic from smaller regional airlines. After the deregulation of routes, it could no longer rely on the traffic from other carriers. It needed to restructure its route system around a hub or hubs so that it could offer passengers more connections from one route to another within its own system. But even with the most intelligently conceived route system, Continental was caught in a sort of sandwich between the larger trunk carriers and smaller regional carriers. The giants of the industry could hope to attract passengers by offering connections and schedules that Continental could not match. The regional airlines were in an even more advantageous position. Generally having lower labor costs and control of feeder traffic, they could invade Continental's most profitable long-haul routes, undercut it with lower fares, and divert feeder traffic to their own flights.

Ironically, Continental would be buffeted in the next two years not so much by the predictable effects of deregulation as by unforeseeable misfortunes. In early June of 1979, an American Airlines DC-10, taking off from Chicago's O'Hare airport, went into a roll and crashed upside down a short distance from the airport, killing all 272 persons aboard. The FAA determined that one of the plane's engines had fallen off because of defective engine mountings and ordered a grounding of all domestic DC-10s. Continental was one of the two airlines most adversely affected by the disaster: DC-10s accounted for 42 percent of its capacity. When the FAA lifted the ban on DC-10 flights thirty-eight days later, public confidence was slow to return; a large body of travelers avoided, and would continue to avoid for months or years to come, flying on the aircraft.

The tragedy, moreover, coincided with economic adversity. The second half of 1979 marked the beginning of a steep rise in fuel prices. Month after month the industry witnessed price increases of as much as 20 percent. Continental did very well in the first half of the year, but by year-end it registered a loss of $13 million in net earnings.

At this time of crisis, Six finally appointed a successor after a long and well-publicized search. His choice, Alvin L. Feldman, age fifty-two, had a record of achievement that justified high expectations. A mechanical engineer by training, Feldman worked briefly for General Dynamics in San Diego and then began a distinguished career with Aerojet General Corporation, a subsidiary of General Tire. He was picked in 1971 to head the parent company's aviation subsidiary, Frontier Airlines, a regional airline based in Denver. Frontier had suffered heavy losses for four consecutive years and operated with poor on-time performance, excess capacity, and losing routes. Although he had no previous experience in the airline business, Feldman quickly turned the company around. Within one year, Frontier was reporting a solid operating income, and it soon emerged as one of the most profitable domestic carriers in the late seventies, achieving an operating profit more than twice as large in relation to revenues as that of most major carriers.

By taking the Continental job in Los Angeles, Feldman was able to be closer to his ailing wife, Rosemily. They had met when they were both engineering students at Cornell, and she was, by all accounts, his emotional mainstay and only personal confidant. Eight years earlier Rosemily had been stricken by cancer, complicated by respiratory problems in the high elevation of Denver. Remembering the happy years of their early marriage in the San Diego area, the couple chose to live in the beautiful seaside town of La Jolla. Feldman commuted during the week to his job in Denver. His move to Los Angeles brought only temporary proximity: on July 15, 1980, Rosemily died. Feldman was deeply shaken by the loss, and he buried his grief in long hours of work.

Feldman soon revealed himself to be a strong leader and a complex human being. A big, bearish man, standing six feet four inches tall, with rather elegant manners, he possessed a quick mind and an articulateness that gave force to his impressive personal presence. As an executive, he easily dominated any gathering. Mike Roach, who worked with him every day as his executive assistant, chooses three words to describe him: rational, private, and ethical. These qualities were combined with a deep sense of propriety and awareness of his leadership role. "Everything he did," Roach recalls, "was with a studied calculation of how what he would do would affect others." Instinctively concerned with ethical issues, he took a genuine interest in establishing a program of compliance with the Foreign Corrupt Practices Act, which prohibits payoffs to foreign officials.

Although Six remained chairman of the board, Feldman assumed full executive powers and imposed a style of leadership —marked by a demand for thoroughness and a passionate commitment to goals—that reflected his engineering background. He liked to have ideas presented in writing and would grill executives until he was satisfied that all options had been explored. At all management levels, he introduced a system of management by commitment. Employees would make annual commitments to their supervisors as to their anticipated performance, and they could be fired for failing to fulfill the commitments they had made.

Perhaps reflecting an engineer's interest in line operations, Feldman's sense of executive responsibility extended to the interests of rank-and-file employees. "He thought of the company as a group of people he was working with," comments a friend. To keep employees informed of management decisions, he introduced the practice of issuing corporate bulletins every week or two. Mike Roach remembers that Feldman edited the bulletins himself and "labored over every word." Widely read and believed, the bulletins reveal a humane side to his personality. Years later a mechanic would fondly recall that Feldman hoped eventually to retire all the employees he had let go in a general furlough. When asked the source of this information, he said, "A management bulletin." Most employees regarded Feldman as a "heavyweight," a miracle worker who had turned things around at Frontier. They were charmed when he followed Six's practice of eating periodically at the employee cafeteria. He would sit down at a table of employees and say, "Hi! I'm Al Feldman. Where do you work?" If the employee worked in the print shop, he might ask, "What are you doing there this week?" His transparent personal integrity on such occasions endeared him to the Los Angeles office employees and contributed to a growing legend of his ability and goodwill.

Under Feldman's management, Continental began to form a dual hub system, centered primarily at Denver and secondarily at Houston. But the airline did not have the type of aircraft that would allow it to retrench into a strong regional position; its wide-body planes were uneconomical on short routes. The best strategy for survival in the era of deregulation appeared to lie in merger with another large carrier. Continental had in fact negotiated a merger agreement with Western Airlines in 1979 that the CAB unexpectedly blocked. Western remained the best candidate for a merger. The two airlines would reduce operating costs by combining stations, consolidating maintenance and other facilities, and eliminating some duplicate flying; and a merged route system could offer better connections which would generate increased patronage. The airlines together would form the largest system west of the Mississippi, accounting for 20 percent of all passengers boarding a plane in the region. Continental calculated that the merger would yield annual benefits of no less than $91 million.

In August 1980, Feldman again opened negotiations with Western Airlines which within two weeks produced another merger agreement that named him as chief executive officer of the combined airline. Continental's CAB counsel, Lee Hydeman, believed that the CAB would approve this second application. The red ink that both carriers had incurred since deregulation would convince the agency that the merger was the means of survival, not regional dominance. The CAB nevertheless required a full administrative review of the proposed merger which was expected to last about eight months. The merger was delayed until May or June of 1981.

While planning for the Western merger, Feldman inherited

a long-simmering labor dispute with the flight attendants that interrupted his business plans. Negotiations with the flight attendants dragged on for eighteen months after the company demanded that they give back concessions they had won in the past. Perceiving the demand as another instance of discriminatory management pressure, the flight attendants finally called a strike on December 6, 1980. A full 90 percent of the union membership joined the walkout; but, contrary to expectations, the pilots and mechanics refused to honor their picket lines. Union leader Darenda Hardy realized that the strike was lost without support of other unions and quickly tried to salvage the best agreement she could. She was forced to accept the basic terms of the company's last offer and the continued employment of 102 flight attendants whom the company had hired during the strike.

The strike lasted only twelve days, but the company did not immediately restore the previous level of operations. Many of the canceled flights were on economically marginal routes, and the approaching winter quarter was historically the least profitable. Feldman chose to restore the prior level of service in stages over a six-month period, changing several schedules and routes. The flight attendants were furious. Not only was their strike used to restructure the route system, but they were forced to work with strikebreakers while their colleagues remained on furlough. It was easiest to take out their anger against the pilots. On some flights, no one would volunteer to serve the pilots in the cockpit. A grievance proceeding concerning a meal spilled on a pilot's lap (the flight attendant was fired!) would have been ludicrous if it were not symptomatic of prevailing tensions.

After the first year of his management, Feldman still had not turned the airline around; the net loss for 1980 in fact increased to $21 million. But the loss was aggravated by causes of a nonrecurring nature—the flight attendant strike, the cost of route restructuring, and the residual effect of the DC-10 grounding. Management projected a profit of $11.4 million for 1981. Continental remained a premier airline, with a valuable fleet and remarkable esprit de corps. The Western merger,

Feldman hoped, would give it the marketing strength to meet the challenges of deregulation.

Continental did not have much in common with the airline that would soon become its challenger, but Texas International Airlines was also led by a man of unusual background and abilities, Francisco A. Lorenzo.

The son of Spanish immigrants, Lorenzo grew up in a working-class district of Queens where his mother operated a beauty parlor. Driven by an uncommon desire to succeed, he worked and borrowed his way through Columbia University and Harvard Business School. When his much-admired older brother, a rising New York investment banker, died of a heart attack at the age of thirty-three, Lorenzo shed forty-five pounds and became a determined long-distance runner. He once ran the marathon in three hours and thirty-eight minutes. Today, at age forty-three, Lorenzo is a slightly built, almost gaunt man, five feet eight inches tall, with deep-set eyes and Hispanic features. Colleagues describe him as quiet, introspective, and cerebral. In formal business conversations and court appearances, he sometimes talks so softly that others have to strain to hear him.

Lorenzo entered the airline industry after graduating from business school by briefly holding jobs as a financial analyst for TWA and Eastern Airlines. At age twenty-six, he founded a financial consulting firm with a business school classmate, Robert Carney. Despite their youth, Lorenzo and Carney became involved in major transactions and earned a reputation for financial expertise. A New York banker was quoted in the *Wall Street Journal* as saying, "Frank Lorenzo is as smart as they come."[3]

Texas International Airlines, a Houston-based airline long known as Trans-Texas Airlines, turned in 1971 to the young financial consultants for help in arranging a plan for financial restructuring. Trans-Texas Airlines began flying in 1947 with a fleet of DC-3s which remained its mainstay into the sixties when they were finally replaced by early models of the DC-9 jet. The airline prospered modestly for two decades but was somewhat of a joke in the industry because of its policy of flying obsolete planes on short, low-density routes. The DC-3s, which were unpressurized and flew at low altitudes, were probably responsible for its popular identity as Tree Top Airlines. Other plays on its initials, TTA, included Thankful to Arrive, Try Try Again, Tinker Toy Airways, and Texas's Threat to Aviation. Despite its unfavorable image, Trans-Texas Airlines was generally profitable until 1967 when it was acquired by MEI, a midwestern bus line operator. An unsuccessful expansion plan resulted in four years of losses, leaving the airline with a negative net work of $4.5 million.

In an improbable transaction, the young financial consultants not only rescued the airline's finances but, with the blessing of shareholders and creditors, acquired for themselves a controlling interest in the company. Before negotiating the deal, they had formed their own company, Jet Capital Corporation, with the view of entering the aircraft leasing business and had attracted $1.5 million in venture capital. During eighteen months of negotiations with the management and creditors of Texas International Airlines, they worked out an agreement to restructure $33 million in debt. As part of the plan, Jet Capital Corporation itself acquired 24 percent of the airline's equity and 58 percent of its voting power in consideration for an investment of only $1.3 million. Certainly the principal asset of Lorenzo and Carney was their reputation in New York financial circles. The hidden hand guiding the negotiations was unquestionably the chief creditor, Chase Manhattan Bank, which wanted a new management capable of salvaging its loans.

The bank's confidence was justified. By cutting unprofitable routes and raising some fares, the new management of TI (as Texas International Airlines was commonly called) sharply reduced losses in 1972 and earned a small profit the next year. Lorenzo, who assumed the position of chief executive officer, began a program of expansion that continued until the time our story begins. The airline's revenue passenger miles increased 327 percent from 1972 to 1980. The financial results of Lorenzo's management were more uneven. After earning very small profits in 1973 and 1974 ($320,000 and $400,000 on revenues of $77 million and $92 million), TI suffered a loss of $4.37 million in 1975 as the result of a strike. There followed four years of prosperity which ended soon after the advent of deregulation in 1979. Operating income and revenues (in millions of dollars) during this period were as follows:

	1976	1977	1978	1979	1980	1981
Operating						
Income	6.0	12.1	16.0	15.3	7.8	(8.9)
Revenues	120	145	180	234	267	277

TI's brief prosperity in the late seventies was greatly stimulated by an innovative promotional scheme, "peanuts fares," which dramatically changed its public image. The airline extended discounts of 30 percent to 50 percent to many off-hours flights and to a designated number of aircraft seats on more heavily traveled flights. Passengers were served only a soft drink and peanuts. The promotion attracted enough passengers to more than offset the reduced price of the fares. Few airlines had ever aggressively pursued discount fares with such success, and TI began to attract attention. Its advertising capitalized on its new image, portraying a smiling winged peanut traversing the sky above the caption, "Lowest Daily Fares, No Strings."

To become a more effective price competitor, the TI management sought vigorously to cut costs. It achieved remarkably high utilization of its fleet; the average daily operation of its DC-9s rose to ten hours in 1978, among the highest levels in the industry. Aided by improvements in fuel conservation and employee productivity, TI's unit costs remained stable in 1977 despite the effect of inflation. But this success in cost control did little to overcome the airline's heritage of poor service. The quality of service was actually of secondary importance to the Lorenzo management. The airline's marketing program was directed more at attracting the cost-sensitive casual traveler than the quality-sensitive business traveler. By design or neglect, standards of service remained low. TI's high utilization of its fleet was accompanied by a poor on-time performance record. On the Denver–Salt Lake City route, it consistently placed seventh out of seven carriers in on-time performance. The airline's Federal Aviation Administration complaint record —another indicia of the quality of service—was also mediocre. From 1978–1980, it received two and a half times as many complaints per one hundred thousands passengers as did Continental. A poll of business travelers, published by *Texas Business* magazine, placed TI last in hospitality and second to last, above Braniff, in overall performance.[4]

Management's efforts to cut costs led to a confrontational approach in dealing with the labor unions which represented 80 percent of the work force. The 1975 strike was of unusually long duration—four and a half months. Later, the company attempted a series of innovations in flight operations that brought it in conflict with the pilots' safety committee. A program to increase payload by "optimum overspeed takeoff" was alleged to have caused eighty-five tire failures between January and June of 1980. Another attempt to increase payload actually involved mounting a rocket on the aircraft. The pilots complained that the DC-9s lacked the cockpit controls to correct weight and balance errors caused by this unusual innovation. Employee discontent with such management practices tended to be directed at Lorenzo himself who was thought to be ultimately in charge. Being most at ease in small gatherings, Lorenzo generally stayed aloof from the work force. Some disgruntled employees began to call him "the brain in the bottle."[5]

These problems did not, however, tarnish Lorenzo's reputation in the financial community. In 1978, he was known as the man who had transformed a nearly bankrupt carrier into one of the fastest growing airlines in the country. Investors' confidence enabled him to stage the first of a series of remarkably successful public offerings. In the largest public offering ever made by a regional airline, TI raised $28 million in April 1978 —$19.6 million in subordinated debentures and the remainder in the sale of common stock. Later in the year, it repeated the feat by raising another $31.7 million—$25 million through a convertible Eurodollar debenture and $6.7 million in common stock. Armed with this war chest, Lorenzo entered into one of the most famous exploits of his career: the bid to acquire National Airlines.

When Lorenzo bought a 9.2 percent interest in National Airlines on the open market and applied to the CAB for permission to purchase a controlling interest, *Forbes* magazine aptly called him Lorenzo, the Presumptuous. National Airlines not only had more than three times the revenues of TI but enjoyed an incomparably stronger financial position; it had only $50 million in long-term debt and a fleet of 727s and DC-10s valued in the range of $600 million. TI had a long-term debt of $154 million, a record of only two recent years of more than marginal profits, and a fleet of old planes appraised at close to their depreciated value of $83 million. But TI had cash and the financial backing of Manufacturers Hanover Trust Company, then seeking a foothold in the aerospace banking market. Lorenzo succeeded in purchasing 23 percent of National's stock for $54 million at an average price of $28.20 per share. National quickly sought a merger with Pan Am, which was interested in a domestic route system to feed its international routes. Eastern Airlines then joined the bidding by making its own offer to National shareholders. At this point Pan Am made an offer of $50 per share for all the National stock. Lacking the financial resources to match this offer, Lorenzo sold all TI's holdings in National to Pan Am, earning an after-tax profit of $34.7 million.

The National Airlines exploit preceded the first years of TI's declining fortunes. The regional airlines, as a group, profited from the first three years of deregulation. Their share of the industry's revenue passenger miles increased from 9.2 percent to 12 percent. But deregulation had an impact on TI similar to that which it had on the smaller long-haul carriers. The airline's profits in 1979 and 1980 rested largely on interest income and the sale of investments. Operating income fell and turned into a loss of $8.9 million in 1981.

Although TI gained a brief advantage as the first discount airline, it was a hard act to sustain. Other airlines soon responded in kind. In particular, TI faced the challenge of Southwest Airlines. Beginning service in 1971, Southwest originally based its operations in Dallas's Love Field, the old municipal airport near the city center, but rapidly expanded in the late seventies throughout the southwestern states and California. Enjoying labor costs well below those of TI, the airline succeeded in maintaining harmonious labor relations with a generous profit sharing and employee stock ownership program; in 1981, employees owned 13 percent of the company's stock. In addition to the advantage of low costs, Southwest achieved a high standard of service. The poll of *Texas Business* magazine, mentioned earlier, placed Southwest first in the quality of service among all the carriers serving the Texas market. Capable of offering lower fares and better service, Southwest presented impossible competition for TI. Increasingly it occupied the market niche in the southwestern states that TI had sought to establish through the "peanuts" fares.

Faced with discouraging prospects of internal growth, Lorenzo continued to look for acquisitions. In September 1979, TI acquired a 4 percent interest in TWA—a carrier eleven times its size—and Lorenzo announced his interest in acquiring control. It was a measure of his personal prestige that he was taken seriously. He engaged in discussions with TWA's chairman, Edwin Smart, which prompted a front-page article in the *Wall Street Journal*, but he soon dropped plans to make the bid, and TI sold its holdings in TWA for a small loss.

A man not easily thwarted, Lorenzo unsettled the industry again in 1980 with another display of resourcefulness. By organizing a holding company, Texas Air Corporation, he created a separate nonunion subsidiary, New York Air, to operate a shuttle service between Boston, New York, and Washington. The new subsidiary recruited pilots for roughly half the salary offered by the major airlines—a newly hired captain was paid $30,000 a year. With low labor costs and a simple route structure, Lorenzo hoped that New York Air could engage in the sort of aggressive price competition that TI itself could no longer pursue. He rapidly passed all regulatory and organizational hurdles. Texas Air was incorporated in June, and New York Air began service on December 19, 1980.

TI transferred the bulk of its liquid assets to the new holding company in a complicated series of transactions. Among other things, TI paid Texas Air a $35 million dividend and gave it a $25 million loan at 7.5 percent interest. Texas Air raised $40 million in a public offering of convertible debentures but invested only $10 million of its financial resources in New York Air which was capitalized largely by a public offering of common stock at $9.50 per share.

The reorganization enraged the TI unions which saw their company's resources for further growth diverted to a holding company and a nonunion subsidiary. The pilots filed a grievance charging violation of the union contract (four years later the grievance is still in litigation) and staged a work slowdown until restrained by a court order. The national pilots' organization, ALPA, responded with lawsuits, vituperation, and boycotts. A suit filed in New York charged unsuccessfully that New York Air was not a "fit" carrier within the meaning of regulatory legislation because of its inferior working conditions and the poor safety record of the TI management. The normally urbane pages of the *Airline Pilot* magazine asserted that New York Air was "rotten to the core."[6] ALPA hired the public relations expert, Ray Rodgers, to organize a campaign of boycotts, picketing, and adverse publicity directed against New York Air and anyone who did business with it. Giving the dispute top priority, the national head of ALPA was himself photographed on an informational picket line protesting New York Air's union-breaking policies.

Lorenzo was easily the most controversial figure in the airline industry at the beginning of 1981. Possessing only a competitively weak regional airline and an unproved low-cost subsidiary, he controlled formidable cash resources. He had carefully planned his next move.

CHAPTER
TWO

THE TENDER
OFFER

While Six was still chief executive of Continental, TI had begun buying Continental stock which it held anonymously in the name of Girard Trust Company. Lorenzo's first overture to the Continental management, however, ended in a rebuff. In November 1979, he arranged a dinner with Six on a Saturday evening in Los Angeles. When he arrived in the city and called to confirm the appointment, Six had forgotten the date. "You've come out on the wrong Saturday!" Six asserted. Lorenzo persisted; he asked if a meeting could be arranged in any event since he had made the trip. Six told him firmly to come back the next week. Lorenzo did return bringing carefully conceived ideas for a merger of the two airlines, but for Six the matter had deeply personal implications. Continental was the proud achievement of his life; throughout the year he had been looking for a suitable successor, and Lorenzo was not among the list of names that he had discussed with the selection committee of the board. Six refused to pursue detailed negotiations or to include other executives in the discussions. A friend of Six's, commenting on Lorenzo's overture, notes that Six had a talent for putting people down. A secretary claims to have seen Lorenzo walk briskly from Six's office with fire in his eyes.

After organizing New York Air, Lorenzo began to lay plans to take on the open market what he could not secure by agreement. He asked Kidder, Peabody and Company and Smith Barney, Harris Upham and Company to study the feasibility of a tender offer to Continental shareholders. The firms prepared similar analyses of financial statements and stock trading history (the Kidder, Peabody report was undated and cryptically referred to as the "Poseidon Corporation"). Both reports contained a critical revelation: 30.7 percent of Continental stock was held by institutional investors who were not likely to pass up an opportunity to sell their holdings for a price, above market value, offering an adequate profit. As fiduciaries who are held accountable for their performance each year, the managers of these institutional funds are necessarily oriented toward the short term; they cannot excuse a bad year by saying that their sagging portfolios have good long-term prospects. Since Continental had been trading in the area of $10 per share for several years, a one-third interest in the airline could be had almost for the asking. It was necessary only to offer a sufficient premium over this market value to afford institutional investors a suitable profit.

The balance sheet analyses also revealed that a tender offer could be financed largely on the strength of Continental's own assets. The depreciated value of Continental's fleet was $290 million, but at current market values it was probably worth over $500 million, and it remained unencumbered by mortgages. The 15 million shares of Continental had a market value of only $150 million. Even with the payment of a premium, a controlling interest in the airline might cost less than $100 million. Lorenzo could find ample collateral in Continental itself to finance a takeover bid of this magnitude without depleting his large cash reserve.

The proposed merger of Continental and Western stood as a major obstacle to Lorenzo's takeover plans, but he still saw an opening. Curiously, the two airlines had decided to postpone a shareholders' vote on the merger until after receiving CAB approval. In 1979, each airline had spent $500,000 in holding special shareholders' meetings before the CAB denied permission to merge. Several advisors, including Continental's general counsel, Edward Cotter, did not wish to risk making this needless expenditure again. With his engineer's inclination to build methodically for the future, Feldman was easily convinced that shareholder approval should be sought later, in proper sequence. This decision, taken for the sake of a $1 million economy, gave Lorenzo his chance.

The impending Western merger nevertheless demanded that TI pursue a takeover strategy inconsistent with CAB precedents. The Airline Deregulation Act, like previous legislation, required CAB approval of an airline's acquisition of a 10 percent or more interest in another airline. The only exception was one that Lorenzo had himself established in the National Airlines acquisition case. Departing from its own precedents, the Board allowed TI to purchase a 25 percent interest in National Airlines provided the stock was placed in a voting trust pending a CAB ruling on the acquisition. The exception was a limited one: the stock in the voting trust had to be voted proportionately to the votes of other outstanding shares on all issues, and TI was denied permission to purchase more than a 25 percent interest. This kind of voting trust would not be enough to permit a decisive bid for Continental. Lorenzo needed more than a 25 percent stock interest, and he had to secure CAB permission to vote the shares against the Western merger.

Lorenzo had good reason to hope that he could, once again, go beyond CAB precedents. He had long enjoyed a favorable image with the CAB. As the head of a fast-growing airline featuring discount fares, he was seen, in the words of Washington lawyer Simon Lazarus as "the embodiment of the spirit of deregulation." In separate opinions the Board had praised TI's "demonstrated commitment . . . to low fares" and its role as a "convinced low fare advocate and practitioner."[1] Lorenzo reportedly had counted on this reputation when he made his bid for TWA. An airline executive was quoted in the *Wall Street Journal* as saying, "I think the CAB would approve, with great glee, a Lorenzo takeover of TWA."[2]

The goodwill of the CAB was enhanced by two corporate appointments. Alfred Kahn, a former CAB chairman and the father of deregulation, consented to serve on the board of New York Air; and Phil Bakes, who had recently resigned as CAB general counsel, accepted the position of vice-president of regulatory and government affairs of the newly organized Texas Air Corporation. Bakes, age thirty-five, was personable, articulate, thoroughly political, and very smart. He carried with him the friendship and extended loyalty of the CAB staff. Continental mechanic Doug Schoen describes him as "the sort of person you wish was on your side." Bakes had worked on the staff of the Senate Judiciary Committee when the Airline Deregulation Act was in gestation and was firmly identified with the cause of deregulation.

On September 18, 1980, the TI board of directors authorized management "to undertake an examination of the possibilities for combination with another carrier." The record of internal memos, thoroughly explored in subsequent litigation, indicates that there was never any question that Continental was the preferred choice. The TI management did not find it necessary to make more than a few preliminary studies of the consequences of a merger of the two airlines, such as route maps, revenue analyses, and pro forma balance sheets. Confident of the business merits of the acquisition, the top executives devoted their energies to matters of timing and strategy. For expert counsel, TI retained the three hundred-attorney New York law firm of Skadden, Arps, Slate, Meagher & Flom, one of the nation's leading practitioners of the art of hostile takeovers. A working paper dated October 20, 1980, and entitled "Project Eclipse, Preliminary Timetable," contemplated the preparation of documents between November 19 and 30 and a public announcement of a tender offer for Continental stock on December 1. Drafts of the principal documents, each referring clandestinely to "Vibrant Enterprises" and "Eagle Enterprises," were in fact circulated among top executives in late November, but Lorenzo then hesitated, apparently influenced in part by a small rise in the price of Continental stock. In December TI sold about 100,000 shares of the 600,000 shares it held in Continental.

Two events in early February of 1981 brought Lorenzo to a decision. On February 3, the CAB administrative law judge recommended an unconditional approval of the Continental-Western merger. Although it had been expected, the decision brought CAB approval of the merger a step closer. It coincided with an opportunity for TI to buy a large block of Continental stock at a favorable price. Smith Barney, Harris Upham and Company had just brought to TI's attention an offer to sell a block of at least 400,000 Continental shares for a small premium over market value. In the course of the next week, a deal was worked out for the purchase of no less than 800,000 shares in two transactions. So as not to disrupt the market, the sales were postponed until the last minutes of trading in the week. On Friday, February 6, TI bought 420,000 shares at $10.75 per share fifteen minutes before closing and another 380,000 shares at $11.25 per share three minutes before closing.

The purchases more than doubled TI's holdings in Continental: it now held a 9.5 percent interest. Lorenzo and other executives considered their next move in intensive discussions throughout the weekend with investment bankers and the Skadden Arps law firm. Lorenzo asserts that he did not reach a final decision to make the tender offer until Sunday night. He then called Six to inform him personally of his intentions and to express the wish that the acquisition could be carried out in a friendly way. Six referred him to Feldman whom he also called. The news caught Feldman by surprise even though rumors had long circulated among the Six management team about Lorenzo's interest in Continental. As a professional manager who had worked all his career for the subsidiaries of large corporations, Feldman had never needed, or desired, to concern himself with matters of this sort.

The next day TI launched on several fronts an intricate and well-planned ambush. In a brief press release, the airline announced its intention to make a tender offer to buy six million Continental shares at a price of $13 per share, about 25 percent above market value. It was enough to increase TI's holdings to 48.5 percent of Continental's outstanding stock. The offer would be conditioned on CAB approval of a voting trust, specially authorized to vote the shares against the Western Airlines merger. The formal offer to purchase was mailed to Continental shareholders on Friday, February 13. It gave shareholders (and Continental management) a deadline: the purchase date of 12:01 A.M. March 7. At that moment, all shareholder tenders of stock would become irrevocable and TI would be entitled to purchase the tendered stock, giving it a dominant interest in the airline.

The five-day interval between the announcement of the tender offer and the formal offer to purchase—the maximum period permitted by SEC regulations—had a well-calculated purpose. The trading in Continental stock increased thirty times on February 9 over the previous Monday. By the end of the week, almost two million shares had changed hands at a price that hovered around $12 per share. The phenomenon was a familiar one on Wall Street. No one doubted that many of the sellers were individual shareholders and most of the buyers were professional arbitrageurs, stock traders specializing in transactions such as tender offers that offer a chance for a small but quick profit. The five-day delay in making the formal offer thus had the effect of drawing as many Continental shares as possible into the hands of investors interested in short-term gains.

Lorenzo's ability to finance the tender offer was never in any real doubt. On Monday, February 9, TI contacted Manufacturers Hanover Trust Company, which had financed its bid for National Airlines. Three days later, the bank signed a commitment to loan $50 million, at a rate of prime plus 1.75 percent to be repaid on September 30, 1981, or if the acquisition were successful, in installments pursuant to an agreed schedule. TI agreed to secure the loan initially by a pledge of its Continental stock, but after acquiring control over Continental, it promised to provide as substitute collateral "a first lien security interest on certain of the aircraft and related assets of the . . . merged entity." Since its own fleet was fully mortgaged, TI was in effect offering the unencumbered fleet of Continental as security for the loan.

The purchase of stock in the tender offer cost $78 million and the purchases on February 5 another $8.8 million. Manufacturers Hanover Trust Company actually loaned TI $48.4 million. Where did TI find the remaining $38.4 million? The record is a complicated one but leads in part to Continental's own lead bank, Chase Manhattan Bank. During the first quarter when the purchases were made, TI did not draw on its cash reserves or short-term credit but reported an $87.4 million increase in long-term debt as a result of four borrowings—the $48.4 million loan from Manufacturers Hanover Trust Company, a $7.5 million loan from Societé Generale, and two loans under agreements with Chase Manhattan Bank. The Societé Generale loan evidently was applied to the stock purchase. In addition, Texas Air briefly contributed $18 million to TI in the form of a preferred stock purchase that it later rescinded in April. Thus, in the first quarter, one can easily account for $73.9 million applied to the stock purchase ($48.4, $7.5, and $18 million). The financing of the balance of the purchase price may have come from the Chase loans. One of the loan agreements was confined to aircraft purchases, but the other agreement, representing a credit of $20 million, was not so clearly limited—the borrowings could be secured by TI's existing DC-9-14 aircraft and applied to "capital expenditures." Phil Bakes asserts that this loan had "no connection" with the tender offer, and Chase Manhattan also denies the link. Certainly, in the second and third quarter, there are other possible sources of funds: the cash reserves of TI diminished sharply, and Texas Air purchased $10 million in preferred stock. But it is a fair interpretation that part of the Chase Manhattan loan was applied, at least on an interim basis, to assist the tender offer.

Chase Manhattan had been Continental's lead bank since 1938 when it helped finance Six's first aircraft purchases. Over the years, Continental became Chase's largest customer in the airline industry. An accountant recalls that Continental executives were "livid" on receiving evidence that Chase had aided TI's tender offer, but another executive observes that relations between corporations are largely relations between people. The longtime manager of Continental's account at Chase had recently retired; his successor, Michel Kruse, was drawn from the bank's European division and had no ties of loyalty to Continental. When the tender offer assumed the appearance of success, Chase had reason to regard the TI management, not that of Continental, as its real client.

The news of the tender spread "like a flash fire" through the ranks of Continental executives as one person called another. Most executives were stunned and apprehensive. Only the executive assistant to the president, Mike Roach, who had recently come to Continental from the CAB, viewed the tender offer as a possibly favorable development. For Feldman, it was an unwelcome interruption of carefully laid business plans. He had come to Continental determined to turn the airline around, and he was convinced that the Western merger offered the best hope. Earlier in the year he had conducted a study of several merger possibilities that showed a combination with TI to be, in his words, the "weakest and least significant possibility." TI could add only a modest increment to Continental's capacity: a combination with TI would increase Continental's available seat miles from 14 billion to 17.9 billion. TI's fleet of thirty-three planes included eighteen antiquated DC-9-10s with an average life of fifteen years; Continental would pick up only fifteen desirable short-haul planes. The annual operational benefits of the merger, in the view of Continental management, were in the range of only $7.5 million to $15 million and vulnerable to increased labor costs often associated with airline mergers. The proposed merger with Western appeared to be far more advantageous.

Feldman acted quickly to retain the nation's preeminent law firm in takeover defense, Wachtell, Lipton, Rosen & Katz. Riding the crest of the wave of corporate takeovers in the seventies, Wachtell, Lipton had grown in a few years from a small New York partnership to a sixty-attorney firm composed of bright young lawyers. Two partners flew out to Los Angeles the next day: Erica Steinberger, an attractive thirty-two-year-old partner and coauthor of the leading legal text on takeovers; and Bernard Nussbaum, a former member of the Harvard Law Review with a warm, unaffected manner that sometimes seems to belie his high professional attainments. Wearing his emotions on his sleeve, Nussbaum doesn't speak of the takeover defense as an intellectual game. "We're not the sort of lawyers that just lay out options," he says. "We fight for what we think the client should do."

For local counsel, Feldman turned to a firm with which he was linked by a personal friendship. For years he had taken an annual vacation to a fishing camp near Jackson Hole, Wyoming, that he shared with Richard Ferris, president of United Airlines, and Rod Hills, a Washington partner of the Los Angeles law firm, Latham & Watkins. Feldman ultimately chose Hills's colleague, George Vandeman, to lead the takeover defense. Vandeman occupied a place on the apex of the legal pyramid beyond the realms of specialization; he could only be described as a business lawyer, an architect of complex transactions. Polished and businesslike, he shared with Feldman a strong sense of personal privacy. Few associates knew (or could have suspected) that he was the son of the prominent television evangelist, the Reverend George Vandeman. Feldman had first met him while planning for the Western merger, and he felt increasing respect for his abilities as well as a personal affinity for his self-contained and rational temperament.

On Tuesday morning, a small crowd of lawyers, investment bankers, and financial executives gathered in the Continental boardroom to consider the takeover defense. In an effort to impose some logic on the situation, Feldman himself stayed away from the first hours of discussion, preferring to wait until the assembled experts had thrashed out some options. He first joined the meeting about 1:30 P.M., dressed as usual in slacks and shirtsleeves. Erica Steinberger remembers that his attitude was restrained: "He was not one of those executives who, faced with a takeover threat, thump on the table and say how can we stop this. He saw himself as a professional, and his real concern was to keep the airline running." He clearly felt an unusual degree of personal responsibility for the takeover defense. "Al was more questioning than a lot of executives," Steinberger remarks. With his quick intellect, Feldman dominated the afternoon's discussions, as he summarized points of view and probed for clarification. "Al did not simply accept advisors' suggestions, or limit his involvement to the 'big picture' and turn over the details to advisors," Steinberger continues. "Even though it was not his area, he wanted to be taken through all the steps and make up his own mind."

In the early strategy sessions, there were some alternatives that were quickly discarded. In particular, Feldman ruled out the option of the corporation offering to buy its own shares at a price exceeding Lorenzo's offer. Such a defense—if it could actually be carried out—would leave Continental financially strapped. In a presentation to the board, Feldman described it as a "scorched earth" defense that might destroy Continental as a viable competitor. But with this option excluded, the defense team offered Feldman a sobering assessment: if the CAB should approve the voting trust, Continental's avenues of defense were either unpromising or undesirable. At best, the company could only blunt the tender offer somewhat by appeals to shareholders. Lorenzo was assured of tenders from institutional shareholders and arbitrageurs that would bring his holdings above 40 percent. A lawsuit challenging the legality of the tender offer was worth a try, but one could not predict a high probability of success. The only alternative to TI's tender offer was likely to be the sale of a controlling interest to another preferred investor, known in common parlance as a White Knight. As George Vandeman observes, "In a cash tender offer, there is no winning. Nine out of ten times the company is sold"—if not to the original bidder then to a White Knight.

For all his determined objectivity, Feldman actually did not hesitate to recommend to the board of directors that it oppose TI's bid for control. Corporations rarely accede graciously to hostile tender offers. Rather, the hostile challenge provokes a hostile (and often self-destructive) reflex. The Continental management was no exception, but in view of its fiduciary duty to shareholders it needed a rational basis for concluding that TI's price was inadequate. Lehman Brothers offered the board an opinion letter which employed a sophisticated analysis, relying largely on the record of other acquisitions in the airline industry, to reach the conclusion that the $13 per share offer was "grossly inadequate from a financial point of view." Fortified by this opinion, the board had no trouble authorizing management to oppose the tender offer.

The proxy solicitation firm of Georgeson and Company, which had long helped to organize Continental's shareholder meetings, was retained to appeal to the airline's 32,290 shareholders. It didn't take long for the Continental management to gain a sense of the problem its solicitors faced in appealing to institutional shareholders. Early in the first week, the financial vice-president, Jack Woodlock, undertook to contact independently the largest institutional shareholders. Acting on instructions, he dutifully began by calling the Dreyfus Fund to extol the benefits of the Western merger. "Are you kidding?" the Dreyfus executive asked. "I've never received a phone call like this. I'm an arbitrageur. I'm going to make $2 per share." Georgeson and Company nevertheless drew on its experience to contact the investment managers who might be most sympathetic. Georgeson executive Peter Harkins remarks, "Sometimes institutional investors will pass up a tender offer, but you may get only three percent of them. They may agree with you, but if they can make a good short-term profit, you don't have a prayer." He found that Continental's institutional shareholders "were sympathetic but they had their own performance standards."

The Continental management was in the strongest position appealing to individual shareholders holding stock in their own name. To reach these shareholders, Georgeson and Company relied mostly on its best resource—graduate students in law and business at New York University. It posted notices offering pay at a rate of $10 per hour and employed as many as fifty people at a time to make calls. The student solicitors, after being briefed and given a sales pitch, found that shareholders were receptive to their arguments. "We did very well with small investors," recalls Peter Harkins. Small investors are generally inclined to support management. Joe Morrow, a partner of TI's solicitations firm, conceded, "When you talk to holders of stock for a long time there are emotional ties. They like to feel the people running their company know what they are doing." In the case of Continental, many shareholders were also passengers who felt ties of loyalty to the airline. Mrs. Teddie Hart of El Paso bought five hundred shares of Continental "after being very impressed by their service on my first airplane trip across the ocean." She didn't like the spectacle of a hostile tender offer. "It may be poor business not to take my money and run," she said, "but I wouldn't do that. That would be very disloyal." Other shareholders perceived Lorenzo as a kind of financial buccaneer, preying on a successful enterprise. "You do not have enough money to purchase even one of my shares of Continental," a Texan wrote to Lorenzo.[3]

All things considered, Continental did fairly well in the shareholder battle but not well enough to gain any advantage. It took TI a month to secure tenders of all six million shares, and the shares of individual shareholders came in slowly toward the end. But on March 12, TI announced that it had purchased a 48.5 percent interest in Continental.

Corporations usually respond to tender offers with lawsuits charging violation of securities laws. "You never know," comments George Vandeman, "whether you will turn up something that will convince some judge." Bernard Nussbaum was a specialist in this litigation, and three days after the tender offer was announced he filed in federal court a complaint that was an impressive display of legal ingenuity. One count alleged, for example, that the offer to purchase was so linked with opposition to the Western merger as to constitute a proxy solicitation made without proper SEC filings. The object of the suit was to obtain a preliminary injunction delaying the stock purchase, but Nussbaum knew he had only an outside chance of success—there were no egregious legal flaws in the tender offer. Feldman himself referred to the lawsuit as "chicken soup"—it might not help but it couldn't hurt. The court set a hearing for March 6, the day before the purchase date, on Continental's requests for a preliminary injunction.

Foreseeing the probable failure of other tactics, the Continental defense team had lost no time to begin a search for a White Knight. Continental could offer a block of authorized but unissued stock to a friendly investor, or it might persuade a desired business partner to top Lorenzo's bid for Continental's shares. In the lists of potential White Knights drawn up in the first brainstorming sessions, Federal Express was an obvious candidate. The previous year it had purchased four of Continental's most valuable aircraft, the cargo convertible DC-10-10, for $95 million—about the same price that Lorenzo was paying for the entire airline. In November, it had allowed options to lapse for the purchase of four more DC-10s at a price of $22 million each. Unless bid up by Lorenzo, Federal Express might acquire control of Continental, thereby gaining use of these four planes and sixty-four others, for a cost a little more than the option price of $88 million. Feldman arranged a meeting with Fred Smith, the chairman of Federal Express, but Smith later decided he was not interested in entering the scheduled airline business and canceled the appointment.

Continental's investment bankers, Lehman Brothers, had by far the widest range of contacts with potential investors and led the search for a White Knight. But two years of deregulation had already transformed air carriers into a troubled industry. It was a bad time to look for a White Knight even among such logical partners as hotel chains. The chairman of Hyatt Corporation, Jay Pritzker, actually sat on the Continental board, but he showed no interest in an airline investment at this time. (Two years later Hyatt would purchase Braniff.) Collectively, the defense team had no shortage of leads or personal contacts. "We didn't leave a stone unturned," Vandeman avers. But in the end it was possible to enter into serious discussions only with Continental's intended partner, Western Airlines.

Immediately after learning of the tender offer, Feldman had contacted Western to discuss ways of salvaging the merger. The folly of deferring shareholder approval of the merger was now painfully apparent, but the defense team thought that a tactical advantage might possibly be gained by calling a special shareholders' meeting to approve the merger at an early date. If TI's purchase date could somehow be delayed, the two airlines might still be able to approve a merger blocking TI's bid for control. Western was willing to go along with the tactic, and on the same day that TI made its formal offer to shareholders, Continental and Western called special shareholders' meetings on the earliest feasible date—March 12.

As Continental's options began to narrow, George Vandeman proposed a plan for Western to intervene as a White Knight. The plan took advantage of the special shareholders' meeting: Western would make a tender offer of $18 per share for 5 million shares of Continental stock, and as a condition of a valid tender, it would require shareholder proxies authorizing it to vote the tendered stock in favor of the Continental-Western merger at the shareholders' meeting. Arbitrageurs and institutional shareholders, who together accounted for more than 5 million shares, would unquestionably choose to tender to Western. Since most individual shareholders remained loyal to the Continental management, Western could easily assure approval of the merger by voting this large block of stock. Subsequently, the combined company would redeem Western's holdings in Continental stock so that the $90 million cost of purchase would be born equally by both airlines. While there was a risk that TI would respond by outbidding Western, it would have to react quickly and make an offer for a controlling interest of 7.5 million shares, not merely 5 million shares.

For the first time, Feldman could personally respond to the tender offer with a clear chance of success, acting in his own element of private business discussions. Under his direction, the financial staff prepared a thorough analysis of the two airlines' financial resources for the counter tender offer. Western's unencumbered fleet of fifteen 737s appeared to give it enough leverage to secure a short-term loan, and Continental's own unencumbered fleet offered ample collateral to secure its half of the indebtedness after the merger. Feldman arranged a weekend meeting at the Western headquarters to present the plan to the two top Western executives,

Arthur Kelly, chairman of the board, and Dominic Renda, president, and to their most esteemed financial advisor, Ira Harris of Salomon Brothers. Feldman talked privately with Harris and the two Western executives throughout most of Saturday and Sunday, breaking away from time to time to go over particular points with three financial executives who stood by in a neighboring room. The discussion continued until 1:30 A.M. Monday morning. Continental's controller, Mike Conway, remembers that Feldman then entered the room where he sat waiting and said tersely, "Come on, let's get out of here!" Though betraying no emotion, Feldman knew he had not succeeded in persuading the Western executives. Kelly and Renda had agreed only to refer the plan to the executive committee of the board. Two days later Renda visited Feldman to inform him that the executive committee had rejected the plan.

Why was Western unpersuaded? When asked the question a Continental executive could only shake his head. The projected *annual* benefits of the merger (89 million) equaled the cost of the proposed counter tender offer. Kelly and Renda objected that the plan would reduce the net worth of the combined company to an undesirable level. Implicitly, they preferred the risks of a weaker route system to the risk of finding themselves with insufficient financial resources as a result of the investment. Whether out of prudence or a failure of leadership, the Western executives were unwilling to stake the financial viability of their company on the clear benefits of the merger that were indicated by their own analyses.

On another front, TI's petition to the Civil Aeronautics Board for approval of the voting trust began an argument, heavily tinged with ideology, that would continue during the next six months. TI posed as an advocate of an objective endorsed by the Airline Deregulation Act—the untrammeled operation of the market. "The Board has committed itself," it noted, "not to interfere in the normal workings of the capital markets." The approval of the voting trust would give shareholders the same opportunity to sell their shares at a premium that would be present in normal market conditions:

In an unregulated industry the shareholders of Continental would indeed have the opportunity to tender their shares for cash at a premium, and the future control of Continental would be determined in the marketplace without the necessity of prior approval of a regulatory agency.

The policy of the Airline Deregulation Act demanded that the Board give shareholders this choice. "The congressional mandate to return the air carrier industry to the marketplace," TI argued, "requires that the Board grant this petition."

In reply, Continental argued that TI was asking for a discriminatory relaxation of regulatory standards. The TI takeover bid did not differ from three previous cases in which the CAB had required voting trusts free of elements of control. Furthermore, Continental strenuously argued that the real effect of the tender offer was to bring into play the activities of arbitrageurs and professional investors; it exploited a short-term bias of the market rather than offering shareholders a legitimate business choice.

The five-member board, which would prove to be so well disposed to TI, provoked more than a little animosity among Continental employees, but it was by no means composed of political hacks. The chairman, Marvin Cohen, was a Phi Beta Kappa and a successful lawyer in Tucson, Arizona; Elizabeth Bailey was a distinguished economist from Bell Laboratories; George Dalley came from a high State Department position; James Smith could claim a successful career in airport administration; and Gloria Schaffer, at the age of twenty-seven, had been the first woman in history elected to the Connecticut state senate and had run as the Democratic candidate for the U.S. Senate in 1976. All the members, however, shared an ideological commitment that they perceived to be embodied in the Airline Deregulation Act: a belief, beyond the reach of empirical analysis, in the beneficent effect of the free operation of market forces. Only Gloria Schaffer at times wavered from this ideological position. At the hearing on the voting trust, Elizabeth Bailey typically remarked,

> Essentially what we're allowing is the stronger of Texas International and Western to be able to merge with Continental and thereby are really letting the marketplace work.

Gloria Schaffer, however, asked,

> Would it be fair to say that this is rather like the battle of, say, the pocket book over the mind? Continental has the opportunity to argue for the minds of people who have tendered stock—to argue that they would be better off holding out and pulling their stock out and voting for the merger—whereas you are saying "we have this cash in hand" and, you know, "you can take it or leave it." In other words, you can enrich your pocket book immediately.

The Board consolidated its consideration of the voting trust and the Continental-Western merger by scheduling arguments on both petitions for the same day, and it promised to deliver a ruling on Monday, March 2, four days before the purchase date. That morning the Board first delivered an opinion laboriously approving the Continental-Western merger; then it announced a decision that barred actual consummation of the merger—approval of TI's proposed voting trust. The decision undertakes a long review of the arguments of both parties, eventually ending up in a final statement of policy:

> Finally, we emphasize that our role in these cases is not to equalize the opportunities of all parties. We will not intervene to substitute our judgment for that of the marketplace. . . . Our decision is meant to insure that the airline industry experiences the disciplines and gains the benefits of the capital markets.

The voting trust should be approved in the form proposed by TI, the Board held, because to do otherwise, would block the successful execution of the tender offer and thus interfere with the free play of capital markets.

Among Continental employees, the general reaction to the tender offer was first one of incredulity. "Texas International was so small!" exclaims flight attendant Pearl Kelly. "It seemed ludicrous." But, as John Bidlake relates, disbelief was quickly overtaken by a sense that "No, this is something serious." Continental employees regarded TI as a second-rate airline, plagued by problems of poor baggage handling and poor on-time performance. Rightly or wrongly, they felt that they were better trained and more competent than their counterparts at TI. Chuck Coble, who now admires Lorenzo, remembers that most employees thought: "We were Continental Airlines. We didn't want to be Texas International." While Lorenzo enjoyed an excellent reputation in the financial press, he was an unpopular figure among airline industry employees. Stories alleging unfair dealings with unions, and high management turnover circulated through the airline grapevine as flight crews passed through the operations center, ramp workers met mechanics, and ticket agents talked to flight attendants at the gate.

The employee apprehensions were intensified when TI took two positions adverse to employee interests in its CAB petition for approval of the takeover. An exhibit implied that TI would not respect existing union contracts:

> It is Texas International's position that it will be necessary to renegotiate existing collective bargaining agreements when a combination of Continental and Texas International becomes effective.

A footnote disclosed that TI would oppose the customary labor-protective provisions. Since 1952 the CAB had conditioned approval of air carrier mergers on acceptance of certain standard provisions designed to protect employees. These labor-protective provisions provided an arbitration procedure for resolving disputes and guaranteed a degree of compensation for displaced employees, such as a "dismissal allowance" to employees who lost their jobs and moving expenses of employees forced to change their places of residence. The provisions were a useful, though expensive, device for smoothly integrating different work forces. No air carrier had ever sought to challenge them, but relying on its credit with the CAB, TI urged that these matters should now be left to private negotiations, free of government interference.

The pilots were the employee group most apprehensive of the takeover. Deregulation spelled the end of an era of job security and elite compensation; and under a Lorenzo management, change promised to come in a peculiarly invidious form. By creating New York Air, Lorenzo had presented pilots with a *fait accompli*, avoiding negotiation and foreclosing career prospects. With reason, a leaflet of the Air Line Pilots' Association stated that New York Air, "the brainchild of Texas International executive Frank Lorenzo, symbolizes the threat every ALPA pilot faces." In contrast, according to pilot Jim Rinella, the pilots "totally trusted" Feldman and were generally convinced of the value of the Western merger.

On February 24, the Master Executive Council (MEC) of the ALPA pilots at Continental met to take action. The pilots anticipated that Lorenzo would have to conduct a proxy solicitation campaign to block approval of the Western merger at the special shareholders' meeting, and they thought they might be able to assist the company by themselves contacting shareholders. A respected pilot outside the union leadership, Paul Eckel, agreed to lead the effort. A devout Mormon, Eckel was deeply imbued with the moral commitment to action that lies at the heart of the Morman tradition. He had always been a leader. As the eldest son in a family of eleven children, he had grown up being responsible for younger brothers and sisters. His family ate in shifts at a small kitchen table where there was not always enough to eat. At school, Eckel achieved early recognition in athletics and academics. He was captain of an all-conference football team at Brigham Young University and finished first in a class of one thousand at the Air Force pilot training school. During much of his career at Continental, he had held management positions: first that of flight manager and then, from 1977 to April 1980, that of chief pilot, a high executive position with responsibility over all flight operations. After returning to pilot ranks following a dispute with the vice-president of flight operations, he chaired the ALPA merger committee that planned technical details of the Western merger.

On Friday, February 27, Eckel presented to Feldman an ambitious plan to aid the company in proxy solicitations. He proposed that during the ten-day period from March 2 through 11 the pilots would attempt to visit personally every shareholder having more than five hundred shares, and to contact other shareholders by telephone. Feldman could only welcome the offer of support, however unlikely a proxy fight actually might be. Over the weekend, Eckel worked around the clock to organize the campaign. Under his leadership, the pilots established a telephone tree, prepared scripts for shareholder solicitations, planned training sessions, divided the country into sections for personal visits, enlisted team leaders, determined the availability of volunteers, and set up work schedules. The project released pent-up emotions. "There was tremendous willingness to do what was necessary," Eckel recalls. In Los Angeles, a hundred people were committed to the effort. But on Monday, when the organization was well advanced, the pilots learned that the CAB had approved the TI voting trust, and there could be no hope of winning a proxy battle. Eckel left for his base in El Paso while other pilot leaders remained in Los Angeles.

In the discussions of pilots congregating in the ALPA offices, Jim Rinella, a former MEC member, urged a change of strategy: the pilots themselves should make a counter tender offer for Continental stock at a price above the Lorenzo offer. Continental had a long history of discussions of employee stock ownership. It was said, however, that the management opposed the idea for "Six" reasons. With paternalistic concern, Robert Six sought to provide employees with soundly funded pensions, not stock of fluctuating value. After the 1976 pilots' strike, Rinella had argued that the pilots should independently purchase stock to gain a place on the board of directors. He thought that the strike had resulted from a failure of communications of the sort that could have been avoided if the pilots had been closer to the inner councils of management. Now at the eleventh hour, he saw the purchase of stock as the pilots' only chance. On his own initiative, he called Eckel in El Paso. "There has to be a way out of this," he said. "Why don't you come out?" On Rinella's insistence, Eckel returned to Los Angeles to attend an emergency MEC meeting on Wednesday morning.

In an emotional debate, the pilots began to listen to Rinella's idea. Eckel relates, "An interesting thing happened in all these conversations. We got out of the 'stop TXI mode' and into a 'let's buy a business' mode. It was a very exciting period of time." Phil Nash, the local executive chairman from Denver, puts it another way: "We were believing anything. We had to. We were scared to death." Most of the discussion envisioned pilot contributions to a trust that would purchase Continental stock. A few calculations were enough to show that the pilots were unlikely to raise more than a fraction of the necessary funds, but Eckel became convinced that, if other employee groups were enlisted in the effort, the goal might be within reach. It was necessary above all to act immediately. He had no formal position in the union but enjoyed the confidence of other pilots. Without bothering to secure clearance from the MEC, he took charge of an intense effort to identify sources of funds and to form an employee coalition.

Accompanied by several other pilots, Eckel told Feldman about his plans for a counter tender offer on Wednesday afternoon. According to George Vandeman, Feldman regarded it to be "a matter of human interest" that they should attempt such a quixotic effort. Only the vice-president of personnel relations, Jack Sage, and the CAB counsel, Lee Hydeman, took the idea seriously. A gregarious man with wide friendships, Sage had pursued tough labor relations policies that provoked two strikes, but he possessed a politician's ability to shift easily from an adversary to a friendly relationship. When the bargaining was over, he could talk with union leaders as colleagues. Being well attuned to employee mood, he sensed that something important was afoot. For his part, the CAB counsel, Lee Hydeman, saw another weapon in the ongoing legal contest before the regulatory agency. There might conceivably be some basis to petition the CAB for a ten-day stay in the order approving the voting trust so as to permit a competing employee tender offer.

The idea of an employee stock purchase found unexpected support the next day in a proposal by the controller, Mike Conway. One of the youngest officers, Conway had been hired by Feldman and felt intense admiration for him. "It was impossible not to respect the man," he says. People inevitably reveal their own values in the praise of those they admire. Conway insists that Feldman was above all a "humanitarian." The description tells as much about Conway as it does about Feldman. Before coming to Continental, Conway had once examined a tax shelter lease of aircraft proposed by Eastern Airlines pilots. The transaction showed him that the employee payroll can, under some circumstances, be regarded as a financial resource. Since the first news of the tender offer, he had been considering how employee opposition to TI's bid could be translated into financial clout, but he was outside the inner circle of management and actually worked in a building a few miles from the corporate headquarters. He was in a position only to recommend his ideas to his boss, chief financial officer, Roy Rawls, who at first showed little interest. On March 5, prompted by reports of Eckel's activities, Rawls asked Conway to put his ideas in writing. Conway quickly produced a memo that proposed a tender offer financed by a secured bank loan and repaid by voluntary employee payroll deductions. Conway acknowledged that "the legal implications are obviously several, not to mention the complex logistics." But the central idea of the proposal had a degree of plausibility.

After a night of frenetic activity, the pilots' search for funds had begun to generate some optimism. The MEC had enlisted the services of Eugene Trope, a Los Angeles attorney with a reputation for wealthy contacts, who soon reported progress in finding investment funds that could be put in a trust controlled by employees. A "Hawaiian investor," purportedly having $30 million at his disposal, said he would fly to Los Angeles on four' hours notice. The credit union was also viewed as a possible source of funds. Although it could only loan to individuals, the idea briefly gained currency that it could tap the resources of other credit unions to make a large-scale offering of loans that could be invested by employees in the purchase of Continental stock.

A more serious proposal revolved around use of the pilots' pension funds. The pilots possessed a defined benefit plan, which provided basic retirement benefits, and a defined contribution plan, known as the B-fund, which paid benefits reflecting the success of its investments. The B-fund had $115 million in assets. Under federal law, the defined benefit plan could invest no more than 10 percent of its assets in the employer's stock, but it appeared possible that the B-fund might be used more freely. A pilot who had served on a national ALPA pension committee, Chuck Cheeld, had some well-informed ideas about possible ways to draw on the B-fund. A psychology major, Cheeld has a reflective mind, molded by a strong Protestant religious background. Though temperamentally very different from Eckel, he shared much of his idealistic motivation and began to work closely with him.

Encouraged by the new ideas for financing a counter tender offer, Eckel shed all doubts and reservations. On Thursday afternoon, accompanied by Cheeld and other pilots, he presented a plan to Feldman. The pilots were prepared to launch a blitz of telegrams to the CAB to support a motion for a ten-day stay of the order approving the voting trust. With the benefit of this time, they could find funds from employee contributions, the "Hawaiian investor," the credit union, or pension funds to finance a counter tender offer. Eckel had already organized a meeting for Friday morning at a hotel near the airport to form a broadly based employee coalition to sponsor the effort. It was perhaps a dream rather than a plausible program, but Eckel had committed himself to the goal of employee ownership with an intensity that promised results. "The whole thing got started because Paul was so darned positive," remarks a pilot, Felix Tomlinson. Feldman agreed to authorize CAB counsel, Lee Hydeman, to file the motion for the ten-day stay.

Feldman may have acted merely out of regard for Eckel's determination and idealism, but he did consider the use of the pension funds to be an idea worthy of examination. The next day Cheeld received a telephone call at his home as he was leaving for a flight. "Chuck, this is Al," said a voice; Cheeld says he will never forget his shock at this newly gained intimacy with the chief executive. Feldman wanted to be briefed on the possibilities of using the funds as a vehicle for employee ownership. As it turned out, Cheeld was unable to persuade him that the company, as administrator, should permit use of the funds for this purpose. Feldman objected that exploitation of the funds in a takeover struggle might leave the employees as "indentured servants" with their financial future compromised for the immediate interests of the company. But the idea of using the funds to buy stock in the pilots' own airline persisted throughout the takeover struggle, and recurred three years later, because it reflected the strong desire of many (perhaps most) pilots.

Hydeman filed the motion for a ten-day stay on Friday, March 6, at the last possible opportunity. The motion could offer no specifics but accurately stated that "it was only yesterday, March 5th, that an idea was discussed by the employees and management of Continental which offers real promise of a viable, competing proposal by the employees." With characteristic optimism, Eckel hoped that the Board would be persuaded to grant the motion by an outpouring of employee telegrams. The telephone tree organized a week earlier for the aborted proxy fight was put into action, and management permitted a general appeal to be sent out on the company teletypes. Two pilots actually went to the CAB headquarters in Washington, D.C., to make sure that the telegrams had arrived. According to varying accounts, the appeal, organized on a few hours' notice, produced between five hundred and two thousand telegrams.

At the Friday morning meeting that he had organized, Eckel spoke to employees about the need for a Continental employees' association. About 150 people attended the meeting, including representatives from all the unions and a few noncontract employees. Eckel's plan had a simple logic: if the eleven thousand employees of Continental pooled their resources and energies, there had to be a way to stop the takeover. The meeting was dramatically punctuated by telephone calls from arbitrageurs who had somehow heard of the proposed counter tender offer. It was all Eckel's show. Expressing a confidence that defied all odds, he was, in his words, "jazzed about the idea of being in a contest and coming out as owner of a company." Another pilot, Dick Engle, remembers that other employees were affected by Eckel's enthusiasm "but underneath we knew we didn't have the time."

At the time of the employee meeting, Texas Air vice-president, Phil Bakes, sat in the Kidder, Peabody office in New York awaiting a visit from Eric Gleacher of Lehman Brothers. He had flown up from Washington, D.C., in response to an invitation of Marty Lipton, the senior partner of the Wachtell, Lipton firm. According to Bakes, their conversation had gone "back and forth" but carried the implication: "Let's bury the hatchet." Bakes watched the New York Stock Exchange tape in the brokerage office to pass the time before the meeting. Suddenly, the news appeared that Continental was considering an employee stock purchase. Bakes immediately canceled the meeting and told Kidder, Peabody to inform Lehman Brothers: "If you're going to call off that sort of thing, we'll talk."

The dream of an employee counter tender offer did not last long. Friday afternoon the CAB denied the request for the ten-day stay. Only two members of the Board bothered to attend arguments on the motion although other members were polled in their offices. The ruling asserts, "No one could properly have relied on the assumption that the Board would turn the trust down. . . . Under the circumstances we see no basis for interfering with TI's tender offer at this late date." Earlier in the day, the federal court in Los Angeles had denied Continental's motion for a preliminary injunction delaying the purchase date.

Eckel's drive for an employee coalition took place against a background of rumor and tension. Earlier in the week Feldman had flown to New York in the corporate jet to meet with Lorenzo in the hope of opening settlement negotiations before a board of directors meeting scheduled on Thursday. Reports began circulating in the corporate headquarters that Feldman, the wonder worker, had found a White Knight. In fact, nothing came of their meeting; Lorenzo talked in generalities and promised only to stay in communication. The board of directors meeting coincided with a very different sort of crisis: a Continental jet was hijacked at the Los Angeles airport. When a flight attendant noticed a boarding passenger carrying a gun, the pilots quickly escaped through a cockpit window, and the gunman responded by holding five passengers and a flight attendant hostage in the grounded jet for eleven hours.

With this bizarre setting, Feldman undertook a difficult task for a man who believed in the importance of fulfilling commitments—explaining the failure of the takeover defense. Turning to his chief concern—settlement negotiations with TI—he reported that his conversations with Lorenzo left him with the impression that, while he intended to combine Continental with TI, he had not worked out the details of such a merger. As recorded by the minutes, Feldman closed the meeting by stating that he was "very concerned about the deterioration of morale of the Continental employees."

When the last defenses failed on Friday afternoon, the pilots' MEC demanded a meeting with Feldman. Phil Nash, who has an uncommon memory, preserves a vivid recollection of the encounter. The MEC, together with Eckel, Cheeld, and a few flight attendants and mechanics, sat in straight-backed metal chairs around a long rectangular table in the conference room of the flight operations center. Feldman, wearing his accustomed gray slacks, blue button-down shirt, and dark tie bearing the Boeing insignia, looked exhausted and troubled. "Your heart went out to the guy," Nash says. Leaning back and bracing a foot on the table, his shirtsleeves rolled up, Feldman said he was there to talk and answer questions. He spoke in a low monotone voice and began to take the employees step by step through everything he had done to fight the tender offer. "I think he's got us," he concluded, as if speaking to old friends. There was a rush of questions, and a flight attendant struck a note of hostility. Feldman responded fully to each question but increasingly displayed a kind of emotional tightness and soon ran out of cigarettes which he borrowed from Cheeld. Finally, Nash asked a question that he ruefully describes as "stupid." "Have you offered to sell us to an airline like Delta?" he asked. The thought that he would have ignored such an obvious possibility was too much for Feldman. He was a man who loved good organization and liked to be in charge. For weeks he had been at the beck and call of lawyers and investment bankers, engaged in a losing game that eluded rational analysis. "You know," he said, his voice cracking, "I'm like the puppet on the string. Everybody has been pulling those strings, and I've been dancing as hard as I can. If you want to pull the strings some more, I don't think there's any more dance in me." Feldman fled the room, pursued by Eckel who tried to offer the group's apologies. Nash and other employees rose and applauded in an awkward attempt to communicate their confidence in him.

That evening Feldman ruminated on the tender offer battle with his executive assistant, Mike Roach. "It's the first time in my life I've ever lost," he said. Feldman was then fifty-three years old.

Phil Nash returned to his hotel room later that evening after commiserating with his friends. "Holy shit," he thought. "Up to now I've always been lucky. Here goes the end of my career." He randomly flicked on the TV and caught the beginning of the movie *Apocalypse Now*.

CHAPTER
THREE

THE ESOP
IDEA

Not caring to rest, Feldman acted quickly to arrange a Sunday dinner with Lorenzo at a restaurant in a Beverly Hills hotel. The dinner meeting—one of their few personal encounters— did not lead to mutual trust. Feldman's executive assistant, Mike Roach, remarks, "I don't think Frank understood Al." But surely Feldman had similar difficulty understanding Lorenzo. The two men possessed very different temperaments and styles of management. Lorenzo acted intuitively and was capable of bold, decisive action and abrupt reversals of direction; he held his cards close to his chest and liked to preserve all options. Feldman approached business dealings as if they were engineering projects that required thorough marshaling of facts and arguments and carefully refined plans. According to Mike Roach, he was "startled" to find that Lorenzo had no studies of merger "synergy," that is, of the operational benefits of a combination of Continental and TI.

The meeting resulted in an incident, well aired in subsequent litigation, but no concrete progress. Lorenzo chose the occasion to make an overture to Feldman. He said that Feldman would make an effective chief executive for the new company and suggested that he was "underpaid" at his current salary of $275,000. He then began to describe his practice of giving equity securities to senior executives. It was not an approach calculated to appeal to Feldman's ego or sense of ethics. Feldman later testified, "I elected to cut off the discussion since I felt it was inappropriate."

Feldman thought that TI had won the takeover battle; by meeting with Lorenzo, he hoped only to begin negotiating a settlement that would serve the interests of his constituents—employees and nontendering shareholders. His objective in serving employee interests was limited to securing the standard CAB labor-protective provisions as part of a settlement agreement. When he asked for a public commitment to respect these provisions, Lorenzo replied that the best he could do was to write a letter, for general distribution, to allay employee fears. Texas Air vice-president Phil Bakes sent a draft of the letter to Continental a few days later. On behalf of management, Mike Roach protested that the letter contained broad generalities but no specific commitments, and he tried to persuade Bakes that a strong letter was important because "the employees were really aroused." The language intended to reassure Continental employees read:

> While we do not normally respond to baseless rumors, I want to assure you and all the Board that any rumors concerning liquidation, dismemberment or similar schemes are completely false.

> [O]ur objective is to seek a merger with Continental, and we would welcome the opportunity to negotiate promptly a mutually beneficial merger agreement. We would expect that the agreement would contain provisions that would protect the most valuable resources of our two companies—our employees. Those provisions would prevail independent of a CAB decision not to impose labor protective provisions.

The Continental management actually distributed the letter to employees weeks later as evidence of the failure of negotiations with TI.

In his Sunday dinner with Lorenzo, Feldman also pressed for what he saw as the best solution—a three-way merger of Continental, TI, and Western. Since Lorenzo's strategy in the tender offer had been so largely concerned with preventing a

Continental-Western merger, it was hard to imagine that he would agree to an arrangement he had fought, but Feldman always expected rational conduct in others and regarded the benefits of the merger to be clearly demonstrable. In fact, Lorenzo did give the proposal a respectful hearing. About a week after the conclusion of the tender offer, Dan Love, Continental's vice-president of futures planning, met with Lorenzo in New York to explain the advantages of the Western merger. Love remembers that Lorenzo "asked some penetrating questions as he can do" and explored the idea of a three-way deal "without making positive or negative expressions." The meeting, however, failed to prompt serious negotiations.

The most critical issue in these early negotiations was the treatment of nontendering shareholders. Mike Roach believes that a settlement would have been quickly reached if TI had advanced a satisfactory proposal on this issue. But the TI management was in no hurry. Phil Bakes explains, "We didn't have a clear idea of what the second half of the deal would be." Since any final agreement would have to await CAB approval of the merger, TI saw no point of rushing to a settlement. The two personal meetings of Feldman and Lorenzo were followed by several telephone calls and by various requests for information passing between the finance departments of the two companies. The Continental management, left dangling like a fish on a hook, was increasingly unhappy with the absence of real negotiations, but TI regarded these early contacts as reasonable preliminaries. "Both sides were feeling each other out," Bakes says.

Continental did receive a proposal of a sort in a meeting on March 18 in New York. The principal spokesman for TI was Robert Hotz of Smith Barney, Harris Upham and Company, assisted by the TI treasurer, Robert Snedeker. Eric Gleacher of Lehman Brothers and financial vice-president Jerome Himmelberg, represented Continental. Hotz opened the meeting by verbally sketching a possible concept for a merger. TI would first transfer its Continental stock to its parent, Texas Air Corporation, but retain the related debt. TI and Continental would then merge; Texas Air would receive 56 percent of the stock in the new company in exchange for its 48.5 percent stock ownership interest of Continental; and Continental's non-tendering shareholders would receive 44 percent of the common stock, plus a preferred security with a stated value of $3.50. Lorenzo and Feldman were brought into the meeting by conference telephone calls. Snedeker says the TI management thought the concept "was appropriate and constructive negotiations could begin." But within the framework of corporate law, a proposal more favorable to the interests of TI's parent, Texas Air Corporation, could scarcely be imagined, and the new company would be financially weakened. After transferring its Continental stock to Texas Air Corporation, TI would have a negative net worth of $40 million. Neither TI nor Continental would receive an infusion of capital from Texas Air Corporation. The vaguely described preferred security was of uncertain value, and, to the extent that the security could be regarded as a form of debt, it would subject the new company to additional indebtedness.

After the meeting, Jerome Himmelberg, a financial vice-president of Continental, called Feldman to say that he didn't see any opening for negotiations. He was particularly troubled by the lack of a precise written description of the preferred security. "It was pretty difficult to see what they intended to do," he says. Feldman asked him to stay another day to press for a written proposal. Himmelberg waited at Lehman Brothers' office the next morning as Gleacher tried to elicit a written statement, but he returned to Los Angeles with only his notes. Lorenzo appeared genuinely surprised by Continental's reaction. After talking to Hotz and Snedeker, he called Feldman that evening to complain that Continental did not appear to be interested in serious negotiations. "We were somewhat frustrated at the lack of response from Continental," Hotz says.

While the Continental management sought a settlement with TI, the pilots resolved to continue the fight. Feldman offered no encouragement to the union leaders. The weekend after the tender offer he told the members of the MEC that they couldn't win, and he would "not have any part of it." But he responded very differently to Eckel and Cheeld who persisted on their own to search for a way out of the apparent defeat. Throughout the weekend of March 7 and 8, they debated new strategies to secure employee control. Knowing that Feldman liked to have ideas precisely expressed in writing, they presented him with a memo on Monday morning. Cheeld thought that "basically he took it because some employees brought it to him," but Feldman displayed a genuine sympathy for their efforts; he questioned them on each section and referred the memo to George Vandeman. The same day he told the board of directors that a "spontaneous employee movement" had emerged to oppose the takeover. Later in the week, Eckel and Cheeld were relieved of their flying duties and given an office and a secretary in the corporate headquarters.

In the next two weeks, Eckel and Cheeld were barraged by ideas coming from all categories of employees. Eckel recalls, "When I got home, I was never off the phone. I would get three hours sleep a night." Often the employees would want to pass on ideas they received while talking about the problem with their fathers, bankers, or brokers. Debating these suggestions in the evening, Eckel and Cheeld composed six or seven memos in a period of ten days. Many of the employee suggestions revolved around direct employee contributions to a trust and the pledge of payroll deductions—an idea that runs afoul of legal restrictions on the assignment of wages by employees. Other ideas included stock bonus plans and sales of unissued stock. Cheeld pursued the possible use of pilot pension funds by drawing on the expertise of the national ALPA office. Feldman continued to see them periodically but soon suggested that they go first to Vandeman. None of the ideas survived Vandeman's scrutiny. "In the first two weeks, we didn't accomplish much except bother Feldman," Eckel says.

Eckel and Cheeld soon learned that they had an ally in controller Mike Conway and talked to him almost every day. Despite the success of the tender offer, Conway saw hope of reducing Lorenzo to a minority position by the sale of unissued stock to employees. On the advice of Leman Brothers, Continental had increased its authorized but unissued stock from 5 million to 35 million in the May 1980 shareholder meeting, specifically for the purpose of giving the corporation flexibility in responding to takeover bids. In two memos, Conway pointed out that a sale of unissued stock might be structured as a contribution to shareholder equity which would improve the company's balance sheet while defeating the takeover bid.

Though making little progress in finding a practical avenue for employee control, Eckel evolved a clear vision, with distinct moral undertones, of what he wanted. Commissioning himself as chairman of a Continental Airlines Employees' Association, he circulated a memo explaining his aims:

March 17, 1981

TO: All Continental Employees

SUBJECT: The Continental Airlines Employees'
    Association

As you are all aware, Texas International has purchased 48.5% of Continental Airlines stock.

In an effort to prevent a takeover by Texas International and to provide a vehicle for employee ownership of a controlling interest in Continental Airlines, the Continental Airlines Employees' Association has been formed.

The employees need to own at least 51% of the stock to block Texas International's takeover move. If we accomplish this, we will be the first employee group to own a majority of the company stock in airline industry history and will begin to accrue the following benefits:

A vote on major decisions affecting our company.

Representatives on the Board of Directors.

Potential receipt of dividend distributions.

An equity position in Continental that can be enhanced by our own efforts.

Major issues in the areas of compliance with securities law, organizational structure, financing and repayment, ERISA, and tax implications are being resolved as rapidly as possible.

If you have any questions, we are located in Room G283 at the G.O. and can be reached on 646-8964, 646-0301, and 646-2846.

We are looking forward to your support and assistance in the employee's fight to save Continental!

Paul Eckel
Chairman
Continental Airlines
Employees' Association

The memo was written in audacious disregard for apparent legal and financial realities—Eckel had devised no feasible means of pursuing his plan—but the day after it was written a solution appeared in a way that Cheeld regards as providential. At a Sunday evening meeting of the administrative board of his Methodist church, a friend told Cheeld about tax qualified employee stock ownership plans, or ESOPs, a new form of employee stock bonus plan permitted by the Employee Retirement Income Security Act of 1974. On Tuesday, the friend called Cheeld to say that the Union Bank was trying to develop business in the field. Cheeld contacted the bank and arranged a Thursday afternoon appointment. Later the same day, while driving home from work, Eckel heard an advertisement on the radio of a Union Bank seminar on ESOPs, and, at the earliest opportunity, he asked Cheeld if they should contact the bank. Cheeld replied, "Paul, you're not going to believe this, but I've already set up an appointment."

Two Union Bank trust officers talked to Eckel, Cheeld, and three other pilots for about an hour and a half and introduced them to the concept of a leveraged ESOP. Though ordinarily a form of employee benefit, the leveraged ESOP could be structured to effect an employee buyout of an employer. The ESOP relied on a trust that would borrow money to purchase an employer's stock on behalf of employees. To support the financing of the stock purchase, the employer would guarantee the loan to the trust and commit itself to make periodic contributions to the trust. The bank officials, Cheeld says, "conveyed a positive feeling that an ESOP could be a vehicle to block a takeover or acquire employee control." Immediately taking their idea to management, the pilots arranged to have the Union Bank representatives return the next day to make a presentation to Feldman and other top executives.

The way for management interest in the ESOP had in fact been prepared. The previous week Alan Batkin, a managing director of Lehman Brothers, participated in a strategy session of executives and advisors. When Feldman mentioned Eckel's employee movement, Batkin remarked that an ESOP could be used to give employees a large equity interest in a company. Feldman asked him to look into the possibility and report back. As it turned out, Batkin never gave his report, and Lehman Brothers played no further role in developing the ESOP idea. The efforts of Continental's own staff outpaced those of the investment bankers.

Most of the credit for the detailed development of the concept goes to Mike Roach, the executive assistant to the president, who began to study seriously the use of employee stock ownership plans the same week that Eckel and Cheeld discovered the idea. Having worked as a legal aide to CAB chairman Alfred Kahn, Roach was a believer in deregulation and was well disposed to Lorenzo. Early in his career, he had drafted the original airline deregulation bill introduced by the Ford administration; at the CAB, he had welcomed Lorenzo's bid to acquire National Airlines. But when Continental failed to engage TI in negotiations, Roach began to consider alternatives. With a sense of intellectual discovery, he perceived employee stock ownership as a takeover defense that was also an innovative response to the challenge of deregulation, a means of enlisting employee support for needed change. Later in the year, Roach explained the logic that brought him to advocate the ESOP:

> A number of approaches are open for existing air carriers to make more efficient use of their work forces. They include:
>
> (1) spinning off assets to create new companies, able to write less restrictive work rules on a clean slate with new employees, such as Texas Air Corporation has done with New York Air;
>
> (2) confrontation with present employees and their union representatives—a course followed in the past by Northwest Airlines to gain productivity concessions; and
>
> (3) giving employees an incentive to greater efficiency by granting them a major share in corporate equity and decision making.
>
> The first two approaches offer management the possibility of more immediate results, but they also carry substantial costs for the American public.
>
> The third approach, sharing corporate equity and decision making, may offer less immediate results; it definitely requires by far the greatest management effort. However, Continental and its employees have elected this approach because of their mutual confidence that together they can build a profitable airline.

The legislation authorizing tax qualified ESOPs had been enacted in 1974 through the initiative of Senator Russell Long. Employee stock bonus plans were already recognized under federal tax law, but borrowing from the economic theories of Louis Kelso, a San Francisco securities lawyer, Senator Long wished to create new mechanisms, facilitating employee stock ownership, that would promote a form of capitalism true to American democratic traditions. Employee stock ownership has spread at an exponential rate since 1974, and if present trends continue, it may fulfill Senator Long's vision of a more democratic capitalism. Between 1975 and 1983, employee stock ownership plans have increased from perhaps three hundred to over six thousand throughout the country. In the latter year, three of the largest leveraged buyouts of U.S. corporations—Dan River, Raymond International and Weirton Steel—were effected by employees through tax qualified ESOPs. But early in 1981, the use of ESOPs to secure employee control of a corporation was still a novelty. The plans were commonly designed on a smaller scale as a fringe benefit, giving employees limited stock ownership to supplement other forms of compensation.

The Union Bank representatives explained the idea of a leveraged ESOP again in a Friday afternoon meeting attended by Feldman and three other executives. The leveraged ESOP offered a financing vehicle with clearly defined tax treatment: the company could deduct its contribution to the ESOP trust to repay the stock purchase loan, the income of the trust would be exempt from tax, and employees would not be subject to tax unless the stock allocated to their account was directly transfered to them. Moreover, the ESOP proposal placed the Continental management in a small but established field of finance. If the company wished to pursue the idea, the Union Bank trust officers recommended that Continental retain Kelso & Company, the San Francisco firm that had pioneered employee stock ownership plans.

A Union Bank representative, Robins Bogue, recalls that the Continental executives were "excited but reserved. They saw that there was a lot of work that had to be done to make it fly." The impact of the meeting owed much to its timing. Two days earlier the Continental executives had received TI's March 18 merger proposal, and they were in a mood to look for alternatives to a settlement.

The Union Bank meeting proved to be the catalytical event that brought about a rapid crystallization of the ESOP idea. Working long hours throughout the weekend with a group of other executives, Mike Roach produced a twenty-three page memo, designated "extremely confidential," that set forth detailed financial projections for an ESOP involving different amounts of employee stock ownership. All the Continental executives believed that the plan made sense only if it were combined with a program of wage and salary concessions. The company's contributions to the ESOP trust to finance the stock purchase represented a form of payroll cost. The management could not justify to its shareholders an increase in payroll expense even if it served to defeat an undesired takeover. The plan could be defended on its own merits only if it were associated with an employees' commitment to forego a portion of their wages and salaries equal to the company's contributions to the ESOP. Roach's memo assumed that the company would make contributions to the ESOP equal to one-half of future employee pay increases up to a limit of 15 percent of payroll expense. The figures worked: this rather modest wage and salary forbearance generated enough funds over six to eight years to carry out the stock purchase. Feldman reviewed the memo on Sunday and, in his words, gave Roach a "very broad delegation" to continue to study the proposal.

The ESOP was weighed against the alternative of a negotiated settlement with TI in a critical strategy session on Thursday, March 26, in a small conference room, opening onto Feldman's office, that was the scene of most discussions of the takeover defense. The room was a converted office with a view of the north runway of the Los Angeles airport and enough room for about fifteen people to sit around a long table. Like other rooms in the executive suite, it contained a prominent blackboard. With his engineer's bent for precision, Feldman liked to visually analyze ideas before reaching a decision. The room was filled to capacity for the Thursday meeting. Lehman Brothers partner Eric Gleacher had come to present a proposal for a settlement with TI. Gleacher argued that Continental should respond to TI's oral merger proposal of March 18 with a counter-proposal asking for nontendering shareholders to receive an upgraded preferred security, having a stated value of $6.00 and a guaranteed 12 percent dividend, in addition to stock in the merged corporation. Mike Roach, normally one of the quietest participants in the strategy discussions, strongly objected to this potentially time-consuming line of negotiations.

Already an advocate of the ESOP, he argued, "We will lose time. We've got to go now!" Feldman finally accepted Gleacher's recommendation, but to keep his options open, he asked Roach to "continue to do spadework" on the ESOP. Feldman was, however, deeply troubled by the financial viability of a merger of the two airlines. After the meeting he plunged into an analysis of financial projections that by the next morning caused him to change his decision.

The bottom line of the Continental executives' analysis of the takeover was insolvency. They believed it was more than a bad business deal: it would result in an airline burdened with debt beyond its ability to pay. Feldman remarked, "Any way I open the envelope, all I see is debt." As analyzed by Lehman Brothers, TI's December 31, 1980, balance sheet, when adjusted to reflect the purchase of stock in Continental, showed a debt of $259.2 million, out of a total capitalization of $311.8 million, for a debt/capitalization ratio of 83/17. In addition, TI had embarked on a much-needed program of fleet modernization, involving the purchase of used DC-9-30 aircraft from Swissair, which would cost $49 million in 1981. Continental itself had a debt of $359 million out of a total capitalization of $560 million for a debt/capitalization ratio of 65/35, and like TI, it needed to replace some of its older aircraft.

How would the combined company pay for its debt? Lorenzo had not offered any infusion of equity. Although Texas Air had $75 million in liquid assets, it was unclear how much cash it could actually spare in view of its commitments and those of its subsidiaries for aircraft acquisition and debt service. TI brought very modest operating income to the combination. In 1980, its operating income was only $7.8 million, and during the seven years of Lorenzo's management, the bulk of its income had reflected gain on the sale of investments (chiefly National Airline's stock) or federal subsidies for small community service (terminated in 1978). Excluding these items, the airline had cumulated income of only $5.8 million or about $750,000 per year over the period of Lorenzo's management.

Continental's financial staff analyzed the merged carrier's ability to pay for its debt under five scenarios. The repayment of the present debt of the two airlines, plus routine capital expenditures of $40 million a year, required operating income of $99 million annually. The operating income of the two companies for their five best years (1974–78) averaged only $52.8 million, and in the previous five years averaged only $29.2 million—much less than needed to service the debt and cover capital expenditures. This basic scenario was varied by assuming the purchase of new aircraft, a stretch-out of debt and an equity infusion. Even under the most favorable circumstances, the merged company appeared likely to be short of funds to meet fixed debt charges and necessary capital expenditures.

Besides affording an alternative to the takeover, the ESOP offered significant improvements in the company's income statement and balance sheet. Both these financial benefits flowed from the assumption that it would be financed with funds that would otherwise be expended on payroll. In the case of the income statement, the ESOP would result in the elimination of the interest expense on existing bank loans. These loans would be paid off immediately with the proceeds from the sale of stock to the ESOP. The company would incur an equivalent obligation to make contributions to the ESOP trust to finance its purchase of stock, but these contributions would be paid out of funds that would otherwise go to wage and salary expenses; the result would be a reduction in interest expense with no offsetting increase in payroll costs. Continental faced estimated interest payments in 1982 of $22 million under its bank loans. If linked to a program of wage and salary forbearance, the ESOP would increase net income by this amount.

The sale of stock to the ESOP trust would also result in an improvement to Continental's balance sheet which would occur over a period of years as the stock purchase loan to the ESOP trust was paid off by company contributions to the trust. Initially, the stock purchase loan to the trust would be treated as a liability of the company since the company would have to guarantee the loan. But as the ESOP paid off the principal on the loan with company contributions, the payments would reduce the company's liability and increase shareholders' equity by a corresponding amount. When the loan was fully retired, the shareholders' equity would be increased by the amount of the stock purchase loan. Feldman at first balked at this accounting treatment. "The whole thing's done with mirrors," he objected. But the controller, Mike Conway, pointed out that the transaction would have real substance as a form of equity contribution by employees to the extent that the stock purchase was financed by wage and salary concessions.

The improvements to the income statement and balance sheet would come at the cost of at least temporary dilution in the book value of stock held by nontendering shareholders. The extent of the dilution would depend on the number of unissued shares sold to the ESOP. The problem of dilution did not bother those who believed that Continental faced a struggle for survival in the period of deregulation. "Nobody ever went out of business through dilution," remarks Mike Conway. But it was still the most vulnerable aspect of the ESOP. One could show with relative ease that the takeover was a bad business deal and that the ESOP would generate certain benefits. The more difficult question was whether these benefits compensated shareholders for the dilution of their interest by the massive issuance of new shares.

In view of this issue of dilution, the most critical factor in evaluating the ESOP—and the most difficult to assess—was the impact of the ESOP on employee productivity. The improvements that the ESOP would bring to the company's income statement and balance sheet were admittedly modest to justify a large increase in outstanding shares, but if the ESOP would promote significant improvements in employee productivity, the issuance of the new shares to employees might indeed be a good investment for other shareholders. In 1981, the record of ESOPs in stimulating productivity varied widely. One study of ESOPs in closely held corporations found that the evidence of improved productivity was inconclusive, but it acknowledged that most of the ESOPs studied were merely a form of fringe benefit, of restricted marketability, that offered no real opportunity for participation in ownership.[1] Another study of the U.S. Senate Select Committee on Small Business found that ESOPs were most likely to have a positive result when employees have either a major stake or a controlling interest in the employer company.[2] Evidently, the impact of ESOPs on employee productivity depended much on the design of the plans.

For a man as careful as Feldman, it was a bold act to propose a plan of employee ownership that, for its success, depended on an untested and unpredictable employee response. He said that he was driven to the decision after studying the financial viability of a combination of Continental and TI throughout the night after the Thursday meeting with Gleacher. The next day he told Lehman Brothers to hold off presenting to TI the counterproposal for an exchange of securities. But how could he propose a plan, intended to enlist employee support for higher productivity and substantial wage and salary concessions, without some evidence of employee support? Feldman decided that he had to conduct an employee poll. The idea was entirely his own and was the first of several decisions that would give the ESOP a uniquely democratic character.

Before proposing the plan, Feldman had to decide the number of shares to be issued to the ESOP. Eckel had long favored doubling the outstanding shares so as to give employees 51 percent ownership. This sort of numerical majority had a value that might generate greater employee support, but it would pose the issue of dilution in the most acute form. For his part, Feldman sought a clean, decisive solution. He later told John Huber, a close friend of Eckel, that he came to a decision while he diagramed alternatives on a blackboard in his office during a discussion with Eckel and several other pilots—he would propose 51 percent employee ownership.

Feldman called Lorenzo on Monday, March 30, to make a last effort to open negotiations, but in a long conversation he was unable to elicit any concrete offer. Lorenzo said the earliest he could set up a meeting for further discussions was on April 10 in Houston. The appointment was never kept. The next day Feldman brought the idea of the ESOP to the executive committee of the board of directors.

CHAPTER
FOUR

THE ESOP
CAMPAIGN

The ESOP was born of a management decision, prompted by the initiatives of Eckel, Cheeld, and other pilots. Can it therefore be viewed as a management-inspired scheme to defeat the takeover? Certainly it was a very tentative plan at the outset. Feldman viewed the ESOP as no more than a possibly viable alternative to the takeover that merited further consideration. He told other executives that there were several mountains to cross, the first being a strongly affirmative vote on the employee poll, and he did not seem to believe that the plan would get beyond this initial obstacle. "He was not at all convinced," remembers Erica Steinberger. "He had to be persuaded by the employees." Until the results of the poll were known, management was authorized only to give Eckel the assistance he needed in the next weeks to present his program to the employees.

Eckel's vision of a Continental employees' association coincided nicely with the tactics of the takeover defense. In any heated takeover fight, the challenger will inevitably raise the charge of management entrenchment which implies that management has breached its fiduciary duty to the corporation by acting to preserve its own position. To give the employee poll a legitimacy, free of the appearance of management manipulation, it was best for the proposal for employee control to be presented by the employees themselves. This was, however, an ideal that could be only partially realized. Eckel did not have a companywide organization or the resources to form one without the help of management. Jack Sage, working with Eckel, developed a tightly packed agenda calling for a brief but intense management effort to bring into being the Continental Employees' Association (CEA) that Eckel aspired to lead. The key elements of the plan were: selection of a CEA board of directors, an employee meeting in Denver to announce the ESOP, a ballot accompanied by a letter from Eckel mailed to all employees, and a series of "corporate update" meetings that would give CEA board members the opportunity to urge a yes vote on the ESOP. A personnel department memo set forth the agenda:

ESOP Campaign

April 2 —CEA orders campaign material
      —Sage sends notice of DEN [Denver] meeting to prospective missionaries
      —Sage schedules roadshow for Feldman and eight management teams 4/13–4/16

April 3 —Rawls reports on banks
      —Feldman briefs executive committee
      —Feldman briefs senior management
      —Levine, Roach prepare first draft of Management Bulletin
      —Eckel, Bidlake, Roach et al. prepare draft of CEA letter

April 4 —Eckel, Levine, Roach et al. meet with lawyer, produce final draft of CEA letter, ballot
      —letter and ballot to printers

April 5 —CEA letter to employees produced, addressed, stuffed with ballots
      —Eckel, Levine, Sage, Duggan, Roach script contents of DEN show

April 6 —Feldman meets roadshow coordinators
      —Roach et al. meet division heads, initiating chain of command communication on ESOP
      —CEA board meets in DEN
      —CEA letter and ballot mailed to employees
      —Campaign buttons and posters delivered to CEA

April 7 —CEA meeting to train missionaries in DEN
        —distribute management bulletins
        —Feldman-Six letter to employees gives them reply
            to Lorenzo
April 8 —Pilots MEC ratification meeting LAX [Los Angeles]
        —Eckel meets with employees LAX [Los Angeles]
April 9 —Eckel meets with employees, LAX (morning) DEN
            (afternoon, evening)
April 10—Eckel meets with employees IAH [Houston]
April 11—Eckel delivers first wave of poll results to Feldman
April 12—Second Management Bulletin
April 13—Management roadshows (Feldman and eight teams
    to 16   hold employee meetings at all Continental stations
April 17—deadline for employees to postmark poll
April 20—CEA tabulates poll results

Eckel asked nine employees to serve on the board of directors
of the CEA after interviewing candidates recommended by the
personnel department. The board represented a cross section
of employee groups, but, as a reflection of Eckel's philosophy
of employee control, none of the employees were prominent in
union affairs. The nine employees who answered Eckel's sum-
mons could not have imagined where it would lead them. They
received their first exposure to the concept of an ESOP in a
training session conducted by the staff of Kelso & Company,
the ESOP consultants retained by the company. Mechanic Rich
Carberry was at first "baffled" by the idea of the ESOP. "Then
the more I understood it," he says, "the more I was sold on it.
I thought it was too good to be true. I think it's the American
dream." To ticket agent Bill Miles the ESOP was a fresh and
exciting idea. "When I first listened to it," he recalls, "it made
all the sense in the world. We had worked for the airline for
years and were an integral part of it. Why shouldn't we own
it?" The training seminar was for him the beginning of an intense commitment that superseded all other obligations. "My
wife says," he recounts, "that I left for the CEA on Friday and
returned in October."

The original plans for the employee meeting in Denver contemplated a gathering of one representative from each of Continental's bases, but marketing executive Barrie Duggan, who spoke at the meeting, notes that the organizers "were overwhelmed by requests of others to come." The list of invitees was expanded to 150, including a representative of terminal services and passenger services from every base. Other employees were told they could come on their own time and expense. Barrie Duggan recalls that when he arrived at the Denver airport he found himself surrounded by hundreds of exuberant Continental employees, wearing buttons and carrying posters. Over 400 employees crowded the conference room in a downtown hotel which had a capacity for only 350.

The employee buttons and posters displayed a theme conceived by a new marketing department employee, Jack Riddle. Searching for a slogan, Riddle thought of Continental's traditional advertising theme stressing pride. He explains, "People would react to that word as a trigger more than any other because there *was* pride in the company." In an audacious anticipation of victory, the first graphic materials that Riddle designed proclaimed, "We're the company pride built (and bought)."

The conference room was decorated with banners as if for a political rally, and employees sat behind signs identifying their cities of origin. The program included speeches by two management representatives, Jack Sage and Barrie Duggan, and brief exhortations by members of the CEA board, but Eckel enjoyed center stage. As he described the ESOP, he spoke confidently, almost triumphantly, and enlisted the audience in a David and Goliath struggle in which they could not fail to succeed. He was interrupted after an hour's presentation by a telephone call from Senator Russell Long. Returning to the podium, he announced that Senator Long was going to speak in favor of the ESOP on the floor of the Senate the next day. Referring to himself as "your chairman," he declared in a tone of evangelical self-assurance:

Your chairman wrote a very gutsy letter early this morning about 6 o'clock that was so persuasive that the most powerful man in the United States, next to Reagan, is going on the floor of the Senate and make a few comments as to what is happening at Continental and how the company can be an example to companies all over the country. You can be very proud of yourself.

Court files have left a detailed record of the meeting, but the most important element, the mood of the employees who crowded the room to hear an utterly unexpected promise of self-determination, is best preserved in two letters. A Los Angeles employee, Betty Roth, wrote to Eckel:

Paul:
I sat in on the meeting in DEN yesterday (4/7) and had to drop you a note about how absolutely dynamite the whole meeting was. In my ten years at CO, I've never felt such a surge of 'pride', esprit de corps, whatever, that I felt on leaving that meeting. And everyone I talked to felt exactly the same way.
We all owe you a big debt for giving us the needed jolt to get us out of our apathy. If there's anything I can do to help, please let me know.
Congratulations! We're all behind you.

Betty

An airport sales agent from Tulsa, Oklahoma, addressed a letter to Lorenzo:

Mr. Lorenzo:
As a Continental Airlines employee for the past 14 years I, with the help of the Continental Employees' Association will do all in our power to stop the current attempt by you to control "Our Airline". If you think the Japanese awoke a "sleeping giant" at Pearl Harbor, just watch what 10,400 dedicated employees at the "Proud Bird" are doing.

*The pride at Continental has extended over 38 years
and millions of dedicated passengers who use Our Airline. I will not standby and see this destroyed for a few
dollars gain by Texas Air Corporation.*

Respectfully,
Gary R. Bilbrey

The ESOP idea had clearly struck a responsive chord among
many employees. The Continental Employees' Association,
which had been Eckel's personal dream, sanctioned and assisted by management, now existed as an authentic employee
movement under Eckel's leadership.

The employees returned to their bases to explain the ESOP
to their co-workers and to form a network of CEA representatives. San Jose ticket agent Pat Simpson found that other employees were skeptical at first but warmed to the idea of the
ESOP as soon as they were persuaded that it was feasible:

> They were skeptical at first. They thought it was some
> harebrained-scheme. But I explained it as they explained
> it to me and then the light went on. After a while just
> about everyone was for it. It gave them a little hope.
> People thought they would be a partner in the airline
> and would have an actual say-so instead of being a
> drone out there. It was a chance to get out to contribute
> something and be a part of something instead of being
> a mere employee. . . . It was super!

Eckel had appealed to employees to chose team leaders; concurrently, Sage notified supervisors of the need for local CEA
representatives. As a consequence of this double appeal, some
team leaders were appointed by station managers and others
were chosen by the employees themselves. In Portland, Oregon,
Craig Adcox became de facto the city captain when he volun-
teered to report about the Denver meeting in two general
employee meetings. There was no formal election, but he
insists, "The supervisors had nothing to do with it." Although

the team leaders sometimes worked with union members, they were without exception noncontract employees.

Since management sought to maintain a low profile, it fell on Eckel to publicly announce the ESOP plan in a press conference on April 8. The ESOP, he declared, presented an issue of human freedom: "This allows us to control our own destiny. We're not selling an investment. We are selling control of their (employees) future."[1] Alluding to the fact that Lorenzo's bid of $93 million equaled three months' payroll at Continental, he explained, "The whole purpose of our association is to gain *some* way to gain control of our destiny. We just resented the dickens out of somebody coming in and taking us over for three months payroll and being in charge of our lives." Eckel mixed his advocacy of the ESOP with a vision of a revivified capitalism: "The way of the future is for American employees to be owners of their companies and we think there is an increment of motivation that will come from that. That is the ultimate expression of deregulation, to let the employees rise up and own their own company. That's capitalism, that's Americanism, that's what we're all about in this country." It must be added that Eckel spiced his arguments with the inflammatory theory that Lorenzo would sell off Continental aircraft. Noting that TI had transferred assets to Texas Air Corporation, he flatly stated, "We're afraid he'll raid our fleet."

Over a thousand employees filled the inner courtyard and crowded around the office windows of the corporate headquarters to listen to Eckel at a rally that followed the press conference. Taking credit for the ESOP idea, Eckel rode the wave of excitement triggered by the Denver meeting. "I've been listening to Eckel for two days now, and he's wonderful," said Jan Appanaitis, a computer programmer. "He's really worked on it, and I believe it would be beneficial." A ramp worker, Robert McCleery, added, "I've come a long way with this company. I'll be damned if I'm going to give it away to a Texas airline."[2] Some employees readily accepted the notion of the takeover bid as a threatened asset raid. "Lorenzo is a snake in the grass," said Joan Kepp, a ticket agent. "He's in this to make money and destroy our airline."[3] But many saw a value in the ESOP quite apart from its effect on the takeover struggle. "I wanted the Continental I knew to survive," says flight attendant supervisor John Bailey. "This seemed to be the only way it could be done in a deregulated environment. It was the only way to get union and nonunion people together." When the rally was in full swing, Feldman was seen watching from the window of a third floor executive office. In response to a spontaneous acclamation of the crowd, he came down to the patio to say a few words. A photograph in the *Los Angeles Herald Examiner* caught the normally self-controlled Feldman smiling broadly in response to an employee question.

As the ESOP surfaced as a viable proposal, the board of directors did no more than authorize the employee poll. The actual design and negotiation of the ESOP was largely deferred until the vote was known. Two meetings of the executive committee on March 31 and April 3 were followed by a meeting of the full board on April 6, the day before the Denver meeting. The Board then gave the green light. A letter of Eckel's, accompanied by a ballot, was put in the mail immediately following the meeting. The letter, which had passed through the scrutiny of a series of executives and lawyers, exposed employees to a muted version of Eckel's rhetoric playing both to the employees' fears and idealism.

April 5, 1981

Dear Fellow Employee:

Many Continental employees are concerned about the future of our airline and our jobs if Texas International is allowed to complete its takeover of Continental.

We don't want to entrust our jobs and our futures to Frank Lorenzo, who has already diverted assets from Texas International in order to start New York Air, an operation known for its substandard wages and benefits. In seeking to combine Texas International and Continental, Mr. Lorenzo has refused to commit to Labor Protective Provisions which have been standard in every airline combination.

As most of you are aware by now, we have established the Continental Airlines Employees' Association to formulate a plan that will enable the employees of Continental Airlines to preserve its independence and to guide and participate in its future.

We have met for hundreds of hours with independent lawyers and financial experts and with management. Now we are ready to propose a plan that would enable the employees of Continental to participate in an Employee Stock Ownership Plan which would acquire a controlling stock interest in the company. If supported by all employee groups and success-fully carried out, this plan would prevent Mr. Lorenzo or any other outsider from unilaterally dictating decisions that will shape the future for us and our airline.

The Employee Stock Ownership Plan, "ESOP" for short, would work like this:

1. Continental Airlines would establish the ESOP by set-ting up a trust for its employees.

2. The trust would obtain a bank loan with which to buy shares of Continental Airlines stock. The company would guarantee the loan.

3. The number of shares purchased would give the ESOP controlling interest in Continental. These shares would be either newly issued stock purchased from Continen-tal, stock purchased from existing shareholders or some combination of both.

4. As the loan is paid off, over a four- to seven-year pe-riod, the shares of stock that are paid for would be credited to each Continental employee.

Nobody wants to take a cut in present pay levels or bene-fits as Braniff employees recently did. Our proposal, therefore, is that the company divert to the ESOP a portion of the funds which it otherwise would use to provide future pay increases to us.

This plan would make our jobs more secure by strengthening Continental Airlines. For one thing, the ownership and control of the company would be placed in the hands of its employees. It would be OUR company, not Texas International's. Since it's our company, we would all have an incentive to work harder and to make it successful. We would be more competitive and better able to protect our company from transactions which would not be in the best interest of Continental, its shareholders and its employees.

The cost will be substantial (perhaps as much as $185 million) and the success of this plan will depend on us, the employees. With success, we will gain an increased stake in the future of our company. But management has indicated that it will recommend this plan to Continental's Board of Directors only if a majority of our employees support this program.

Before you mark the enclosed ballot, consider the alternatives.

If Texas International succeeds in taking over Continental on terms which they have proposed to date, the result will be an airline in worse financial shape than Braniff. We believe that our future would be as precarious as that of Braniff's employees.

On the other hand, by committing part of our pay increases over the immediate future in an independent Continental Airlines, we can secure our jobs and control the future of our airline by our own efforts.

If you want more information, please attend the meetings that the Continental Employees' Association will be holding throughout the system during the next two weeks.

Then, . . . VOTE!

The decision is yours, as it should be. Any questions that you may have should be directed to the Continental Employees' Association at (213) 615-0411.

> *Sincerely,*
> *Paul Eckel*
> *Chairman*
> *Continental Employees' Association*

A ballot enclosed with the letter presented the question:

As a Continental employee would you be willing to forego a portion of your future pay increases to participate in an employee stock ownership plan that would give Continental employees the controlling interest in Continental Airlines?

☐ Yes ☐ No

Although he wished to remain publicly aloof from the ESOP, Feldman took a big step toward committing himself to the plan by mailing to all employees a copy of his letter to Lorenzo opposing a merger with TI. The ESOP was, after all, the only remaining alternative to the takeover. The letter explains Feldman's concern that the merger would lead to a weakened carrier:

April 3, 1984

Mr. Francisco A. Lorenzo
Chairman of the Executive Committee
Texas International Airlines
P. O. Box 12788
Houston, Texas 77017

Dear Frank:

Thank you for your letter of March 13, 1981, describing your plans for the merger of Texas International and Continental. I appreciate your assurances that you do not intend to liquidate or dismember Continental. Thank you also for your kind words about Bob Six and myself. I especially appreciate your expression of respect for Mr. Six. All of us at Continental stand in his shadow.

As you know, I do not believe that a merger of Texas International and Continental makes good business sense. Since I came to Continental, we have studied every reasonable alternative to help us complete the transition precipitated by deregulation, including possible mergers with several other airlines. Of those we have studied, a Continental-Texas International merger has always finished last. The consistent conclusion of our analyses has been that a merged Continental-Texas International would not be a substantially stronger company, that it could do nothing that Continental alone cannot do as well or better.

Neither airline would lend significant traffic support to the existing operations of the other and the merger would produce no major cost savings. But the successful integration of two very different operations, our separate labor forces, our fleets and facilities would be a costly enterprise. In the absence of a significant increase in revenues and/or a substantial reduction in expenses as a result of the combination of our two systems, I can see no justification for incurring the expense and disruption of a merger.

. . . .

We cannot accept a proposal that is not fair to our remaining public shareholders. Any merger must be fair as well to our employees. Continental's employees have borne the largest burden in building our great airline and must not be treated as pawns in a financial transaction.

We have received through your investment bankers an outline of your plan. As I understand your proposal, you intend to effect the consolidation of the two airlines through a two-step transaction. In the first step, you would pass the 48.5% of Continental's stock now owned by Texas International up to Texas International's parent, Texas Air Corporation, while leaving the cost of that stock an obligation on the books of Texas International. The result of that first step is to reduce your equity in Texas International by about $93 million. Since Texas International has a present net worth of only $53 million, that would leave Texas International with a negative shareholders equity of $40 million.

In the second step of the transaction, Texas International and Continental would be merged into a new company in which you expect to receive 56% of the common stock—in exchange for Texas International's negative net worth and your minority

position in Continental—while Continental's public shareholders would be diluted from their present majority position
to 44% of the common stock, plus shares of a non-voting
preferred. In effect, the new company would end up paying off
the debt Texas International incurred to buy its Continental
stock.

Your proposal hardly seems fair. But, more important, the
resulting company would be very weak. I believe its chances
for survival would be poor. Even before it purchased Continental's stock, Texas International was a highly leveraged
company with $183 million in debt and only $53 million in
equity. When you add to Texas International the burden of the
additional borrowings you made to purchase the Continental
stock, the situation becomes almost intolerable. The combined
company would have long term obligations of $642 million,
and equity of only $142 million. This results in an 82:18 debt
to equity ratio, which is worse than Braniff Airways at the end
of 1979. More importantly, the debt service coverage requirement, including the dividend on the preferred stock you propose, approaches $150 million annually. The operating profit
required to service this debt is more than our two companies
together have ever earned. Even a modest program of fleet
modernization would result in a further serious burdening of
an already overburdened company. . . .

It may be possible to salvage this situation but only by selling off a major part of Continental's fleet so as to realize the
market premium over book value. Such a course of action would
be in direct conflict with your assurance to me that you do not
intend to dismember Continental. The possibility of a planned
partial liquidation of Continental as a mechanism for the new
company to pay off the costs of your stock acquisition looms
large in our people's minds as a possible explanation of your
continued and adamant rejection of the standard Labor Protective Provisions. I believe these provisions are appropriate to
provide a safety net for the hard working and loyal employees
that might be adversely affected by your plans.

· · · ·

Finally, I must tell you that each day more of our employees come forward to manifest their resolve to reject your bid for control of Continental. They are determined to oppose you with every means at their disposal. In the face of their determination, it may not be possible to merge our two airlines.

Sincerely,

A. L. Feldman

"The ESOP caught us totally by surprise," says Phil Bakes. TI issued a press release promising that it would "redouble its efforts, if necessary, to complete its acquisition of Continental Airlines."[4] The next day TI sent each Continental director a telegram several feet long that set forth grounds for charging him with personal liability: it alleged that the plan was a scheme to "entrench and protect current management" and that it violated the directors' fiduciary duties under civil and criminal provisions of securities law, the Railway Labor Act, and the Employee Retirement Income Security Act. "You could almost see the directors physically react as they read the telegram," Mike Roach remembers. TI gave the directors four days to order Feldman to kill the ESOP.

In the words of Julian Levine, vice-president of public relations, Continental's board of directors was "largely a function of Six." The seven outside directors were Six's personal friends who possessed a degree of wealth that made compensation for their services unimportant; they received an annual stipend of only $4,800, plus a fee of $100 for each meeting attended. Six's wife, the former actress Audrey Meadows, was an advisory director. For a group that had little personally to gain and much to lose in the struggle, the board showed considerable backbone in standing up to the threat of litigation—an attitude that was no doubt fortified by the fact that the company carried fiduciary liability insurance. The day before the deadline the executive committee of the board reaffirmed its previous decision to authorize the employee poll. As Lorenzo had threatened, TI filed an action in federal court on April 17 seeking to enjoin the ESOP and charging the directors and management with personal liability.

Before filing the lawsuit, Lorenzo responded to Feldman's April 3 letter in a forceful statement of TI's case. He now retracted the oral merger proposal that had been offered by Hotz and Snedeker on March 18, characterizing it as a "strawman":

April 14, 1981

Mr. A. L. Feldman
President
Continental Air Lines, Inc.
7300 World Way West
Los Angeles, California 90009

Dear Al:

I am in receipt of your letter of April 3, which was hand delivered to my office on April 8, 1981, after I learned of its contents from news services. While normally we would not respond to such an obvious publicity stunt, the false and misleading statements contained in your letter require a response in order to provide a more accurate picture to Continental's employees, directors and shareholders, as well as the general public. As a consequence, we are publicly releasing this letter.

As you know, I believe a merger of Continental and Texas International would make good business sense. As I have already outlined to you, Continental lacks some of the basic strengths of Texas International, which if added to Continental could forge an attractive entity for the deregulated 1980's.

Two of Texas International's most important strengths are its fuel efficient fleet of short-haul twin-jet aircraft, and its already well developed hub and spoke system, particularly at Houston. Texas International is one of the few carriers in the business that did not burden itself with substantial orders for large aircraft which deregulation and a downturn in the economy have made increasingly difficult to fill. Rather, we chose to increase and emphasize one basic efficient aircraft type.

As you are aware, we have emphasized a hub system which would be extremely compatible with Continental's longer haul operations at Houston and provide the opportunity for a better use of Continental's long-haul aircraft. Texas International's DC-9 aircraft would make attractive and profitable substitutes for some of Continental's expensive short-haul flying with large aircraft never designed for that purpose. The DC-9 aircraft would also contribute passenger feed for Continental to other hubs such as Denver.

In addition, Texas International has important financial strengths. As you know, we have a low cost structure which could help moderate Continental's already high costs. Also, our financial structure is particularly sound. While your letter says that we have an unfavorable debt-equity ratio, it avoids mentioning that most all of our pre-acquisition debt is long-term relatively low-interest rate debt and that the Company holds substantial cash balances and short term investments.

We have no evidence that you have studied the benefits of a combination of our two companies with an open mind. Yet, you claimed in your letter that Texas International never ranked very high in your so-called "merger studies". I have repeatedly asked you for the studies that gave rise to your assertion that you are not excited about a Texas International-Continental combination and you have repeatedly referred me to your CAB submission, which, of course, shows that Western Airlines is the answer to all of Continental's problems.

Your letter leaves the impression that Texas International has prepared and submitted a formal merger proposal to Continental through our investment banker. As you know, no such proposal has been submitted. In fact, the only prior written communication between our companies that contained anything remotely connected with a merger proposal was my letter to you of March 13, 1981, which apparently you chose not to make public. I attach a copy to refresh your memory.

In creating and then knocking down a strawman—the so-called merger proposal—your letter mischaracterized the few discussions that we and our investment bankers did have in which we suggested a number of concepts that might form the basis for negotiations leading to a Continental-Texas International amalgamation.

This sudden uprising on the part of Continental's employees in support of your management and opposed to a Texas International acquisition is being fueled by the promise of an employee stock ownership plan.

The stock ownership plan currently being promised to the employees of Continental is instead a management protection plan. If successful, the plan will operate to entrench current management, dilute existing shareholders by 50%, create a corporate liability on your balance sheet of $185 million, jeopardize the company's ability to finance itself in the future and its status as a New York Stock Exchange listed company, and subject the company and its directors to civil and potential criminal liability. It is a base perversion of the ESOP concept.

It is unfortunate knowing your fine record at Frontier Airlines, that you would help lead such a scheme—all for the avowed purpose of maintaining top management control of Continental. In our view, the scheme is not only a waste of corporate assets and opportunities, but a cynical and very unfair use of your employees—a dedicated and professional group of men and women who deserve better.

Al, I must say how surprised and disappointed I am at where we find ourselves today. I was confident that patient and intelligent negotiations conducted in good faith by us were about to begin and would have produced a sensible merger agreement benefiting our shareholders, our employees and our companies. Our goal remains the same and we will pursue it as diligently and responsibly as we can.

Sincerely,
Frank Lorenzo

After mailing the ballots for the employee poll, the Continental management staged a series of corporate update meetings that gave CEA representatives an opportunity to advocate a yes vote. The company had long followed the practice of holding these meetings two or three times a year, but the meetings in April 1981 were unique in organization and scale. Nine teams —consisting of an executive, a member of the personnel department, a freshly commissioned member of the CEA board of directors and a representative of Kelso & Company—were formed to visit thirty-three cities in a ten-day period. The two-hour meetings followed the same agenda: the executives gave a briefing on Continental's financial situation, alluding to the unfavorable aspects of the takeover bid; a CEA board member then took the floor to explain the ESOP with the aid of a slide show; and a Kelso & Company representative stood by to answer technical questions. The Wachtell, Lipton lawyer, Erica Steinberger, established guidelines for the presentation of the ESOP to employees. The CEA representatives were to avoid statements opposing the TI takeover and any speculation as to the value of the ESOP as an investment but rather were to advocate the plan as an experiment in corporate democracy.

"It was a blockbuster for us presenting it," says dispatcher Ron Aramini. "People were very inquisitive." In Midland, Texas, the city manager, Chuck Logue, arranged for extensive press and TV coverage. "I'm excited about it," he told a reporter. True to his guidelines, Chuck Widel, the CEA board member, insisted, "Texas International has nothing to do with it. We're just trying to control our destiny."[5] Plainly touched by the outburst of employee emotion, Feldman edged toward a personal commitment to the ESOP. Seeking further reassurrance, he went again and again through the logic behind the plan in private discussions with advisors, but as he took the plan to employees, he seemed to be swept by degrees into the current of general enthusiasm. He originally planned to give corporate update presentations at the major bases unaccompanied by any CEA representative, but at the last moment he allowed Eckel to speak after him in Denver. Elsewhere, he offered personally to answer questions about the ESOP. Attributing the idea to Eckel, he prefaced his answers with the disclaimer, "To the best I understand it. . . ." When pressed about his position, he adopted the ruse of saying, "Well, I really can't say that but . . ." Here, to the delight of the crowd, he stretched back his shoulders and revealed a CEA button pinned to his shirt, proclaiming "Continental the Airline Pride Built (and Bought)."

As employees marked their ballots, Bill Miles believes they "were voting on emotion—on a chance to own the company." Jeannette Martin remarks that many corporate headquarters employees were willing to "go along" with the ESOP because of the tacit support of management. Whatever the mix of motives, the employees supported the ESOP with extraordinary unanimity. The accounting firm of Peat, Marwick, Mitchell and Company received unopened all ballots sent to the CEA office, and it announced the results of the poll on April 21. With 85 percent of employees voting, 96.7 percent voted to forego a portion of future pay increases to secure a controlling interest in the company.

CHAPTER
FIVE

THE ESOP
TAKES FORM

The ESOP would not only cause Continental to be, by some measures, the largest employee-owned company in the United States, but it was designed to have certain uniquely democratic features. Roland Attenborough, special counsel to Kelso & Company, describes it as "far and away the most liberal ESOP in the country."

ESOP provisions regarding trust administration are commonly drafted to avoid any real concession of control by management. The trust holding the employer stock purchased on behalf of employees is ordinarily administered by a management committee which has full power to vote the stock. The Continental ESOP departed from the pattern. The administrative committee consisted of representatives of seven employee groups. More important, the individual employees rather than the administrative committee controlled the voting of stock held by the trust. As the loan was repaid, stock would be allocated to individual employee's accounts with full voting rights, and the administrative committee would vote the unallocated stock in the same proportion as the employees themselves voted the allocated stock. In determining this proportion, the committee would ignore the actual number of shares voted by individual employees and would instead give each employee one vote. Thus, the unallocated shares would be voted on the principle of one man, one vote.

The provisions regarding vesting and participation completed the democratic design of the ESOP. The term vesting refers to the acquisition of nonforfeitable rights to benefits; participation refers to the eligibility of employees to begin to accrue rights to benefits. As an employee benefit plan subject to the Employee Retirement Income Security Act, an ESOP must adhere to certain minimum guidelines with respect to these matters. The vesting provisions, for example, must meet one of three minimum schedules under which stock allocated to individual accounts becomes nonforfeitable after a period of time. The provisions of the Continental ESOP were very simple: all stock allocated to an individual's account became immediately vested, and all employees from their first day of employment began to accrue rights to stock ownership.

The Kelso & Company attorney, Roland Attenborough, who has helped design over three hundred ESOPs, says that the employee-controlled administrative committee was "new in my experience." He adds that the provision that unallocated stock would be voted proportionately to allocated stock was "more liberal and democratic than any voting provision I had seen in any ESOP in the country." Management may have supported the startlingly liberal one-man-one-vote provision partly to dilute pilot influence. From the first days of Eckel's movement, according to Mike Roach, management rejected every scheme—and there were a number—for pilot control of the airline. The top executives agreed that this generously compensated group should not be given the power to aggrandize its position. The pilots represented 11.8 percent of the work force but 28.5 percent of the payroll. The one-man-one-vote rule gave pilots the power to vote only 5.9 percent of the outstanding stock in the first year of the plan. But the democratic character of the ESOP also reflected a desire of management to keep faith with employees. The three executives most responsible for the design of the plan—Feldman, Sage, and Roach—believed they could best retain employee support for wage concessions and productivity improvements by giving employees the rights they might expect to have as shareholders, free of the limitations customarily hidden in technical ESOP provisions. Only one CEA representative, Chuck Cheeld, actually participated in the design of the plan. He remembers the series of drafting sessions as being "brainstorming sessions," rather than negotiations, in which he enjoyed common interests and objectives with other participants.

The negotiation of the ESOP financing proceeded in a separate sphere, having little connection with the design of the plan. Continental's banks had been contacted as soon as the ESOP emerged as a possible alternative, and with the notable exception of Chase Manhattan, their response was generally favorable. The ESOP would involve an additional extension of credit, but it would also give the banks an opportunity to improve the quality of their existing loans. Continental had a bank debt of $150 million which it could pay off by selling stock to the ESOP trust. The trust would presumably borrow from some of the same banks to finance the purchase of the stock. Thus, the banks could finance much of the credit by merely shifting their loans from the airline to the ESOP trust. The total cost of the ESOP—representing the current market value of 15.4 million shares—was estimated to be $185 million, only $35 million more than the bank debt.

As it turned out, Continental entered into negotiations with nine of its twenty-five banks which then held 55 percent of its bank debt. Management had expected Chase Manhattan, which held 30 percent of the bank debt, to go along with the ESOP. But Chase was, according to some observers, increasingly committed to TI and refused even to consider shifting its existing $45 million in loans from the airline to the ESOP. Chase's decision represented a gamble that TI would prevail. If the ESOP were consummated, Continental would retire all Chase's loans with the proceeds from the sale of stock to the ESOP trust, ending the bank's long business relationship with the company.

Continental could not hope to interest the banks in the ESOP without offering a guarantee of the ESOP loan supported by a mortgage of aircraft. The mortgaging of Continental's valuable fleet was, however, a concession that management would have to face anyway in its next round of bank negotiations. Most other fleets in the industry were fully collateralized. The previous year, Chase Manhattan had secured the closest thing to a pledge of the fleet: a pledge not to offer a security interest in the fleet to another party without its consent. In February 1981, Continental had already fallen in default under one of the financial covenants. Management knew that by offering a portion of its fleet as collateral it would be giving voluntarily a concession that it could not long postpone.

Even without Chase Manhattan's support, the company obtained financial commitments for the ESOP loan with unexpected ease. In the week following a lenders presentation on April 8, Continental received tentative commitments of $195.5 million from the nine banks—more than it had sought. The commitments contemplated a secured loan of $185 million extending over a six- to seven-year period. Two major breaks, Security Pacific National Bank and the First National Bank of Chicago, offered credits of $43 million and $40 million respectively. In an apparent bid to replace Chase Manhattan as Continental's lead bank, they agreed to serve as co-agents of the transaction. One of the nine banks, the Bank of America, offered to do little more than shift its existing loan from the airline to the ESOP, but the other banks contemplated large additional extensions of credit. The commitments of Security Pacific and First Chicago both entailed an additional $28 million credit above their existing loans of $15 million and $12 million.

According to the controller, Mike Conway, the bankers were mainly concerned with the business rationale of the transaction. "We had to convince them of the business merits of the ESOP," he says. For the conservative bankers, the attraction of the transaction lay in the reduction of debt, not in employee ownership. Richard Simons of Crocker National Bank wrote:

> The major business risk associated with the ESOP centers around labor's increased power. With the employees having a 51 percent interest in the company, there is the risk that management would be hampered in its ability to negotiate future labor contracts or to initiate cutbacks in operation when faced with economic downturns.

Daniel Stebben of Security Pacific actually visited a CEA meeting at the corporate headquarters on April 17 to obtain some firsthand impressions. He reported in a memo to file:

> There was standing room only in the cafeteria and balcony with overflow into the hallway. The employees did not appear intimidated or shy in terms of asking pointed questions and the spontaneous response indicated a very upbeat, motivated group.

The banks contemplated this major extension of credit at a time when Continental was under financial pressure; it was seeking to loosen its financial covenants to avoid default at the same time that it was asking for more credit. The bankers found some reassurance in the value of the fleet as collateral, but they relied chiefly on Continental's projection of a financial recovery. The company had indeed suffered a $21.8 million loss in the first quarter, traditionally the poorest quarter in the year, but the loss would have been considerably less if it had not included the cost of restoring normal operations after the flight attendant strike. The company had actually done better in the quarter than indicated by its own financial projections. The airline was well along in a process of restructuring its routes to a dual hub system which, it was believed, would allow it to compete in the new deregulated environment. The market planning department expected a $25.3 million profit in the third quarter resulting from increased traffic and higher yields. The projection assumed that, as in the past, the increased demand for air travel in the summer season would lead to an easing of price competition. By year-end, the projections predicted $11.4 million in net earnings. The banks were convinced that this financial outlook was realistic. In an internal memo dated May 6, Daniel Stebben of Security Pacific wrote, "We are comforted that their projections are conservative."

By April 15, the financial structure of the ESOP was well enough defined that the transaction could be referred to the commitments committee of Lehman Brothers. As a practical matter, the blessing of Lehman Brothers was as important as the approval of any government agency. The Continental board of directors, attentive to its fiduciary responsibilities, would not act against the advice of its chief financial advisor. After two meetings, the commitments committee declared itself prepared to offer a favorable opinion, affirming among other things that the transaction would create a financially stronger company.

The evaluation of Lehman Brothers, like that of Continental's bankers, relied heavily on the fact the ESOP would strengthen Continental's balance sheet by making a $185 million contribution to shareholders' equity over a six and a half year period (see Continental's balance sheet in appendix 1). But the impact of the ESOP on book value per share was more equivocal. The issuance of 15.4 million shares would immediately slice in half the book value per share, but over the term of the ESOP the book value was expected to improve, as indicated by the following year-end projection:

1980	1981	1982	1983	1984	1985	1986
12.44	6.93	8.52	10.86	13.66	16.88	19.35

Moreover, if Continental should default on the ESOP, the pre-ESOP book value per share would be restored since the ESOP stock would be retired or held as treasury stock. On either assumption—repayment or default—the shareholders would eventually come out whole, despite the initial dilution in book value per share. Accordingly, Continental's accounting firm, Peat, Marwick, Mitchell and Company, offered the opinion that the ESOP would not "effectively" dilute the shareholders' interest.

By eliminating the existing bank debt, the ESOP would sharply reduce interest expense and thus significantly improve Continental's reported income. In 1982 alone it would boost income by $22 million. The impact on earnings per share, however, was not so clearly favorable. Management distributed the following projection (all figures in millions):

	Net earnings before ESOP	Earnings per share	After tax interest saving	Net earnings after ESOP	Earnings per share after ESOP
1981	12	.78	11	23	1.00
1982	14	.91	22	36	1.17
1983	16	1.04	19	35	1.14
1984	19	1.24	13	32	1.04
1985	23	1.50	13	36	1.17
1986	27	1.76	13	40	1.30

But what would be the impact on the ESOP on employee productivity? Having experienced costly pilot and flight attendant strikes, Jack Sage, the vice-president of personnel relations, was strongly disposed to pursue a cooperative rather than a confrontational approach to labor relations. He thought that a democratically designed ESOP would be a promising alternative:

> We needed productivity gains in order to price our product on a competitive basis. We had investigated a number of ways to do this. We had looked at Japanese methods of management, looked at European methods, we had even developed a plan to begin a quality circle approach to improved productivity. We had also negotiated with our pilots the first clause that I knew of in any pilot agreement, which set up a committee of management and pilots to explore all possibilities of productivity improvements. The ESOP appeared to be a new and better alternative to establish a platform for improved productivity.

In later CAB testimony, Sage tried to make a defensible estimate of the productivity improvement that would flow from the ESOP. His estimate was very conservative—the potential productivity improvements in each employee group were far greater—and it was based on detailed plans and actual discussions with two of the three major unions. The causal connection was, however, uncertain; one could argue that the same improvements could be effected without an ESOP or, conversely, that the ESOP would lead to larger improvements. Sage's estimate was really only a conjecture, but it served to illustrate that labor productivity was a large enough factor to make a critical difference in evaluating the ESOP. If the estimated productivity improvement were added to estimated savings on interest expense, the ESOP would have a clearly beneficial impact on earnings per share:

Earnings Per Share

	No ESOP	*With ESOP*	
		Interest Savings	*Employee Productivity Added*
1981	.78	1.00	1.00
1982	.91	1.17	1.30
1983	1.04	1.14	1.48
1984	1.24	1.04	1.55
1985	1.50	1.17	1.87
1986	1.76	1.30	2.24

Wall Street reacted to the ESOP with apparent ambivalence: the announcement of the ESOP and the later news of its fortunes had little effect on the price of Continental stock. The published comments of stock analysts, however, were often favorable. Continental retained the financial public relations firm of Kekst and Company to arrange a presentation of the ESOP to stock analysts in New York. The meeting was well attended, and a number of analysts were evidently persuaded of the merits of the plan. David P. Campbell, first vice-president at Wheat First Securities, remarked, "I'm not worried about the additional shares that will be issued because the plan would improve the company's financial structure and balance sheet." Similarly, Betsy Synder, analyst at L. F. Rochschild Unterberg Towbin, advised, "Shareholders should just hold on to their stock as it seems holders will benefit from the ESOP."[1] An unidentified analyst quoted by *Aviation Daily* stressed the issue of productivity: "That productivity is the most important part of this whole thing, and we're talking about an industry that has had both union and productivity problems in the past. Any improvements achieved this way would have to be beneficial."[2]

TI discounted the idea that the ESOP would lead to productivity gains and advanced a contrary thesis: the ESOP would sanction uncontrolled wage demands. Attorney Peter Kreindler declared, "Defendant's (Continental) fatuous assertion that the employees will not use their voting control of the company to exact higher wages . . . merits only a brief comment." In a more extended statement, Douglas Tansill, an investment banker for Kidder, Peabody, argued that all the financial benefits of the ESOP were "illusory" because they depended on the assumption that employees would forego future pay increases equal to the company's contribution to the ESOP. Instead, he suggested that ESOP would lead to increased labor costs that would in turn cancel out other benefits:

> In my opinion, however, the employees—many of whom are represented by unions—would have a strong incentive . . . to seek to boost their wages by more than they would have without the ESOP in order to cushion the effect of the ESOP contributions on their take-home pay. More than that, with voting control of the company and four representatives on the board of directors, the employees should be able to obtain such wage increases.

These increased costs might force cutbacks in the work force which would further upset plans to fund the ESOP out of projected wage increases.

The criticisms of the TI spokesman indeed focused on the

most critical question: the employee capacity for self-determination. It was a question that really turned on differing views of human nature, and in the heat of the struggle, the sides divided into optimists and pessimists. The Continental management looked optimistically to the democratic character of the ESOP as a guarantee of employee trust. Management knew it lacked any enforceable guarantees that employees would actually consent to the wage concessions approved in the employee poll. The amendment of union contracts offered only a short-term solution since the ESOP extended well beyond the term of the contracts. Moreover, management had exacted no specific productivity concessions. The theory of productivity gains rested on the untested premise that, if employees were given a more direct stake in the airline, they would take the action needed to safeguard their jobs in the rigorous competitive climate of deregulation.

Three years after the struggle, Phil Bakes still feels driven to an interpretation of the ESOP that appears to reflect a pessimistic, Hobbesian view of employee self-determination. In the course of an hour and a half interview, he repeatedly referred to the employee movement as a "Frankenstein." Adopting the same premise as Jack Sage, he stressed that the airline faced a need for dramatic improvements in productivity. "The real question," he says, "was: how do you reduce labor costs? how do you bring reality to a work force that had been so pampered?" The ESOP, he insists, was exactly the wrong answer because it would have put the very employees whose payroll needed to be trimmed in control of the enterprise. Carrying the argument further, he takes the surprising position that the ESOP would put the unions in a controlling position. "It was clear that if the ESOP succeeded the company was dead," he says. "The labor negotiations would be handled by a company controlled by unions." Lorenzo similarly saw employee democracy as an "absurd" response to the need to cut Continental's labor costs—a step in the wrong direction. During the takeover battle, he predicted that Continental would "die on the vine" if the ESOP were adopted. What was needed was to secure concessions by confronting employees with economic realities. "We're going to bring the real world to them, in terms of seeking increased productivity," he asserted. "And that's something they have to face up to. This company's not going to make it with mirrors, but with honest, realistic dealings with employees."[3]

Despite the abundance of financial analyses, the prospects of the ESOP ultimately rested on the probable employee response to the opportunity of self-determination. Were the optimists or the pessimists correct? If any significance can be given to the indifferent response of the stock market, it is that the two arguments were a wash. Jack Sage himself will say only that the democratically conceived ESOP was well worth trying:

> There were a variety of prognostications about the effect of the ESOP. Some thought it would do away with the unions; others that it would do away with supervisors. Some thought it would bring about a kind of egalitarianism that would lead to reduced executive salaries and the elimination of executive perquisities. Nobody knew. It was going to be a wonderful experiment. We thought it was well worth trying and it might be revolutionary.

CHAPTER
SIX

THE APPEAL
FOR
PUBLIC SUPPORT

Not long after the ESOP emerged as a viable defense, Feldman found a remarkable career opportunity offering a personal escape from the battle. Denver oilman Marvin Davis, who had just negotiated an agreement to purchase Twentieth Century Fox for $800 million, offered him the job of chief executive officer of the motion picture company, then expanding into soft drink bottling, telecommunications, and resort operations. Davis wanted a strong, impartial executive to impart a sense of direction to the company's management which was then divided into feuding factions. The offer appealed to Feldman's self-image as a professional manager. He told Robert Six that he liked the idea of taking a job outside the airline industry —he had indeed turned Frontier Airlines around without any previous experience with air carriers. But he could not bring himself to abandon the company at this time. Deeply conscious of his responsibility in leading the takeover battle into a new phase, he felt personally committed to the struggle. George Vandeman, who privately encouraged Feldman to take the job, recalls that he "was not willing to make a move until he had brought the takeover defense to a conclusion he could live with."

Feldman pressed hard for a winning strategy in endless discussions with professional advisors in the small conference room next to his office. Unlike Lorenzo, who traveled restlessly around the country, hosting press conferences and cultivating personal contacts in the centers of financial and political power, Feldman wanted to conduct the defense in a private manner at his own command post in the corporate headquarters. Apart from a few trips to New York, he stayed within a narrow perimeter of the executive office in Los Angeles. In resolving the complicated issues of the takeover defense, he relied chiefly on a small corps of lawyers: executive assistant, Mike Roach; CAB counsel, Lee Hydeman; lead counsel, George Vandeman; and the Wachtell, Lipton lawyers, Erica Steinberger and Bernard Nussbaum. Other advisors or executives were invited if the discussion related to their area of responsibility.

The strategy sessions often opened with a few moments of banter—Nussbaum could be counted on for a note of ebullient good humor—but the mood of conviviality did not last long. Always conscious of his position and responsibilities, Feldman dominated the meetings with a controlled emotional intensity: presenting questions for discussion, cutting in to ask for clarifications, and seeking an intense examination of every issue. The talented defense team possessed a chemistry that guaranteed lively, free-flowing debates, but Feldman wished to give some structure to the discussions. He liked Vandeman's style of laying out alternatives, and he would often try to summarize a point before allowing the conversation to proceed with another. Indeed, he approached the defense strategy in much the same way as he dealt with other business decisions. "He treated the takeover defense as a rational problem," CAB counsel Lee Hydeman remarks. "He needed to go through all the options, and he wanted to see that he had done a thorough job."

Accepting the takeover defense as a professional challenge, Feldman was as much concerned with means as with ends. In strategy discussions, he often raised questions of ethics and spoke of "doing things with dignity." "The question of right and wrong was extraordinarily important to Al," notes Mike Roach. This sense of professional propriety somehow excluded resort to political action. In an early planning session, Roach suggested that Continental should develop a political capability to defend the ESOP. "Why?" objected

Feldman. "This is an internal corporate affair." The Continental representative in Washington, Harvey Wexler, senior vice-president of governmental affairs, never received any authorization to lobby on behalf of the ESOP.

The pilots saw the political dimensions of the takeover battle much more clearly. As early as March, the MEC retained a Washington lobbying firm, Alcalde, Henderson, O'Bannon, Bracy & Williams, paying an initial fee of $250,000. Two partners of the firm, Susan Williams and Terry Bracy, had both served in government as assistant secretary of transportion for legislative affairs. The vice-president of public relations, Julian Levine, who acted as the management liaison with the Alcalde firm, remembers that Feldman wished to avoid closely involving management in the firm's political campaign. "He was very concerned that the company not do anything that would cast discredit on it. The company couldn't and wouldn't do itself what the pilots and Bracy and Williams were doing," Levine says.

The Alcalde firm found, however, a ready ally in CEA leader Paul Eckel. Without questioning the CEA's right to act independently, Eckel began to work closely with Williams and Bracy. The Continental management cooperated to the extent of granting employee leaves and giving the CEA unrestricted use of the teletypes. Making the most of Eckel's support, Williams and Bracy sought to enlist all employees in a broadly based grass-roots campaign. They knew how to translate the ground swell of employee emotion into political pressure, and with their guidance, the employee cause began to attract attention.

The original focus of the political campaign was on the CAB proceedings which still threatened to cut short plans to establish the ESOP. TI had filed a motion to create a "reverse trust" that would give its parent, Texas Air, immediate control over Continental. Alternatively, it asked for broad powers to vote its Continental stock held by the voting trust at the annual shareholders' meeting on May 6. Although the CAB was not subject to direct political pressure, Williams and Bracy thought that it might be more disposed to adopt a full administrative view, attesting to the careful discharge of its responsibilities, if it were put in the public spotlight. What the employees sought was only the time that a full review would afford. No one expected the CAB to disapprove the acquisition.

After the employee poll, the employee leaders had only a week to rally support in congress before the CAB hearings on the proposed "reverse trust" and expanded voting powers, but they already had an important ally in Senator Russell Long, the architect of ESOP legislation. The senator had written a letter to Eckel that proved to be one of the most helpful expressions of support in the public relations effort. "The employees of Continental Airlines," he wrote, "have an opportunity to create a showcase airline—one in which the employees themselves become the major stockholders in the company. If you are successful in your efforts—and I hope you will be—your company may well become the model airline in the industry—the one to which other carriers will look when seeking a formula for success." Senator Long agreed to introduce a Senate resolution a few days before the CAB hearing which would urge the agency to "proceed with consideration of such merger under its regular procedures."

The CEA appealed to employees for letters to senators and representatives and unleashed a flood of correspondence, which was collected at the Denver and Los Angeles offices and carried on Continental planes to the capitol. The bags of letters (ten thousand by one estimate) were sorted in an all-night work session and personally delivered by pilots and Washington employees to legislative offices the next day. Later, in a press conference and employee rally on the Capitol steps, Senator Long appeared at Eckel's side to give visible support for the cause. A concerted lobbying effort accompanied this grass-roots campaign. In one of the few political initiatives of management, Jack Sage came to Washington to testify before the House task force concerned with industrial productivity. The ESOP consultants, Kelso & Company, retained three lobbyists who had been active in the cause of employee ownership and knew potential supporters. And the members of the

Alcalde firm, accompanied by Continental employees, made the rounds of their best contacts in Congress.

The employee letters written at this time provide a poignant record of employee sentiment. An uncommonly eloquent letter was written in Spanish by a Miami employee to the director of the Latin Chamber of Commerce, asking him to intercede with the CAB. As translated, the letter pleads,

> We, the employees of Continental Airlines, do not wish to lose our jobs, or, much less, our airline. I say "our" because it is the sweat of our brows, the unceasing effort of years of service, that has made possible the achievements of Continental. By buying 51% of the stock of the company, we can keep our airline.
>
> We don't want to change Continental. To the contrary, if we have this chance, we will strive harder than ever to make it better.
>
> Do not forget that our success is also the success of our families.

The effort was as successful as could be hoped. Fifty congressmen and twenty senators wrote the CAB urging a full review of the merger case, and the Senate resolution gained fifteen cosponsors. "The lobbying effort," notes lobbyist, Wayne Thevenot, "raised the Continental issue to high visibility. It dominated conversation for a while." In one week of well-coordinated effort, the employees' case in the CAB proceeding became a matter of widespread political interest.

In the next phase of the grass-roots campaign, the Alcalde firm planned one-day visits to thirty-three cities by a team that usually consisted of an Alcalde partner, two members of the CEA board of directors, the local station manager, and other interested local employees. The primary objective was to bring the story to the local press, but the teams also contacted mayors, airport managers, and heads of the chambers of commerce in the hope that they could officially intercede with the CAB. "We started the day with 7:30 A.M. meetings and at sundown, the door of an airplane slammed us in the rear as we went off to another town,"[1] says pilot Chuck Sullivan. On May 8, he and Bill Miles had the following agenda in Peoria, Illinois:

9:00	Greater Peoria Airport Authority
11:00	Editorial briefing, Peoria Journal Star
1:00	Mayor
2:30	President, Chamber of Commerce

It was one of their best days. A week later the airport authority, the city, and the chamber of commerce jointly intervened in the CAB proceedings.

The employees knew that they had a story in the best American tradition. "We're experiencing an emotional high right now," said pilot Gus Wenzel. "We think we've got Lorenzo on the run. You've got to have happy employees. The American dream is to have a piece of the action, and the ESOP is our dream."[2] Though sometimes voicing antagonism to TI, the employees repeatedly expressed the themes of self-determination and productivity. "We're not doing this just to get rid of Lorenzo," said Gerry Gilbert, Casper, Wyoming, station manager. "The employees want to control their company and have a voice in their future. Productivity will definitely increase with the ESOP. Employees will be constantly thinking of ways to save Continental a buck. Our employees have a hell of a story to tell. We'll continue talking to the press, and if the ESOP goes through you'll see service like you've never seen before. The people of Casper have already seen the difference between Continental and Western and Frontier. But you'll really see an expression of our pride now."[3] The employee spokesmen were buoyed up by the friendly public response to their enthusiasm. In a Denver press interview, pilot Jim Martin remarked, "The total spontaneity is amazing." And customer service agent Tom Purta added, "TIA's got the lawyers and the money, but we've got something even better. We've got public sentiment and the employees."[4]

For reporters, Eckel was a refreshing and newsworthy personality. Solidly built with biceps that show even through a business suit, he presented a tough, passionate image. As the founder of the employee movement, he appeared as a man with an idea, motivated by his sense of what was right. "It's wrong for a company that was as strong and as beautiful as Continental Airlines to be picked off by a speculator," he said. "I think ESOPs are an idea whose time has come. It will provide an increment of motivation we didn't have before. Now, we're going to be dynamite motivated, not to ask for a raise, but to make our company so profitable that we all share in the results. This is a way of infusing new capital into American business, and when it catches fire, get out of the way!"[5] Eckel's life was now entirely taken up with the public relations effort. "This is the most exciting thing I've ever been involved in," he told a reporter.[6] But Bill Miles notes that he always had time for people; he never refused a phone call or failed to listen to an employee idea.

In many cities, employees worked independently to gather local support. In Portland, Oregon, ticket agent Craig Adcox spoke to the chamber of commerce, contacted local legislators, and traveled to Washington for two days to speak with the Oregon delegation. Washington ticket agent Donna Shaffer became fully absorbed in the political struggle. She played a part in all the lobbying effort at the capitol and attended every CAB hearing, trading work hours with other employees. At the airport, she kept an alert for legislators—sometimes even going to the United Airlines ticket counter on breaks— and offered a few words to promote the ESOP as they passed through waiting lines. In Los Angeles, Carol Mitchell, an in-flight supervisor, was released from other duties to devote full time to the job of city captain. She formed a local CEA committee with representatives from all departments, co-ordinated a letter-writing campaign, and participated in an effort to contact most newspapers in the state. "We're gambling on ourselves," she told the Los Angeles *Herald Examiner*. "I can't think of a better bet."[7] When the Continental vice-president of civil and environmental affairs, Tom Currigan, failed to make an appointment with Mayor Tom Bradley, Mitchell arranged to have a delegation of employees meet him. Bradley wrote to the CAB and sponsored a city council resolution supporting the ESOP.

The political campaign set the stage for one person's crusade that eventually would cause the takeover struggle to take an unexpected turn. When Williams and Bracy outlined strategies in an early planning session, pilot Larry Schlang raised his hand. "What about the defense and foreign policy implications of the transfer of Micronesian routes?" he asked. No one had thought of this obscure angle. Styling himself Pacific Affairs Advisor of the CEA, he took on the assignment of cultivating official concern about the consequences of the takeover on American interests in Micronesia. After being excused from flying duties, he gave his all to the effort. He says that at times he typed until his fingers hurt. Schlang is confident of his intellectual abilities—he can type rapidly and mail, uncorrected, letters worthy of a Washington lawyer —and he is used to being an outsider. At the naval academy, he was one of a small group of Jewish cadets and even smaller cadre of Jewish pilots. He often rejected the advice of management and attorneys and did not always keep others informed of his activities. Acting alone with persistence and resourcefulness, he exploited every angle of this narrow and implausible issue. CAB counsel, Lee Hydeman, who worked as closely as anyone with him, notes that he was "terribly, terribly useful." Perhaps no one contributed more to the takeover defense.

The Trust Territory of the Pacific Islands covers an area about the size of the continental United States with a population of 130,000 people scattered on 2,100 small islands. After the United States assumed control of the region under a United Nations Trusteeship, it was divided into four partially autonomous republics—the Northern Mariana Islands, the Federated States of Micronesia, Palau, and the Marshall Islands. The American possession of Guam lies on the northern edge of the region.

The control of such a large part of the earth's surface near the eastern edge of Eurasia is of obvious military importance. The island of Truk was the headquarters of the Japanese fleet. The numerous military facilities on Guam make it a major logistics base, much used during the Vietnam War, and give the United States a capacity to guard important shipping and aviation routes. Other islands hold the Pacific Missile Range Facility, a Coast Guard navigation facility, a chemical and biological warfare storage facility, and more installations of a classified nature.

An affiliate of Continental, Air Micronesia, operated two relatively antiquated 727-100s in a route that served nine islands and provided connections with Japan. Employing 209 Micronesians, it was by far the largest enterprise in the Trust Territories and supported a major tourist industry on Saipan in the Northern Mariana Islands, which had direct connections with Japan. As the only transportation link between the small islands, Air Micronesia was of considerable importance to the military because it fostered good community relations and directly served military facilities by moving cargo, mail, and personnel.

Continental could claim a strong commitment to maintaining this air service. It had operated Air Micronesia for thirteen years, incurring losses every year but two and a cumulative loss of $13 million. But what reason was there to suppose that TI would jeopardize the air service? At first, Continental had only the argument that the takeover was so financially unsound that it would lead to the bankruptcy and dismemberment of the airline. Then, not foreseeing the issue, the TI management played into its hands. At a CAB hearing, Lorenzo said it would be "irresponsible" to make any advance commitment to continue air service to Micronesia. When questioned about the routes, TI's vice-president for planning, John Stelzer, said, "I don't think the public interest side of an airline requires it to lose money." A Continental subpoena of TI records produced a memo concerning pros and cons of the acquisition of Continental which listed among the cons:

"Pacific Operations—(could be positive import if suspended.)" Other evidence disclosed that TI planned to replace the 727-100s which were uniquely suited for the long distances and the small coral runways of the routes.

To capitalize on this tactical error, Continental's first objective was to persuade the governments of American territories to intervene in the CAB proceeding. Schlang had valuable contacts on Guam. While in the naval reserve, he had acted as a recruiter for the naval academy. His proudest achievement was to secure the admission of nine Guamanians into the academy, more than had been admitted in the previous history of the island. When he visited Guam's representative in Congress, Won Pat, he found a willing ally who wrote Governor Calvo of Guam a letter explaining what Schlang had done for Guamanian boys. With this introduction, he visited the governor's office accompanied by a group of Guamanian employees of Air Micronesia. "Governor, please help save my job!" one employee pleaded. Calvo agreed to file a petition to intervene in the proceedings.

CAB counsel Lee Hydeman had represented Continental's interests in the Pacific for most of his career, but he was sometimes at a disadvantage as a management representative. Acting independently, Schlang complemented his efforts. In a month's time, the Federated States of Micronesia, Palau, Northern Mariana Islands, American Samoa, and the state of Hawaii also intervened. The intervention of six Pacific governments effectively interjected the issue of Pacific routes as an issue, broadening the scope of the CAB review. Since Continental needed only the time afforded by a complex proceedings, it was no small accomplishment.

As TI pursued its CAB petition to effectively cut short the takeover battle, it elaborated plans for the "reverse trust" that would allow its parent, Texas Air Corporation, to take control of Continental during the course of the CAB proceeding. It was an imaginative tactic: Texas Air Corporation would acquire TI's stock in Continental free of the voting trust, and TI itself would be put in the hands of an ostensibly independent trust during the CAB review period. In this way, it was argued, Texas Air would comply with the regulatory law forbidding common control of competing airlines without CAB approval. It would exercise control only over Continental. By means of the "reverse trust," the parties would abruptly shift sides in the CAB proceeding. Continental, under Texas Air's control, would become an advocate of its own acquisition; TI, under the control of independent trustees, would presumably take a neutral stand. TI argued that the trust could be designed to place a "Chinese wall" between Texas Air and TI. The claim, quipped CAB counsel Lee Hydeman was "an insult to oriental architecture." The ties between a newly formed corporate parent and its subsidiary could not be so facilely separated.

In its notice of hearing, the CAB directed attention to TI's alternative request for broad powers to vote Continental stock at the annual shareholders' meeting. Among other things, TI asked for the power to vote its stock in support of a resolution forbidding issuance of stock to the ESOP and the power to elect a majority of the Continental board of directors. TI argued that these powers—even the election of directors—fell short of the control over Continental forbidden by section 408 of the Airline Deregulation Act.

On April 29, the CAB hearing room was crowded by a hundred or more Continental employees who had flown out to attend. Senator Russell Long sat near the front row to put his prestige as minority leader of the Senate Finance Committee behind the employee cause. To represent the employees' interests, the CEA had retained its own legal counsel, Simon Lazarus, a White House aide in aviation matters under President Carter, who was then associated with the prestigious Atlanta law firm of Powell Goldstein Frazer & Murphy.

Four members of the Board seemed receptive to TI's requests, even to the curious "reverse trust" proposal. Chairman Marvin Cohen, who dominated the hearing, asked:

> What we've tried to do is focus on the narrow responsibilities that the CAB has here . . . to what extent should we interfere with the operations of the market-

place, including the exercise of shareholder rights. . . .
How is it anti-competitive in your opinion for us to
go along with their reverse trust?

Cohen appeared to accept TI's criticism of the democratic
structure of the ESOP:

What's to prevent the new contract between labor,
which is now owner of management, and management
from including enough increase so that the so-called
benefit to the company really doesn't exist because it's
all built into the wage increase?

The CAB members generally viewed the TI motions as consistent with the Board's policy of returning the industry to
the marketplace. Only Gloria Schaffer appeared unsympa-
thetic to TI's case. "Are you not coming to us and asking us
to bail you out?" she asked a TI lawyer.

The CAB decision three days later stated the issue as one
"of balancing our duties under section 408 with our desire to
avoid unnecessary government interference in the capital
markets." Did the employee effort tip the balance? One can
say only that it helped. The 4–1 decision denied the "reverse
trust" but, over Gloria Schaffer's dissent, it gave TI some additional voting powers to block the ESOP. TI gained the right to
offer and vote shareholder resolutions regarding the issuance
of stock to the ESOP, although it was not allowed to elect directors. This concession of voting rights would have a critical
impact on the takeover struggle. Since TI held 48 percent of
the airline's stock, the CAB decision made it impossible for
Continental to call a special shareholder meeting to approve
the ESOP—a matter that would later assume great importance
—but the ruling would not affect the scheduled shareholders'
meeting on May 6. The Continental management had received
an opinion from their Nevada counsel, the state of the company's incorporation, that it could rule out of order any resolution regarding issuance of stock to the ESOP. If TI should offer
a resolution opposing the ESOP, it could be gaveled down.

Then, its only recourse would be to argue in court that its shareholder rights were violated.

The shareholders' meeting became a celebration that many employees remember as the emotional high point of the ESOP campaign. Denver city captain Chuck Coble, working with the pilots, planned to transform the meeting into a demonstration of employee support for the ESOP, but it became more of a party than a political rally, extending from early morning to evening. About seven hundred employees from throughout the system, in their Continental uniforms, came to the meeting and a preparatory rally. Chuck Coble recalls, "There was nothing we couldn't do—that was the way we felt. There was a togetherness that emerged from this that was really tangible. If an employer could tap this residual energy, all his motivational problems would be solved."

Employees sang as they were taken in double-decker buses, draped with banners, from the airport to the Denver civic center. Along the route from the airport, the organizing committee had rented ten or twelve billboards that proclaimed, "We built it. Let us buy it." Two pilots flew above the downtown area in a small plane that pulled a banner with the words, "Pride in the Sky—Continental." The pre-meeting rally featured music and speeches, stimulated by live television coverage. As at other rallies, Paul Eckel was the main attraction. "Paul was the guy who made it believable," observes marketing employee Jack Riddle. Leaning back with one arm outstretched, he spoke with a personal charisma derived from his evident idealism and his role in originating the ESOP. Employees saw him, in the words of pilot Gary Webb, as "enthusiastic, optimistic, sincere, and honest." In his exhortation, the ESOP was raised above the level of a business proposition: it became a call for renewed loyalty and dedication. While the Continental theme song was being played after Eckel's appearance, a Continental 727 flew over the rally. Without a trace of melodrama, Houston reservation agent Karen Harvey says, "There was not a dry eye in the rally."

At 11:00 A.M., the employees marched four blocks to the Brown Palace Hotel where most were given proxies that enabled them to attend the shareholders' meeting. The room was filled with placards and banners. Some bore the professional mark of Jack Riddle's work and struck a positive note, but many homemade placards, especially those carried by pilots, bore epithets directed against Frank Lorenzo, such as "Don't Bank on Frank." Others alluded to TI's much-publicized peanuts fare by saying, "You Can't Buy Pride for Peanuts," or, more aggressively, "Proud Birds Eat Peanuts." Despite this evidence of hostility, Bill Miles insists that it was not an anti-Lorenzo meeting. "Little by little Frank took a backseat," he says. "The whole takeover became secondary. Ownership became foremost in their mind. They thought, 'Hey, I have a chance to own my own company.'"

On entering the hall, Phil Bakes had a somewhat different impression. "I remember being in a sea of very unfriendly persons," he says. "A couple of us were worried about our security." Indeed, Bakes had traveled to Denver accompanied by two burly bodyguards who were more commonly seen at Lorenzo's side on public occasions. But leaving the bodyguards outside, he and an attorney made their way alone into the room.

The patriarch of the airline, Robert Six, opened the meeting in his capacity as board chairman. He told of his recent heart surgery and, to laughter and applause, announced that he had received medical advice not to chair the meeting since it might be a "very stressful and very emotional meeting." On taking the gavel, Feldman strove to orchestrate the meeting in a dignified and formal manner. Keeping close to his script, he spoke in a controlled, modulated voice and invariably responded to questions, whether friendly or critical, with expressions of personal respect. (For example, saying: "Please proceed," and later: "Thank you, your remarks are appreciated.") A few incidents brought a brief smile and a flash of self-deprecating humor. When a shareholder questioned the tax implications of a measure, he remarked, "I wish we would make enough money so that we would have a tax problem!" While carefully maintaining a dispassionate composure, he seemed sensitive to the employee mood of good feeling. One of the regulars at Continental shareholders' meetings was a well-liked mechanic, Harry Methner, who entered into every discussion. On taking the microphone a third time, Mr. Methner interjected, "First of all, I have a question. I have two and a half years of perfect attendance, no sick leaves, no tardiness. I'm supposed to be at work in two and a half hours. I ask permission to be excused from tardiness." Feldman replied, "Mr. Methner, we have no choice but to love you."

At the anticipated moment, Feldman asked if there was any further business. With considerable poise, Phil Bakes took the microphone to present TI's motion directing the board not to issue stock to the ESOP. After he had finished, Feldman began, "The chair rules your motion out of order as a matter . . ." Here, Jack Riddle recalls, "The roof came off. It was like bedlam." Feldman finally restored order to explain his position that the motion improperly interfered with the powers of the board of directors. Bakes immediately moved to appeal the ruling and was informed that it was not appealable.

At this dramatic moment, the leader of the TI pilots, Dennis Higgins, approached the microphone, accompanied by four other TI pilots, and read a prepared statement to the gathering:

> We, the pilots of Texas International Airlines, have come to this meeting at personal risk to tell you some hard truths about dealing with Frank Lorenzo.

> The truth is this: Mr. Lorenzo is a brilliant man. . . . We are here, however, to tell you that he is also a man who has done nothing to show that he cares one whit for the 3,400 TXI employees who work for him.

> An airline is a service business—only as good as the people who make that service work. We are compelled to report that Mr. Lorenzo's current employees are a dispirited group. Amendable dates have expired in three of the five basic work agreements with TXI. We enjoy not even the elementary job protections that are

standard in the industry. We have encountered no evidence at all of good faith in the bargaining process. And we see no end in sight for the resolution of these fundamental matters.

Now Mr. Lorenzo proposes to take control of Continental, increasing the work force under his control to almost 15,000. As we are troubled about our own situation, we are deeply concerned that these problems will not be resolved if we are joined by 11,000 Continental employees.

Take a careful look at one more issue—the Continental fleet. In the case of New York Air, Mr. Lorenzo did not purchase new equipment, but channeled TXI equipment and money into the new venture. Does Mr. Lorenzo intend to maintain the Continental route structure, or instead, to prop up his debt-ridden, equipment-short empire by continuing to raid the TXI fleet and now the Continental fleet?

We are not against a proper merger; we are against labor chaos and the dismemberment of any competent, established airline. For a merger of that kind creates not benefits, but only victims—the employees, the stockholders, and the American public.

Higgins did not exaggerate when he said he came to the meeting at personal risk; the next day all five pilots were indefinitely suspended from their jobs. After filing a grievance, they were reinstated several months later as part of a contract settlement.

The employee participation in the shareholders' meeting amply succeeded in its objective of drawing sympathetic media coverage. The CEA hoped to repeat this success by staging a rally at the TI shareholders' meeting later in the month, but the plan was partly frustrated when TI changed the location of the meeting at the last moment. The rally turned out to be a quiet gathering of 150 to 200 employees who listened to a bluegrass band and the classical guitar of an Alcalde associate, Jim Benfield. Many wore T-shirts saying "Pride won't let me work for peanuts," produced by a reservation agent, Kathy Roden, who worked in a small business on the side. A group of TI pilots, carrying placards, such as "Will Rogers never met Frank Lorenzo," joined the rally to give moral support to the Continental employees.

The contrast between the TI and Continental shareholders' meetings, as told by Continental employees, might seem to be a caricature if it were not attested by videotapes. A group of TI employees passed out a leaflet at the door protesting that they should not be treated as mere spectators to corporate decisions affecting their future:

> We have invested heavily of our working life's blood in this company. It is in all of our interests to build a well managed and profitable airline. As in the past, we stand prepared to make our contribution. All that we ask is to be respected as employees, valued as people and trusted as partners in enterprise.

Lorenzo did not respond to the complaint that his policies offended the human dignity of his employees. The issue, he insisted, was a purely economic one: adjustment to the competitive environment of deregulation. He argued,

> The facts of life in a deregulated business are that the low cost producer can have the lowest prices and highest profits. With the onset of deregulation . . . we must make a major change in our labor costs. Perhaps unfortunately, our job is the job of a messenger. Today we are being criticized because some of those in our pilot group don't like the message that we're forced to deliver. And they blame the messenger for the message.

Lorenzo treated the Continental ESOP as a gross impropriety, almost a crime. In his principal address to shareholders, he described the ESOP as "perhaps the most desperate anti-takeover prevention scheme concocted in modern American business."

The meeting proceeded in a raucous and disorderly atmosphere. A group of about two hundred TI employees, all wearing blue "Love TI" T-shirts, cheered Lorenzo and management. The remainder of the room was packed by dissident pilots and flight attendants who introduced a series of hostile resolutions and booed Lorenzo, shouting "Answer it!" and "You're a liar!" as he stated his positions. In fielding critical questions, Lorenzo spoke bluntly, with an impatience to move on, and dispensed with expressions of conventional courtesy. Frequently consulting with his general counsel, Charles Goolsbee, he abided the dissident spokesmen for a necessary interval before cutting them off. When one interlocutor asked by what rules he conducted the meeting he replied, "I've been elected chairman by the board, and I'll call the shots as I see them." An outsider might have divided sympathies for the two sides, each denying the other the normal respect due in social intercourse. But the division seemed to reflect a less civilized corporate culture than that of Continental. A Continental pilot, Dan Murphy, who attended the meeting, remembers saying to a friend, "If this is what we have to look forward to, Jesus!"

The takeover battle between TI and Continental became one of the year's most newsworthy business stories. The media coverage was nearly always sympathetic to the employee cause—even in Houston. The employees were attractive spokesmen in a story of a successful underdog. Referring to the employee effort, the *San Francisco Chronicle* commented, "Maybe it will bring another result always favored by Americans: a batch of little guys, ordinary people, taking on the high and mighty and coming out ahead."[8] Bill Schoneberger, a CEA public relations adviser, says that most reporters had the attitude of "Go get them." Carole Shifrin of the *Washington Post*, who had covered CAB proceedings during the period when Phil Bakes was general counsel, reported the allegations of TI's federal court lawsuit challenging the ESOP in detail and gave Continental only thirty words of rebuttal.[9] After a glowing description of TI's "reverse trust" proposal, she commented, "The unusual petition to the board comes from a company and officials who have stunned the airline industry and Wall Street with unusual moves in the past."[10] Shifrin's reporting was TI's major public relations victory. In Washington, it went far toward neutralizing the employees' many successes elsewhere, since legislators and bureaucrats may regularly read all the *Washington Post* and give only sporadic attention to other newspapers.

The campaign for public support fed on its own momentum. Press reports generated more press reports as the employee movement was perceived as a major story. The extensive press coverage prompted the cooperation of local politicians and officials who sensed a politically advantageous cause. The series of resolutions by city councils, chambers of commerce, and airport authorities resulted in more publicity. Seven cities, a county, several chambers of commerce, and two states actually intervened in the CAB proceeding. The city of Denver, in particular, took an aggressive part in the hearings and written arguments. In an early ruling, the CAB had seen only two technical issues worthy of further investigation—labor-protective provisions and Mexican routes. Barraged by letters, resolutions, and petitions for intervention, it found itself dealing with a well-publicized and politically sensitive case.

CHAPTER SEVEN

CORPORATE STRATEGIES

When Phil Bakes traveled to Denver to attend the Continental shareholders' meeting, he carried with him six alternative letters, each signed by Lorenzo, offering terms for a negotiated settlement. Lorenzo would tell him in the morning which approach he had finally decided upon. After calling Houston, Bakes visited Feldman in his hotel suite a few hours before the shareholders' meeting to deliver the selected letter. Feldman remarked, "I wish I had seen this earlier." It was the first written proposal Continental had received. Feldman refused to acknowledge the proposal in response to a pointed question at the shareholders' meeting, but Lorenzo had no desire to keep the overture in confidence and released the proposal to the press the next day.

The letter made a startling offer to purchase all the outstanding stock of Continental for $13 per share in cash. The offer expired on May 21 and was conditioned on TI's receiving "formal commitments" for financing the purchase by May 19. A week later Lorenzo announced that he had obtained adequate financial commitments for the cash offer. On May 19, he increased the offer to $14 per share "to make it a little more attractive" to the Continental board. While announcing the sweetened terms in a breakfast press conference in New York, Lorenzo made clear that the cash offer was good for only two more days. "Our offer expires on May 21, and when it expires, it expires," he said.[1]

Among Continental executives, the cash offer met with

frank incredulity. It would cost TI another $115 million to purchase the stock at $13 per share. They had questioned TI's capacity to carry the debt associated with the $93 million tender offer. Should they now seriously consider a proposal involving $115 million additional debt? If TI should borrow this amount to finance the cash offer, the resulting airline would have $707 million in debt and only $52.6 million in equity. "They should have called Lorenzo's bluff," says a top Continental executive who asks to remain anonymous. The public announcement of the cash offer did indeed serve a tactical purpose. In the ongoing CAB and court proceedings, TI's lawyers compared the offer favorably to the price of stock issued to the ESOP, and TI mailed the offer to all Continental shareholders in an effort to rally support for its takeover bid.

Lorenzo did not disclose his claimed financial commitments to the Continental board, but in a confidential CAB hearing, behind closed doors, the TI treasurer, Robert Snedeker, was required to respond—over the objections of TI's counsel—to a few questions about the financial support for the offer. He revealed that Manufacturers Hanover Trust Company had given a written commitment for a further $20 million credit. Texas Air Corporation, he asserted, stood ready to contribute another $50 million from its cash reserves. For the balance of $45 million, TI had solicited expressions of interest from its existing bank creditors. It had secured no loan agreements or letters of understanding, but two foreign banks—Societé Generale and Bank of Montreal—had responded positively to a TI proposal. "They certainly indicated a desire and willingness to look at a financing for the purchase," said Snedeker, who refrained from disclosing the proposed nature of the financing. Snedeker's testimony revealed that TI did not have the financing in hand. Was the cash offer then a bluff? Lorenzo is a man who values his credibility in financial circles. Surely the foreign banks were prepared to honor his offer in some manner. In later testimony, however, Charles Goolsbee, TI's general counsel, stated, "My opinion is that no merger could have resulted at that price."

The Continental board of directors held a special meeting

on May 20 to consider the TI proposal. As a matter of principle, it was not easy to justify rejecting the $13 cash offer. The board of directors' fiduciary duty extended to shareholders, not to employees or to the corporation as an entity. By taking the $13 per share, the shareholders would get more than the actual or prospective market value of their stock. Mike Roach believes that, whatever their private feelings, they would have felt compelled out of a sense of fiduciary responsibility to accept some price, say, $18 per share. The doubtful financial support for the offer suggested the need for a conditional acceptance, not an outright rejection. But the board's advisors now included committed advocates of the ESOP, such as Wachtell, Lipton lawyer Erica Steinberger and Mike Roach himself, who were able to make a persuasive case for rejecting the offer. When TI increased the offer to $14 per share, the board was already in a rejecting mood, and it was not enough to prompt reconsideration. On May 21, Six and Feldman cosigned a letter rejecting the $14 offer as being below the real value of Continental stock.

The prospect of a negotiated takeover had at least temporarily vanished, but negotiations could also take the opposite direction of arranging a buyout of TI's interest. From the beginning, George Vandeman saw a buyout as Continental's best chance of remaining independent. While a buyout could preserve the ESOP in some form, the employee movement, in his view, chiefly served the tactical purpose of pressuring Lorenzo to come to the bargaining table. Near the end of May, Feldman and Vandeman had their first opportunity to suggest the possibility of a buyout to Lorenzo and Bakes during a brief conversation in New York, but they failed to find common ground. Continental would consider a buyout only at TI's cost while TI wanted a 25–30 percent profit.

With negotiations stalled, the parties played out a complex game to secure advantage. "Our resolve has no end," said Feldman. "We're prepared to fight this in the courts as long as it takes, because we're convinced we're doing the right thing for our shareholders."[2] But it was a lawyer's game, involving regulatory agencies as well as the courts, over which Feldman had little control. While he was speaking, TI was carrying the battle to new fronts.

Continental's securities lawyers were early concerned with obtaining SEC clearance for the ESOP. As a routine precaution, they applied to the SEC on April 10 for a "no-action letter" under the Securities Act of 1933. According to Randy Bassett of Latham & Watkins, they received "indications" from the staff that the letter would be granted; but when TI challenged the ESOP in federal court, the SEC invoked its policy of not issuing opinions on matters under litigation. About three weeks later, the enforcement division of the SEC —apparently prompted by TI's complaints—inquired about the ESOP. After two meetings with Continental's lawyers, the division was satisfied that there were no securities law violations.

Federal law, however, does not necessarily preempt state law in this field. TI carried the attack to the eighteen states where Continental did business. In such a broadly directed offensive, some errors are understandable. A letter from the New York law firm, Davis Polk & Wardwell, to a Florida official cites Illinois law. Three states began investigations of the transaction. The Oklahoma Securities Administrator later said he was "embarrassed" to find that he had acted on mistaken information, but the Washington State Business and Professions Administration and Texas State Securities Commissioner pursued proceedings that became a source of minor concern.

In California, TI found a tactical opportunity that Continental's lawyers could not easily counter: it retained Willie Barnes, the former state Corporations Commissioner, to present its case. Barnes writes with unusual energy and lucidity and is well respected by professional colleagues. A prominent San Francisco securities lawyer describes him as a "solid craftsman"; Randy Bassett calls him "a straight shooter." In the early sixties, a white law student of his abilities would probably have joined a major metropolitan law firm, but like many talented blacks, Barnes found his best opportunity in government. He rose through the ranks of the Department of Corporations, and when Governor Brown considered candidates for the normally political appointment of Corporations Commissioner, Barnes had earned the job. After a successful tenure in office, he left in April 1979 to become a partner in the politically powerful law firm of Manatt Phelps Rothenberg and Tunney, where he was associated with such political notables as Chuck Manatt, Democratic National Committee Chairman; John Tunney, former California senator; Jim Corman, prominent former member of the House Ways and Means Committee; Mickey Kantor, premier Democratic party fund raiser in southern California; and Pete Kelly, rising young Democratic party leader. Barnes's successor as Corporations Commissioner, Geraldine Green, has been described as his protégé, but she was appointed eight months after his resignation, and the two had little personal acquaintance. Barnes's real influence lay with the staff of the Department of Corporations which knew him well as a colleague and boss.

While the employee poll was being conducted, Barnes met with the staff of the Department of Corporations to urge that it issue a cease and desist order to block the ESOP. The presentation of the plan to employees, he contended, constituted an illegal promotion of a security. Under California law, a beneficial interest in a stock bonus plan is regarded as a security unless the plan qualifies for special tax treatment under the federal Internal Revenue Code. The Continental ESOP would not so qualify, Barnes argued, because it was proposed as a takeover defense rather than a plan for the exclusive benefit of employees. In addition, he claimed that Eckel's letter to employees and other employee communications violated the disclosure requirements of California securities law because they failed to state material facts "necessary to make statements . . . not misleading." The issuance of stock to the ESOP, Barnes pointed out, would raise another set of legal problems. He argued that the exemption of stock bonus plans from state jurisdiction did not apply to leveraged ESOPs. The only other possible exemption was that for stock traded on the two national stock exchanges. If Continental should fail to list the ESOP stock on a national stock exchange, he contended that it would have to apply to the California Corporations Commissioner for a permit to issue the stock to the ESOP.

While not accepting all of Barnes's case, the staff was won over to the view that the Continental ESOP presented an enforcement problem. There was no improper influence here. Stung by later criticism, Chief Deputy Commissioner Steven Gourley says with apparent sincerity, "We were only trying to do our job." Having heard TI's criticisms of the ESOP, the staff was genuinely convinced that it was a questionable transaction. Gourley summoned Continental's lawyers to a meeting early in May and told them to call off the "hoopla" accompanying CEA activities. The company should not make any more presentations to employees, he said, until it obtained a tax ruling or a permit to issue the stock. Turning to the question of the need for a permit, Gourley aggressively advanced Barnes's contention that the stock bonus plan exemption did not apply. The California Corporations Commissioner had never actively sought to regulate leveraged ESOPs, and specialists in the field generally followed the practice of implementing the plans in reliance on the stock bonus plan exemption; but the wording of this exemption, if literally construed, did not easily fit leveraged plans. Gourley decided to take a stand on the Continental ESOP to establish the jurisdiction of his department. He told the Continental lawyers that the company would have to apply for a permit to issue to the ESOP unless it qualified under the exemption afforded to stock traded on the two national stock exchanges.

The staff's position presented an unforeseen obstacle that could have been largely avoided. The Union Bank of California had been selected as trustee without thought of legal implications. As a Nevada corporation, Continental in the past had conducted certain transactions in Nevada to put them beyond the reach of California securities law. The selection of a Nevada trustee for the ESOP would have given Continental a strong claim to be beyond the jurisdiction of the California Corporations Commissioner, particularly if the transaction were negotiated and closed in Nevada. But in May the delicate negotiations with the banks were well under way. It was then undiplomatic—and of uncertain legal effect—to switch in midstream to another trustee and pursue further negotiations out of state. Moreover, the Continental lawyers were increasingly optimistic that the company could list the ESOP stock in the New York Stock Exchange where Continental stock was traded.

Continental's right to list ESOP stock on the New York Stock Exchange presented a close and novel question. Although a private organization, the New York Stock Exchange is closely regulated by the SEC; and its rules incorporated in a "Company Manual," have much the same practical effect as government securities regulations. The Company Manual provides that shareholder approval is required for the issuance of stock "resulting in a change in the control of a company." When the CAB gave TI power to vote its stock against the ESOP in early May, Continental effectively lost the option of seeking shareholder approval of the ESOP. Having 48.5 persent stock ownership in Continental, TI could easily defeat the ESOP in a shareholder vote. But did the ESOP involve a "change in the control of a company"? It was hard to say that the issuance of the 15.4 million shares transferred control to any person or group. The voting rights to the stock would be exercised by eleven thousand individual employees, scattered throughout the country and representing diverse interests. The administrative committee exercised no control over voting, and the employees had no common agent to cast their votes in a block. Continental had a good argument that the issuance of stock to the ESOP was most closely analogous to the sale of equity to the public at large and thus fell outside the Exchange's rule.

Few people were as well qualified to present Continental's case to the New York Stock Exchange as Feldman's friend and fishing companion, Rod Hills, now a Washington partner of Latham and Watkins. Hills had served as chairman of the SEC during the Ford administration and had worked closely with officials at the top levels of the national stock exchanges. He retained a personal acquaintance with many of the officers and directors of the New York Stock Exchange; and throughout the spring, he kept them informed about the ESOP negotiations. Finding them to be sympathetic to the plan, he gave Feldman encouraging reports of his conversations. Continental finally applied for listing of the ESOP stock on the Stock Exchange on June 1 when the documentation was in order. George Vandeman had earlier warned management of the problem posed by the Exchange rule, but he says that his firm was then "cautiously optimistic" that the stock could be listed.

No serious obstacle emerged as the details of the ESOP financing were hammered out. The ESOP loan was priced at prime rate plus .25 percent, subject to customary provisions for fees and compensating balances. Over the term of the loan, the effective interest rate was very close to that of the bank loans it would replace. The loan was to be repaid over six and a half years pursuant to a schedule that followed the timing and amount of future pay increases. The size of the loan repayments gradually increased during the first years until the company's contribution to the trust rose to 15 percent of payroll. It was a more advantageous schedule than that of the existing bank loans; not only did the ESOP loan extend over a longer term (the average Continental bank loan had a term of only 4.6 years), but the repayment of principal was heavily weighted toward the end of the term. The amortization schedule was based on the participation in the ESOP of two of Continental's major union groups—the pilots and flight attendants. As we will see, the IAM refused to negotiate an amendment of its collective bargaining contract, but its participation was not essential for the ESOP.

The ESOP financing was part of a somewhat larger package. The ESOP leaders also offered a $50 million revolving credit agreement to cover Continental's prospective cash needs. In addition, Continental negotiated amendments to an existing loan agreement, having an outstanding balance of $48.6 million, with a group of institutional investors led by Connecticut General Life Insurance Company. The company was in default under a financial covenant of the loan agreement, and it would violate another technical covenant by issuing stock to the ESOP. In these negotiations, nearly all the fleet was divided up as collateral. Only two cargo convertible DC-10s, which Continental was negotiating to sell to Federal Express, were to be free of mortgage.

The willingness of the lenders to put together this major financial package dramatically revealed their confidence that Continental was passing through a difficult transitional period from which it would emerge with its former financial strength. The transactions contained common financial covenants that explicitly contemplated this financial recovery. Thus, the airline promised to maintain a mimimum net worth that would rise from $165 million on June 1, 1981, to $400 million on January 1, 1988. Feldman believed that, with the benefit of his route restructuring program, the airline could meet these conditions. Referring to first-quarter losses, he told a reporter, "I don't anticipate any other quarter that bad. Hopefully this summer we'll find we made the right strategic moves, and we'll begin to see the benefits of it."[3]

The financing of the ESOP was conditioned on Continental's obtaining "a favorable determination letter from the IRS on or before December 31, 1981." If Continental did not receive this assurance of favorable tax treatment, the banks could amend the plan or rescind the transaction, but they did not wish to be put to this choice; they were prepared to extend the credit only because they were persuaded that the favorable determination letter would be given. The Continental employee benefits counsel, Gerard Kenny of the Los Angeles firm of Gibson Dunn and Crutcher, recalls that the Los Angeles staff of the IRS "went out of their way to be cooperative and agreed to the unusual step of a prefiling conference with Continental lawyers." Relying in part on his contacts with the staff, he offered an opinion letter that optimistically assessed the prospects of obtaining the tax ruling. The transaction did have certain unusual features that could raise doubts about tax qualification, but Kenny assured the bankers that they did not present issues of substance.

As the ESOP negotiations came to a close, the Continental board of directors prepared to consider final approval of the transaction. The board had earlier referred the ESOP proposal to a special committee of four outside directors which retained its own investment bankers, Bear Stearns and Company, to study the plan. The committee members had small holdings in Continental stock and major business interests elsewhere. Jack Wrather, a friend of President Reagan devoted to conservative political causes, was chairman of the Wrather Corporation which controlled extensive investments in the hotel, television, motion picture, oil and gas, and cable TV businesses. Marion Jorgensen was the wife of Earle M. Jorgensen, the chairman of Earle M. Jorgensen Company, a manufacturer of heavy steel and aluminum forgings with sales of $280 million. Samuel Butler was president of Phillip T. Sharples Oil Company in the Denver area. The chairman of the special committee, Joe Kilgore, the only lawyer among the outside directors and a former U.S. congressman, was the partner of an Austin, Texas, law firm. The four directors, acting under the threat of personal liability, had nothing to gain in taking chances; they would be off the hook if their advisors' verdict was negative. One may easily believe that they were disposed to give the ESOP a critical and independent review. But Bear Stearns and Company actually took a somewhat more aggressive stand in support of the ESOP than did Lehman Brothers. The firm was prepared to state unequivocally that the ESOP "is fair, from a financial point of view, to the shareholders of Continental." With Bear Stearns's endorsement, the way was paved for board approval of the ESOP.

There was little drama when the ESOP came before the board in a special meeting on the morning of June 1. The meeting had been very carefully prepared to lay a basis for the board's proper exercise of its fiduciary responsibilities. Eight executives and advisors gave presentations covering every aspect of the transaction and answered questions. Erica Steinberger of the Wachtell, Lipton firm delivered the fiduciary liability lecture to the board. Accustomed as a corporate lawyer to working with men, she remembers her pleasure in addressing other women on the board. The Continental board had three women directors, including advisor director Audrey

Meadows Six. The outside directors met separately in the early afternoon to receive the report of the special committee and to confer with their own advisors out of the presence of the management directors. What reluctance they may have felt was tempered by the fact that they had rejected the available possibilities of settlement. Upon reconvening, the full board of directors gave management authority to implement the ESOP.

The matter of employee representatives on the board of directors—a key element of the plan for a more democratic corporate organization—was discussed in the meeting but deferred for later decision. There was no doubt, however, that the board would accept four employee directors. Jack Sage remembers, "From day one Feldman encouraged and fostered the idea that there would be four employee representatives on the board of directors, one for each of the three union groups and one for noncontract employees." To accommodate these four directors, the number of management directors could be reduced from five to three and the total number of directors increased from thirteen to fifteen. There were, however, few precedents for the selection of employee directors, and none seemed appropriate for Continental. As a practical matter, the method of nomination was critical. Continental did not have cumulative voting in which all of a stockholder's shares can be voted for one candidate. An employee (or union) would have little chance of successfully challenging an officially sponsored candidate at the annual shareholders' meeting.

In conversations with CEA leaders, Feldman appeared to be moving toward acceptance of a unique plan that would be an experiment in corporate constitution making. A pilot, John Huber, who acted as a liaison between the CEA and management, played a role in developing the idea. A political conservative who conceals a sharp mind behind a gruff and taciturn manner, Huber had served on the ALPA negotiating committee but was no friend of unions. He drew a distinction between ALPA ("It's really a professional association," he says) and most other unions. During the takeover struggle, he was in daily contact with management. When Feldman asked for his thoughts on a way to choose employee directors, Huber mentioned a plan that he had discussed with Eckel: individual employees (not unions) would submit résumés to a nominating committee of the board composed of outside directors; after narrowing the field to three or four candidates for each of the four positions, the committee would poll the four employee groups to determine their preference among these candidates; and barring any unusual problem, it would then nominate the employees' choice; the employees finally elected to the four positions would be required to resign any union posts as a condition of serving on the board. Huber recalls that Feldman said, "I like it. We'll do it that way. Write it up." At the June 1 board meeting, Feldman briefly sketched a procedure for selecting employee directors that included most of the elements of this plan.

The plan was clearly part of a bid to reduce union influence in the company. It was hoped that the ESOP would undercut union power, not by confrontation, but by introducing alternative means of representation. Eckel was quite explicit on this point. "What we probably would have come to would be an airline much less dependent on unions than it was at the time," he says. "We felt that owners simply didn't have as great a need for unions as they had in the past." The pilots were prepared to follow Eckel's lead. In an MEC meeting, Jim Rinella had complained that ALPA would have no role in the structure of voting and representation under the ESOP. Eckel responded by putting his personal prestige on the line. Rinella recalls that Eckel said, "If you do it Rinella's way, I quit." And that was the end of the discussion. The flight attendant leadership was not consulted on this issue, but no one doubted that it would oppose any plan of circumventing union authority. When Pearl Kelly, the flight attendant on the CEA board, was selected for the administrative committee of the ESOP, the union objected that it wished to choose its own representative on the committee, and management yielded by appointing the union nominee. The episode had minor importance in itself—the committee had few discretionary responsibilities—but it revealed that the strong and democratic Union of Flight Attendants was not likely to relinquish passively the right to choose flight attendant representatives.

The selection of employee directors by the nominating committee would preserve the vital independence of the board, but would it satisfy aspirations for self-determination? The ESOP campaign had awakened a vision of corporate democracy based in part on the role of employee directors. Chuck Cheeld tells that while he was working fifteen hours a day meeting the press, talking to employees, and taking a plane on an hour's notice, he felt that he was doing something of historic importance. "We all sensed," he says, "that it was a movement of evolutionary proportions in the respect that a lot of other people would be able to move forward doing the same sort of things. It was a step beyond the old forms of labor management confrontation. We would go from a 'we and them' concept of management and employees to an 'us' concept. It would boost productivity and at the same time bring the company together as a human community in which everyone's personal dignity would be respected." The idea of working through the nominating committee was perhaps a reasonable compromise—but a compromise nonetheless—between this idealistic vision and the realities of corporate management. It reflected the belief that a responsive trusteeship, giving outside directors a pivotal role, is the most practical approach to self-determination for a business enterprise.

The ESOP plainly demanded strong leadership: it would bring management into uncharted waters and make it responsible to a more complex constituency, composed of outside shareholders and employees. Employee support for the plan was closely linked with confidence in Feldman. "He was seen as the leader who would make it work," notes dispatcher Ron Aramini. The takeover battle had brought Feldman closer to the work force by multiplying the occasions when he met and talked with employees. Now appearing at Eckel's side in press photographs, he visibly identified himself with the employee cause. The employees saw him as a leader who had cast his lot with their own. "He had come to bat for us, and we were in it together," remembers Carol Mitchell. Rumors that he had rejected a job at Twentieth Century Fox added to the general belief in his dedication to the common cause. Responding to the employee expectations, Feldman now promised success. When he spoke to the annual meeting of marketing employees, he stated flatly: "the takeover will not happen." The marketing employees, all subject to his system of management by commitment, knew that he spoke with utter seriousness —he intended the statement as his own personal commitment.

Publicly, Feldman acquired something of the enthusiasm of a convert. He described the ESOP as being "simple and elegant." "It is ironic—it is ironic—that this willingness to sacrifice was inspired by a hostile takeover," he continued. "But whatever its origins, it now appears to be a remarkably sound business transaction." When he visited El Paso to give the corporate update, he met with Howard Putnam, president of Southwest Airlines, which then had the only extensive program of employee ownership in the industry and enjoyed the best return on sales and equity of any airline. Putnam's message was that his employees did not want "to burden their company with the layers of costs that other airlines found themselves stuck with"[4]—they wanted to be productive. Feldman similarly came to see an employee-owned company as offering exciting possibilities for competition in a deregulated environment. He told a reporter, "If Lorenzo flew off into the sunset and the employees were still willing to take a 15 percent pay cut, I would go ahead with it. Probably the greatest mystery to me is why everybody hasn't used ESOP."[5]

The employees' faith in his leadership seemed to touch something vulnerable in Feldman's complex and private personality, breaching the inner reserve apparent behind his polished manners. In social conversations, he strove to be attentive and affable, using his eyebrows expressively for emphasis, but he commonly stood with both arms folded, even after shaking hands. While mingling with a crowd, he tended to avoid direct eye contact. Close colleagues felt his reserve most acutely; Mike Roach dreaded the silence that would ensue after they had finished discussing business matters on plane trips. But speaking before employee groups, Feldman felt free to display a warmth that he withheld on other occasions. In a lighthearted moment, he told a group of employees that the company owed a debt to Lorenzo for having elicited the ESOP idea. "In fact, when the ESOP is established," he quipped, "we may name one of our DC-10s the Francisco A. Lorenzo. Of course, it will be the one we will sell to Federal Express!"

CHAPTER
EIGHT

THE
EMPLOYEE
MOVEMENT

Julian Levine, the former Continental vice-president of public relations, is a man who sees the good in other people. He speaks well of Lorenzo and found it easy to work with him after the takeover. Although he favored the ESOP, he was only marginally involved in promoting the plan. Most of the active public relations effort was carried out by the pilots and the CEA. As media attention grew, his department limited its role to answering inquiries and issuing statements explaining particular corporate actions. Reflecting on the struggle three years later, he is not so much interested in the issues as in the qualities of the people involved. In particular, he remembers the leaders who emerged from the rank and file of the work force. "Dedicated people appeared out of the woodwork," he remarks.

Of the people Levine singles out for praise, Jack Riddle has already been mentioned. "A classy guy," Levine says. Riddle describes himself as a "corporation man," but with his tieless attire and relaxed posture he seems to belong to an artistic milieu like that of his wife, a commercial free-lance artist. For eighteen years, Riddle had operated his own small advertising agency in Denver. Later, he took a job with Continental and worked his way up to a staff-level position in the marketing department concerned with the distribution of promotional materials. He says he liked the idea of the ESOP from the beginning. One of his former clients in Denver told him that, after establishing an ESOP, "he could take a vacation for the first time in thirty years without worrying if people would turn off the lights." Working on his own time, Riddle designed a stream of buttons, bumper stickers, billboards, newspaper advertisements, and posters that proclaimed the employees' goals. After the first Denver meeting, employees plastered one of his posters urging a yes vote on walls throughout the system. He soon joined the CEA leadership by becoming an advisory director of the CEA board and could be counted on to deal with a supplier, organize a rally, or quickly dash off an appropriate banner. Riddle does not, however, attribute his efforts purely to dedication. "It was a hellacious lot of fun," he says. "There was no problem to get anybody to do anything. Impossible things were done. You could ask for something the next day and get it. The enthusiasm level was so high."

Riddle expressed the best in the movement, avoiding anti-Lorenzo sentiment. He remembers that the employees "were actively caught up with the idea that the airline could be something fantastic." In composing an employee pledge, he tried to capture this enthusiasm:

We, the employees of Continental Airlines
    (soon to become its co-owners)
Do, this 18th Day of June, 1981, pledge and affirm;

    our dedication renewed
        to our company,
        to each other,
        to ourselves—and
        to the again proven creed "It Can Be Done."

    our realization of our combined
        ideals, purposes and commitments
        to serve—proudly—
        those who have given us the opportunity to serve—
        our customers.

our visible display of our pride in our company
and its history,
    in our own attitudes and actions,
    in our dress, our words and our efforts
    to provide for those customers
    (and for ourselves)
    a genuine uplifting of the spirit—
    enjoyment, satisfaction—and
    the knowledge that they
    (and we)
    have been treated to "The Best."

our understanding of our place in history
    as daring innovators—
    as a model to others who strive
    to reach up.

Our collective pride has been judged and found to be genuine.

For those of us who have been—who are now—who will be
Continental Airlines—
Today is our beginning.

Come World and LET US SERVE YOU NOW!

As the ESOP neared implementation, Riddle began thinking
of using the attraction of employee ownership as a marketing
tool. He designed an array of advertising materials featuring
Continental employees as proud owners. Two years later
Eastern Airlines would adopt a similar advertising theme. In
a memo to the CEA board, he discussed one poster:

> Over the past months, Continental Airlines has gained
> an asset that many companies have spent fortunes and
> corporate lifetimes trying to achieve—an almost over-
> whelming public awareness and support of this com-
> pany, its employees, and the monumental struggle still
> being undertaken to effect their own destiny.

It is important that we be fully aware of this support. It is here *now*, it is solid, and it is coming from the most important people possible—our present and potential customers. From a purely marketing standpoint, this highly perishable support must be answered!

The enclosed layout of a suggested designation poster assumes victory. Using real and identified employees as the spokespeople, the message is clear—"This is my airline, I own it, I'm proud of it. I live, work and play in Los Angeles, and I'm also proud of my city. Come fly *my* airline to my city. And (unstated), because I now have a vested interest in its profitability, I will do everything possible to assure customer satisfaction." Not only our posters, but our ads, ticket jackets, time-tables, brochures, point-of-sale materials, and especially our employees' themselves can help tell the story.

The poster was actually printed and placed in tubes for mailing, but it was never used.

Levine describes Houston reservation agent Karen Harvey as "one of those who wrapped their life in the CEA." A tall woman with a nurturing physical presence, she had worked over ten years for Continental, but when the ESOP was announced, she had never visited the corporate headquarters or had substantial dealings with a corporate officer. The CEA suddenly vaulted her into a position to influence others and communicate with the public. During the first employee rally in Los Angeles, she took the microphone after Feldman. "Only at Continental," she said, "would a reservation agent be talking after the president of the company." It was a typical display of poise and good humor. In the early days of the ESOP campaign, she coined one of the CEA's best slogans, "ESOP is no fable." Later, she met TI executive John Carlson, on a Houston talk show and acquitted herself well enough to draw appreciative letters from listeners.

Harvey worked for the ESOP out of loyalty to Continental. "I have the logo in the veins," she says. "I thought we were different and should remain so." Blessed with a gregarious and energetic personality and a joyful religious faith, she made the ESOP credible among her peers because she was personally trusted: employees thought that if she was for it, there must be something in it. "People did believe me," she admits. Her wit and Southern turn of phrase inevitably drew the attention of the press—she became one of the most quoted CEA spokespeople. Before large groups, she had an ease born of actual experience in public speaking in her Baptist church congregation.

After being appointed to the CEA board, Harvey left her two young boys with her mother. They were excited, she says, to see her on television and in the newspapers. She managed to return home every weekend, but she spent most of her time on the road, eating her meal every night on an airplane and talking during the day to employees, the press, local officials, chambers of commerce, airport boards, and other groups. "It was a true grass-roots effort, and it was exciting to be in it," she remembers. Two other Houston reservation agents, Cindy Burns and Fay Kendal, sometimes joined her in Los Angeles on their days off. On one occasion, she shared her hotel room with five other employees. Back home in Houston, she helped organize political contacts, fund-raising activities, letter-writing campaigns, and a major rally. "Everyone felt involved," she says. "If you let it be known that you needed help, you would get volunteers up the ears."

The third person whom Levine mentions is ticket agent Bill Miles. Neatly dressed with a shock of brown hair reaching for his eyebrows, Miles could be mistaken for a young urban professional, but one soon discovers that he is a man deeply oriented toward family and friends. In 1970, Miles took time off from premed studies to work at Continental; he stayed to put his wife through college; eleven years and four children later, the temporary job had become a career. Director of personnel John Bidlake remarks, "He was a real sleeper. He was viewed as one of the better Denver employees, but he didn't emerge as a leader until the ESOP." As a member of the CEA board, Miles displayed a special talent for explaining the technical complexities of the ESOP. He presented the plan to employees in the corporate update meetings, entered the grass-roots political campaign and later found a unique, educational role in the movement. After the initial euphoria had dissipated, many employees began to ask what the ESOP would do for them, and a few notes of disillusionment crept in. Miles remembers that most commonly employees "would say they were for it, but they wanted to know about the impact on their pocketbook." To answer these questions, the CEA organized a series of informal workshops on the ESOP during a five-week period in late May and June. Miles worked "almost nonstop" on these sessions which, he says, were "very well attended."

Miles was a man who had put his family before his career, but he found himself drawn away from Denver, week after week. He tried to return on weekends but usually made it back only one day a week. One day in June, his wife saw a headline in a local newspaper, "Plot to Free Man Wanted in Colorado is Foiled in LA," that gave her an opportunity to lodge an ingenious protest. Clipping the headline from the paper, she affixed it to the top of a mock news story.

DENVER—Continental Airlines employee Bill Miles separated from his family since March, 1981, is wanted in Colorado.

Mrs. Jeri Miles and the couple's four children tearfully talked about their long battle to return Mr. Miles to Colorado. "We begged him to come home, but he donned his white hat and rode off into the sunset," Jaime Miles, 8, stated. Kimberly Miles, 6, noted that her father told her, "Good guys always win." Sean Miles, 3, said nothing but was seen nearby smashing peanuts under the heel of his cowboy boots. . . . Mrs. Miles, changing baby Christen's diaper, folding laundry, washing dishes, cleaning the house, tending the garden, mowing the lawn, fixing dinner, making beds, taking out the trash, and grooming the dog, was unavailable for comment.

The CEA office was often the scene of intense and emotional activity. "You can't imagine how electric it is around here," Chuck Cheeld remarked when the ESOP was first announced. CEA secretary Patrice Boyd says that as soon as she would put down the telephone it would generally ring again. Three times she lost her voice after a marathon series of conversations. When not answering calls, the employees staffing the office distributed materials, sent out teletypes, prepared code-a-phone messages that gave employees day-by-day news of developments, and made travel arrangements for employees —often fifteen or more on a given day—who were traveling to promote the cause. As airline employees, the CEA representatives could usually travel free or at sharply reduced fares on other airlines. The CEA incurred expenses, without management authorization, as if it possessed financial independence, but the company actually underwrote most of its activities by paying a share of the bills (and recording the items as receivables) and by lending use of teletypes, telephones, office space, and printshop.

To support the CEA's professed independence, Eckel appealed to employees for contributions. Many pilots responded with checks for $100 or $200. Other employees gave small contributions for odd amounts that indicated that they had examined their budget to see what they could afford. A secretary wrote a check for $7.25. In several cities, employees organized fund-raising activities. The takeover struggle was perhaps the first in history to include a baked potato sale among the arsenal of defense tactics. The Houston reservation agents donated the potatoes and fixings to their team leaders who cooked them in microwave ovens during lunch breaks. Dallas employees held a raffle for a color TV. In Portland, Oregon, ticket agent, Craig Adcox, says, "A lot of people put in a lot of time and effort" into a weekend garage sale of household items held in the air freight department. The sale was well attended by employees of other airlines who appeared interested in the ESOP.

With widespread media coverage, unsolicited contributions came from unexpected sources. H. S. Finkelstein, a Houston oil executive, gave $500 expressing the hope that "the employees of Continental Airlines will be able to chart their own destiny." The widow of one of Continental's first employees also sent a check for $500 with the following letter:

Mr. Paul Eckel, Chairman
Continental Employees Association
Continental Airlines
7300 World Way West
Los Angeles, California 90009

Dear Mr. Eckel:

I am the widow of Joseph F. O'Connor who until his death four years ago, had worked for Continental for 33 years and that was the love of his life.

I enclose a check for $500. for your association in your fight for control of the company. I think it is a really wonderful idea not only for the company, but also for each and every one of you who are making sacrifices toward your goal.

I feel that not only are you going to win control, but you are each of you going to win some values for yourselves and the company which will make you the most unusual and best operated airline in this or any other country as you build back up again.

I know my husband would have been a part of this had he lived to see it, so I am doing this as a memorial to him.

Sincerely yours,
Mrs. Adger K. O'Connor

By July, the CEA seemed to be doing well—it had contributions of $60,000 and expenses of $80,000. A month earlier the company had distributed a payroll deduction form to all employees that promised a steady flow of contributions. But the largest bills from the CEA law firm, Powell Goldstein Frazer and Murphy, had not yet arrived; and they would eventually total about $200,000. In reality, the contributions were only enough to give some credence to the CEA's claim of independence.

Eckel remained the undisputed leader not only of the CEA but the potentially independent pilot effort. Among the Continental work force, he was nearly always perceived as an employee leader, rather than a spokesman of pilot interests. Mechanic Rich Carberry says, "I don't know anyone who didn't like Eckel." But in day-to-day activities, Eckel tended to rely most on his pilot friends: Felix Tomlinson, who organized field operations; John Huber, who worked in the CEA office; Chuck Cheeld, who was the best public spokesman of the pilots; and Gary Thomas, who was chairman of ALPA's Fight TXI Committee. The prominence of pilots in Eckel's entourage avoided any division between the independently funded pilot effort and the broadly based CEA organization, but it raised questions about pilot dominance of the employee movement. Most rank-and-file employees were not much concerned about the pilots' role, although it was occasionally cited as an objection to the ESOP. "It was not seen as a pilot-sponsored movement," says Jack Riddle. "Maybe it should have been but it wasn't seen in that light." But management and flight attendants—in unusual agreement—perceived pilot dominance to be an important issue. Speaking for management, Jack Sage says, "We were all very concerned with the influence of pilots in the movement, but we thought that the design of the ESOP minimized the problem." Among top executives, financial vice-president Jack Woodlock, emerged as an outspoken critic of the ESOP. His principal objection: threatened pilot dominance. "The company was being run for the benefit of the pilots," he says. Despite the dilution of the pilot vote by the one-man-one-vote rule, he thought the pilots would be able to use the employee organization as a means of defending their privileged position.

The pilots unquestionably gave the ESOP the fullest measure of support. In one day of negotiations early in April, the negotiating committee agreed to forgo over a period of one year pay increases amounting to 15 percent of their payroll. Not waiting for approval of the ESOP, the negotiators consented to the conditional withholding of a 9 percent pay increase scheduled for April 1, 1981. The pilots were able to make such a large front-end wage concession because they had recently negotiated large pay increases to bring them up to a level of parity with other major airlines. While their wage concession involved only a modest financial sacrifice, the pilots did give up the traditional parity with other carriers that they had gone on strike in 1976 to maintain.

The flight attendants, with their history of conflict with management, present a separate story. A large majority—influenced by the unfavorable reputation of TI and the promise of self-determination—had voted for the ESOP in the employee poll, but there was a latent opposition; only 62 percent of the flight attendants returned their ballots and 13.8 percent voted no. Some of the yes votes reflected a soft support that fell off as the summer approached. Of the five Houston flight attendants who went to the Denver employee meeting, Sheri Pennington was the only one who continued to support the plan. Undeterred by others' loss of faith, she promoted the ESOP with a crusading spirit, even lobbying passengers on her days off. An energetic woman with a bright glance that invites repartee, Pennington knows her own mind and accepts controversy, but her commitment was unique among her employee group at Houston. Few flight attendants wore the pro-ESOP buttons that were found everywhere among other employee groups.

The disenchantment of many flight attendants with the ESOP owed something to latent antimanagement feeling, but it was stimulated above all by the prominent role of pilots in promoting the plan. By June, the plan came to be widely identified with pilots and management. In Los Angeles, Ricki Canalstein turned strongly against the ESOP after cooperating in the early stage of the ESOP campaign as a public relations spokesperson for the union. Deeply stung by the defeat of the flight attendant strike, she boasts three years later that she still will not talk to pilots who crossed the picket line. In the spring of 1981, she was particularly bitter about the continued furlough of striking flight attendants, displaced by new personnel:

> The company was using the scabs it hired during the strike while my friends were still out of work. I couldn't believe that the company wanted me to support the ESOP when it was doing this to me.

She thought that Eckel was "personally very nice but very anti-union." The ESOP was "an impractical pilots' scheme" to create a "pilot dominated company." The pilots were "trying to save their jobs at anyone's expense." She was unwilling to give up one-half of her pay increases to finance such a plan:

> Those people who supported the ESOP were fools. It gave us no job protection. We would just be pouring our salary into an airline run by pilots. If I had my choice of working for an airline run by pilots or Frank Lorenzo I'd choose Lorenzo.

As the flight attendant representative on the CEA board, Eckel appointed Pearl Kelly, an uncommonly beautiful Englishwoman whose soft-spoken manner reflects a deep sense of personal dignity. The choice again showed Eckel to be a fine judge of persons. She fought hard and effectively for the ESOP. After the employee poll, she decided to become an American citizen. "The vote was the result of everyone spontaneously reaching out and touching," she said. "It's unusual for a large corporation to act like a close family. I just want to be part of the same company for the next twenty years."[1] Relieved of flying duties, she displayed intelligence and personal charm as a public spokesperson for the ESOP, but she often ran into resistance promoting the cause among other flight attendants. "Most people had difficulty seeing it as anything other than a pilot project," she acknowledges. She and Sheri Pennington became the only flight attendant leaders deeply committed to the cause.

Union leader Darenda Hardy found a way to reconcile the flight attendants' ambivalent attitude toward the ESOP with her own collective bargaining objectives. When Jack Sage asked her to support the ESOP after the employee poll, she replied, "Well, Jack, I'm not saying that we will or won't, but we have to get a new contract." By late May, management was prepared to talk. In only six days of intensive negotiations, the parties reached agreement on a new three-year contract providing for annual 10 percent pay increases, one-half of which would be forgone if the ESOP were put into effect. The union did not seek to recover the major concessions it had made in the 1980 strike settlement, but it got a number of other minor concessions relating to schedules, passes, uniforms, daily bonuses for international flying, and other matters. The negotiations were really the last round of the December 1980 strike negotiations.

The Union of Flight Attendants, always attentive to democratic procedures, took a month to conduct an election on the new contract. Darenda Hardy recommended acceptance. The union had referred the ESOP to an accounting firm, Katz and Company, and received a very favorable verdict. "This ESOP is one of the most liberal yet implemented," the firm concluded. But Hardy was never won over to the ESOP itself; she saw a value only in the three-year contract term. "We didn't like the ESOP. We didn't want to do it," she says, "but the contract promised a period of peace and stability for the union." The vote, administered by the American Arbitration Association, was 794 in favor to 435 opposed, with many votes declared invalid as a result of an internal dispute over assessments. The contract was universally popular. The no votes of 22 percent of the membership were directed against the ESOP.

The tension between the ESOP and union loyalties occurred in a markedly different context among the mechanics, kitchen workers, and cabin cleaners represented by the International Association of Machinists (IAM). Apart from the pilots, no employee group responded to the ESOP with such unanimous and wholehearted support. "Everyone was really gung ho," says landing-gear mechanic Charlie Sands. Only 55 no votes were cast by 2193 IAM members in the employee poll. In general, the support was not based on fear of the takeover. Lorenzo was well regarded by union leaders and little known among the rank and file. It was rather the prospect of self-determination that had particularly strong appeal among the IAM membership. Electrician Gene Pica typically says, "I myself thought it was a tremendous opportunity to be an owner and to have somebody who is working on the board. You would have an inside seat."

The IAM's policy toward the ESOP, however, would not be decided by the Continental employees. The company's request for negotiated wage concessions was given to the district chairman, Lanny Rogers, who handled relations with nine airlines from his Houston office. Rogers followed instructions of the president of the IAM, William Wimpisinger, who categorically opposed ESOPs as an employee benefit intended to instill company loyalty. The remote union leadership made no distinction for the democratically designed Continental plan. John F. Peterpaul, the general vice-president of the IAM, dismissed the ESOP as a management ploy in a letter to Hal Alexander, president of the Continental local:

> It appears that the reason Continental Airlines is demanding compulsory payment into their ESOP program by all our mechanics and related employees is to make them captive to corporate strategy and dilute their collective bargaining strength, preventing future wage and benefit improvement.

The first response of the IAM leadership was to try to reassure the membership about the takeover. A delegation of union leaders visited Lorenzo on April 30, a week after the employee poll, and the union sent to all the membership a transcript of his answers to a list of questions. Lorenzo acknowledged that he "did not intend to continue the extremely high pay of pilots," but he reassured the IAM leaders on matters related to their own interests. Off the record, he is said to have told them: "the IAM is not the one I'm after. My problem is with the pilots." Hal Alexander was persuaded. In a letter to pilot leader Larry Baxter he said,

> On the subject of Frank Lorenzo being anti-union and some kind of monster wanting to destroy Continental to make huge profits. . . . It appears the Pilots WAR with Lorenzo is because New York Air pilots are non-union. To this I say, If you want them in your union, *Organize* them.

Three years later, disillusioned with both Lorenzo and the IAM, Alexander has changed his opinion.

In late May, the IAM headquarters in Washington dispatched an official, King McCulloch, to explain the union's opposition to the ESOP. He focused his criticism on the economic value of the investment in Continental stock and stressed the cost of interest payments on the ESOP loan. To buy Continental stock at the market value of $10.50 per share, employees would have to forgo wages of $18 per share to repay both principal and interest on the stock purchase loan. McCulloch argued that this investment should not be mandatory. In conversations with mechanics, one finds a different explanation of union opposition to the ESOP: the union was afraid of losing power under an ESOP-controlled company. "Who would strike a company they owned?" asks building maintenance worker Phil Bussey.

By opposing the Continental ESOP, the union leadership issued a challenge to the membership that would soon stimulate rank-and-file opposition to the union. At Denver, King McCulloch spoke at a series of special meetings in the union hall which included mechanics from neighboring cities. Rich Carberry, himself the secretary-treasurer of the Denver local, remembers that McCulloch faced a "pretty hostile" crowd. "There were a bunch of questions," he continues. "It got pretty hot and heavy. They were mad, and they're still mad." Often viewed as a self-serving bureaucracy, the IAM lacked credibility among its members. Many mechanics saw the leadership in much the same light as management—a well-compensated elite concerned with its own perquisites. "It's a business for them," concedes Hal Alexander.

Among the local membership, the ESOP did have one articulate and convinced opponent, Milt Burdick, chairman of the IAM political action committee in Los Angeles. Burdick believes in unionism with an idealistic zeal—once he ripped off table covers at a union banquet because they bore the mark of a nonunion manufacturer. A democratically designed ESOP had no place in his categories of thinking. Burdick fought hard to defeat the ESOP, but he admits he didn't persuade many members:

> We didn't have any luck. They were brainwashed by Eckel and management, and we couldn't persuade them otherwise. They had the American dream in their eye. They thought "We helped build the company and it is going to be ours. We'll have a representative on the board of directors and control it."

The union leaders tore down pro-ESOP posters and tried to make opposition to the ESOP a test of union loyalty, but only a small minority of the membership—15 percent by mechanic Charlie Sands's estimate—was won over to the union's position, persuaded especially by the argument that participation should be voluntary.

Electrician Gene Pica circulated a petition in the hope of pressuring the union leadership to change its position. He gathered 531 signatures with ease by mailing a few copies of the petition to Houston and leaving others in various work areas in Los Angeles. But he never received a response from the union leaders. Local challenges to the national leadership have never succeeded in the IAM. Hal Alexander notes that a mechanic cannot rise above the level of grievance chairman without the support of the national office.

A well-known Houston mechanic, Doug Schoen, who had

served as negotiator and chief steward for many years, also tried to rally opposition to the union policy, but he soon became convinced that the only solution was to leave the IAM:

> I spent years of my life with the union, and I expected them to support us. After they told us, "We know what is best for you," I was determined to break the IAM. It was in direct opposition to what the people of Continental wanted.

Schoen obtained leave to take his case to the Los Angeles employees. He says, "I toured the maintenance areas in Los Angeles on my own initiative and talked to all the shops. The people in the shops listened to me. Only union people were opposed." He envisioned forming a kind of "autonomous organization, not really a union," and thought that he was "picking up disciples." In Los Angeles, there was also a movement to charge union affiliation to the Teamsters who were known to accept ESOPs. Some mechanics kept piles of Teamster representation cards in their work area and many signed. The Teamster organizers gave them some encouragement by passing out literature at the airport, but they had a no-raid agreement with the IAM and did not attempt a full-fledged organizing campaign.

The union officially left the door open for the negotiation of a voluntary ESOP. Jack Sage says that management considered the voluntary ESOP to be a possible option that it might pursue with the IAM after the principal plan was in place, but it would require an entirely different design and it might generate ill feelings since the Continental stock was not likely to be a good investment. Milt Burdick says, however, that the union's talk of a voluntary plan was only a "smokescreen"; the IAM actually would reject any form of ESOP. "With an ESOP you're bargaining against yourself," he points out.

CHAPTER
NINE

APPARENT
VICTORY

The battle had been running against TI throughout the spring. While visiting the Paris air show on June 10, Lorenzo called syndicated business columnist Dan Dorfman to vent his feelings. Dorfman neatly summarized the conversation:

> Among other things, he (Lorenzo) suggested that (1) Continental's chief Alvin Feldman was a liar, (2) that Continental's management was knowingly feeding lies to its employees, (3) that Feldman was incompetent, and (4) that Continental had the potential to go bankrupt if it continued on its current course.

Lorenzo hotly denied to Dorfman that he had offered Feldman the job of running a merged airline. "The guy's nuts," he said. "What do we say to him? You lost $25 million, stick around, fella!" He blamed the employee movement on the company's "scare tactics": management was "feeding them a lot of propaganda that we're going to liquidate parts of the airline and sell off its assets." Lorenzo warned that he was not going to be easy to defeat. "I've put in $93 million, and I'm in to the end," he said.[1]

In early June, only the federal court ruling on TI's motion for a preliminary injunction loomed as an important hurdle. Rod Hills, the former SEC chairman, was confident that the New York Stock Exchange would not block the issuance of stock to the ESOP, and the CAB was engaged in the sort of broad, time-consuming investigation that Continental had sought. The pressure on Continental executives began to let up. The vice-president of financial planning, Jerome Himmelberg, who suffered a major heart attack later in the year, recalls that many executives began working long hours, six or seven days a week, in mid-1979 when the airline first ran into difficulties; the takeover battle intensified the atmosphere of crisis. "It was wearing people out," he says. Feldman now advised his top executives to take one week vacations. Setting an example, he left for the fishing camp near Jackson Hole, Wyoming, that he shared with Rod Hills and Dick Ferris, the chairman of United Airlines.

This summer, however, Feldman found it impossible to relax, even at this propitious moment, and he cut short his trip after a couple days. Before coming to Continental, he had been a regular weekend tennis player. His condominium at Marina del Rey enjoyed access to every facility for the sybaritic southern Californian life—pool, tennis courts, massage parlors, and Jacuzzis. But he now had little time for recreation. Vandeman, who had become his closest advisor, remarked, "Al's going too fast." Other things besides the takeover struggle preyed on his mind. He had found little time to concern himself with airline operations in the past months. Now, financial results were beginning to fall below projections, raising the possibility that Continental might not have the profitable third quarter that he had expected.

As the employee leaders anticipated the approaching victory, they continued to pursue their public relations campaign. The appeal for public support was their one handle on the levers of power, and they intended to use it until the end. In mid-June, the campaign focused on the California legislature. Both houses passed a resolution, sponsored by the president *pro tempore* of the Senate, David Roberti, and by the Speaker of the Assembly, Willie Brown, that expressed support for the employees' cause. In one of the minor epics of the campaign, the Austin, Texas, employees also succeeded in securing a resolution of both houses of the Texas legislature that commended the Continental ESOP. In effect, the Texas legislature went on record as opposing a major out-of-state acquisition by a Texas airline. The resolution had a respected sponsor, a legislator from El Paso who was a frequent flier on Continental, and it breezed through the legislature with only a little lobbying. The Austin employees talked of wanting to buy their own company and avoided mentioning the takeover bid. TI didn't get word of the resolution until it was on the governor's desk. "It was a surprise. We came up from the rear," says Arnette Knippa, city captain for Austin.

For pilot Larry Schlang, assigned to spread concern about the effect of the takeover on Micronesian routes, this was a period of incessant activity as he tried, in his words, "to fan an ember into a flame" The affairs of Micronesia and Guam are governed by a constellation of government entities. No fewer than twenty-one federal departments and agencies have direct responsibilities in the region. They are overseen by House and Senate committees of the interior, defense, and foreign affairs. The responsibility for military programs in the region is dispersed through another complex set of bureaucracies. With no official position, Schlang entered this bureaucratic maze aided only by perseverance and an ability to write coherent letters that demanded serious attention. One interview followed another as he sought out persons who might offer a valuable introduction or pass on a report to a higher level.

The results of this patient spadework would come to fruition later, but Schlang did score a notable public relations triumph at this time. Arriving at a meeting of the U.N. Trusteeship Council as a private citizen with a few personal references, he applied for permission to address the council and, to his surprise, was given the opportunity to speak immediately after a delegation of Marshall Islanders presented a petition that had drawn an impressive assembly of the world press: they demanded $450 million in damages from the United States government for the destruction of the Bikini atoll in hydrogen bomb tests. Schlang's story of TI's alleged threat to Pacific air service was also picked up by the national press and made the front page of two newspapers widely circulated in the Pacific, the *Honolulu Advertiser* and the *Pacific Daily News* of Guam.

This unexpected bonanza of publicity gave Schlang great satisfaction. A cultured man, he describes his feelings with a Homeric allusion. "It was one time," he says, "when I thought I put a stick in the eye of Lorenzo."

In the federal court lawsuit, TI could not wait for a court trial. Its one chance was to secure a preliminary injunction, based on extensive affidavits and exhibits filed with the court, that would block the closing of the ESOP prior to trial. If it could not postpone the sale of stock to the ESOP, it would have every incentive to bail out with a settlement that would best salvage its investment. As the TI attorneys took depositions and pursued requests for documents, they were convinced that they were putting together a strong case. Phil Bakes remembers, "We thought we had a pretty good case. We were confident about our court position." The heart of TI's case rested on *Klaus v. Hi-Shear Corp.*, a precedent from the ninth circuit where its lawsuit was filed. The facts of this decision, which involved a kind of dogfight for the control of a small business, were easily distinguishable from those of the Continental case, but TI thought it could meet the legal test enunciated by the court. The decision held that corporate officers and directors breach their fiduciary duty to shareholders by establishing an ESOP to defeat a tender offer, unless they show that the ESOP serves a compelling business purpose.

TI had a simple explanation for the origin of the ESOP that on its face was at least as plausible as the complex story we have followed. "I attribute it to Alan Batkin," says Phil Bakes. "The ESOP was an anti-takeover device proposed by an investment banker." In CAB testimony that might seem to call for reticence, Batkin made much of Lehman Brothers' apparently minor role in the origin of the plan. Among other things, he said that Lehman Brothers was asked "to assist in developing the structure of a sale of a substantial block of equity to employees." TI believed this was the critical revelation of what had really happened. A TI brief states: "Of the many scenarios devised by Continental to thwart TI's attempt to take control of Continental, the one finally selected was an Employee Stock Ownership Plan." Having selected the plan, the Continental management began "fomenting antagonism against Texas International." Lorenzo similarly complained, "The Continental employees have been given a whole fear scenario." The financial analysis of the takeover, he said, was "a lot of flagellation" designed "to whip up employees."[2]

TI had only ridicule for Continental's contention that the ESOP served a compelling business purpose. "The whole thing was a never never land," says Bakes. "What we're looking at," declared Lorenzo, "is a hall of mirrors."[3] The TI briefs characterized the ESOP as "simply a desperate device to dilute Texas International's voting power to prevent it from exercising control over Continental." Admittedly, the logic of the plan depended on one's understanding of employee motivation. Chuck Cheeld thinks that TI's perception of the ESOP was rooted in its history of difficult labor relations. "Lorenzo always viewed employees as a problem," Cheeld remarks. "He couldn't believe that the ESOP was real because he never understood that employees could love a company."

Federal district judge Lawrence Lydick promised a ruling on TI's motion for preliminary injunction within three days after a hearing scheduled on June 15. To avoid a temporary restraining order, Continental voluntarily agreed to defer the ESOP closing until after the ruling. This concession was not expected to delay significantly the closing of the transaction. Continental also had to await New York Stock Exchange approval of the issuance of stock to the ESOP which was expected the same week as the ruling.

On June 16, Judge Lydick filed a terse order denying TI's motion for a preliminary injunction. The next day he discussed his decision from the bench while ruling on a motion of the TI attorney, Frank Rothman, for a stay pending appeal:

> I spent four and a half days reading two huge boxes of depositions. . . . Four and a half days. I have reviewed every affidavit fully and come to some conclusions. . . . You see, you approach the matter, Mr. Rothman, as a basis for every argument that you make, that the ESOP is a device of management created and fostered to de-

feat the legitimate takeover plans of your client. Now I have already decided that I don't think that has yet been proven. I see the ESOP potentially as an alternative to your plan, which may very well be in the best interests of the company and its shareholders.

The ruling was not a decision on the merits of the case; in considering a motion for preliminary injunction, a federal court considers only the equities of the injunction and requires a showing of "a strong likelihood of success on the merits." The Continental employees, however, saw the ruling as a decisive vindication of the ESOP and the product of their own efforts. From the first days of the ESOP campaign, the CEA leaders had predicted success. The CEA now issued a teletype announcing, "We did it! We won!" and organized a "victory" rally at the corporate headquarters. Eckel had promised success when it appeared impossible. "Rightness is against him (Lorenzo)," he once said. "We will not fail regardless of how many things go wrong for us."[4] After the federal court ruling, he could not refrain from gloating. "We've essentially kicked the wizard in the backside," he said."[5]

After being consumed for months by the takeover struggle, Feldman began to think about the changes in management style that would follow employee control. He told his executive assistant, Mike Roach, that employee expectations had been raised and would have to be satisfied by a new orientation toward worker involvement. It was an unexplored frontier for Continental management, but Feldman was able to formulate a few thoughts in a speech to in-flight supervisors entitled, "Life after ESOP," which was taped and circulated to other supervisors. With improved morale and increased peer pressure for good job performance, he believed management could relax many existing controls and thin the ranks of lower level supervision; the one hundred in-flight supervisor jobs were among those to go. Under the ESOP, Feldman hoped that such plans, which might otherwise cause grumbling, would be willingly accepted. He expected the most resistance from middle managers, reluctant to make new delegations of responsibility to employees, but David Miho, city manager for Honolulu, was enthusiastic about the idea of worker involvement. "One of the residual hangovers companies have as a result of continued economic growth and prosperity in the U.S. over the past forty years is a control management mentality," he commented. "Decisions tend to be made at the top of the hierarchy, which alienates employees from the company. They tend not to care about profitability."[6]

The administrative committee of the ESOP began to meet in anticipation of the closing and elected as chairperson Karen Harvey, the representative of ticket agents and reservation agents. It was unquestionably the first time that a reservation agent had risen to a position of leadership in the company. The committee actually had very limited discretionary functions— it controlled, for example, the trust's investment of the company's semimonthly contributions during the periods between quarterly loan payment dates—and it retained E. F. Hutton and Company to advise it on these matters. Its principal function was to oversee the actual performance of the sequence of administrative steps outlined in plan documents and to explain the operation of the plan to employees. As chairperson, Harvey had no financial background, but she possessed the skills in communication that were needed to maintain employee confidence in the administration of the plan.

The assumption of victory was so pervasive in June that the airline began to function for a while as an employee-controlled company. Jack Riddle notes, "We could feel what it would be like if it had succeeded." Would employees, as TI predicted, have sought pay increases? Bill Miles says that employees raised the question repeatedly in the educational sessions he conducted. Each group was on guard against the other groups. Employees would typically say, "I know my group is not going to do this but I'm going to watch these other guys." The probable result, Miles believes, is that each group would have policed the others. "People were going to be very careful of what is given to the other guy," he says. Since employees generally regarded pilots as overpaid, employee control might have effectively curtailed their future compensation. The pilots themselves never contemplated this outcome, but the pilot leaders in the CEA were prepared to work with management for work rule changes that, in the absence of expanded operations, would mean painful furloughs of junior officers. John Huber says that Feldman had "plans" to enlist him and Eckel "as allies in productivity." Eckel publicly stated, "I think the pilots will agree to fly 20 percent more."[7]

The meetings of the CEA in June turned spontaneously into brainstorming sessions on productivity. Eckel explains, "The hue and cry was productivity. It seemed to us that if there was to be a value in employee ownership that had to be it—productivity and motivation." The employees saw possibilities for marked improvements. "In Denver," says mechanic Rich Carberry, "there were a hell of a lot of things to do." Many of the ideas were small matters of the sort that higher management might overlook. Carberry questioned whether it was necessary to throw away certain expensive bolts each time they were removed. Other ideas involved a degree of employee sacrifice. Dispatcher Ron Aramini, considered the possibility of increasing the dispatcher's 219-day work year. Flight attendant Pearl Kelly was concerned with the number of "ways of not flying" under her present contract. "As an employee owner, I would have wanted to see some of these loopholes tightened," she says. Some employees came to CEA leaders to win acceptance of new ideas. At one meeting, an employee presented a very technical plan to assure that engines delivered the optimum amount of thrust for the temperature; he hoped in this way to extend periods of time between engine overhauls.

The CEA had been formed as an *ad hoc* organization for a particular purpose, but with victory near it was not inclined to disband. The board members sensed that the democratic goals of the ESOP required a line of communication from management to employees. The representation of employees on the board of directors was some guarantee that their interests would be heeded, but employees needed channels at lower levels through which to express ideas and complaints. The search for higher productivity similarly might be aided by a forum in which employees could offer suggestions without fear of criticism. Management was somewhat skeptical of the value of continuing the CEA in its existing form. The director of personnel, John Bidlake, points out that effective decision making can be impeded by expanding the circle of those who must be consulted. As an alternative, Jack Sage introduced the CEA board to the Japanese concept of quality circles, workplace committees that serve to enhance effective teamwork. The committees might be linked at a higher level to an employee council or councils. Sage's idea of building on the CEA to form a "quality circle airline" was enthusiastically received, but events overtook efforts to implement it.

Many employees describe vividly a heightened esprit de corps stimulated by the apparent victory of the ESOP. "When victory seemed near," says John Clayton, "everyone felt this overwhelming sense of pride and camaraderie. It seemed to vindicate the belief that we were invincible." Clayton's perception of employee mood was perhaps colored by his own enthusiasm for the ESOP. This enthusiasm was not always shared. Los Angeles employee Jeannette Martin estimates that by midsummer 20 percent of noncontract employees were reluctant to make the contemplated pay concessions, and only 60 percent were still solidly in favor of the plan. But accounts of high employee morale are corroborated by persons, like Chuck Coble, who now doubt the practicality of the plan. "All traditional administrative lines had been crossed. All those lines dissolved," he says. "Pilots talked to ramp men and flight attendants to reservation agents and ticket agents to cabin cleaners. It was magic. There was united and defined purpose." The ESOP rarely provoked resentment, although one anonymous employee told a reporter: "The company has been sneaky and underhanded in the way it's gone about the whole thing."[8] Even in sectors of the company where the ESOP was least well received, one finds reports of a wholesome change in atmosphere. Flight attendant supervisor John Bailey says that relations between management and the union improved noticeably for a while.

The changed social environment, John Bidlake thought, might break down "jurisdictional concerns that impede productivity." But quite apart from its effects on business operations, the ESOP offered the promise of a more humane environment in which social ties would be strengthened and barriers to friendship removed. At least a half a dozen songs were written for CEA rallies. They do not celebrate new vistas of productivity, but rather an awakened sense of community. Jim Waters of El Paso put these words to a country and western tune:

The Continental Family

Verse 1 (solo)

I bought this airline
It belongs to me
I am this airline
And I'm proud as I can be
I love what I'm doing
And it's all for you and me
I'm a member of the Continental Family

Verse 2 (solo)

I bought this airline
It's my company
I love this airline
And I want the world to see
I'm flyin high—the sky's no limit—
We're in it, you and me
And I want you to join the Continental Family

Chorus 1 (group)

We bought this airline
It belongs to us
We are this airline
And we're people you can trust
We're flyin high—the sky's no limit—
We're in it, you and me
So come along and join the Continental Family

Chorus 2 (group)

We bought this airline
It's our company
We are this airline
And we want the world to see
We're flyin high—the sky's no limit—
We're in it, you and me
So come along and join the Continental Family

A sense that the ESOP would soon go into effect spread to the other side of the struggle after the federal court ruling. Stunned by the unexpected decision, the TI management took stock of the prospects of being caught as a minority shareholder on Continental. TI faced great pressure from Manufacturers Hanover Trust Company, which had extended $48 million on the strength of Continental's assets, and it was absorbing interest payments of about $1 million a month on the financing of the tender offer. Continental had fallen below financial projections in the second quarter—its projected profit for May turned into a loss—and its stock had dipped as low as $9.75 per share. As a minority shareholder, TI might suffer losses of the same order of magnitude as the profit it had made on the National Airlines bid.

Very soon after the ruling, George Vandeman received a telephone call from Phil Bakes. Vandeman recalls, "Bakes was exceedingly anxious to sell stock and wanted to come out to Los Angeles to talk. He made no concrete offer but seemed willing to entertain any proposal. I thought he might even be willing to sell TI's stock for a loss." Bakes confirms, "We would have loved to be out at that time. It looked like the ESOP might go through." It was the moment that Vandeman had awaited. He had tried to prepare Continental's management for the possibility it might have a chance to buy Lorenzo's stock before the ESOP was consummated. Then, the ESOP would be used to purchase outstanding shares at an advantageous price, with no problems of continued litigation or possible dilution of stock value. Vandeman remembers saying, "That would be the ideal situation for the ESOP to purchase stock. That is

the transaction we ought to do if the opportunity is presented."
But when he announced that the moment of opportunity had
arrived, Vandeman was dismayed to find that no one—not even
the Wachtell, Lipton law firm—now shared his view. "I was
totally taken aback," he says, "when Feldman's advisors concluded that Continental should not deal. Too many people had
got too committed to the plan we were on. There was too much
momentum behind the ESOP as proposed."

Mike Roach tries to analyze why he and other advisors
opposed negotiation:

> There was a feeling that having won the federal court
> decision, we had won. Lorenzo and company had as-
> sumed mythic proportions as the enemy. George pro-
> posed that we should give back something that we had
> won. None of us was emotionally prepared to do this.
> We wanted unconditional surrender. Only Feldman
> was sympathetic. The rest of us wanted blood.

There was also a fear that the company might compromise its
commitments to employees by negotiating with TI. Roach says,

> It really seemed to me that the way the negotiations
> might come out would amount to reneging on the
> ESOP plan. I had gone over to the side of the employ-
> ees. Some of the possible outcomes of negotiation would
> not give the employees what they had bargained for.

Although Vandeman could not offer to negotiate, Bakes said
that he would come out anyway. In the three or four days between Bakes's first call and his visit, Vandeman argued tire-
lessly for a settlement. He says, "I'd argue all day. By the end
of the day, I'd surrender. But in the morning I'd drive back
with renewed determination." Feldman seemed close to accepting Vandeman's arguments. "I think he knew I was right,"
says Vandeman. But a favorable New York Stock Exchange
decision was anticipated in a few days; it was an audacious
idea to abandon an elaborately prepared transaction, on the

threshold of closing, in favor of an improvised settlement. In the end, Feldman took the apparently safer course recommended by other advisors.

Accompanied by Robert Snedeker, the TI treasurer, Bakes came to the forty-third floor conference room of Latham and Watkins in the hope that his journey to Los Angeles would stimulate the negotiation of a buyout. Vandeman says, "I then regretfully advised them I had no authority to deal." There was nothing more to say, but the Continental attorneys tried to make small talk for about eight minutes. Bakes and Snedeker then left. Not knowing the struggle that preceded his visit, Bakes thought the attorneys had treated his initiative lighly. "They laughed at us and threw us out," he says. "I remember the scene very vividly. It was pie in the face." Vandeman also remembers the scene clearly. "We had it in the palm of our hand," he says.

CHAPTER
TEN

THE ESOP
RUNS INTO
TROUBLE

Feldman took personal responsibility for handling the New York Stock Exchange application, working directly with his friend Rod Hills. As a private organization, the Exchange handles applications informally through *ex parte* discussions. In the words of a Los Angeles securities lawyer, it is "almost like dealing with a country club." If not actually a member of the club, Hills belonged to the same milieu as the top Exchange officials and knew many of them personally. Feldman believed that Hills could deliver a favorable ruling through reasonable conversations with responsible officials. This was the sort of private and dignified way of doing business that Feldman liked. He asked the employees to stay out of the proceeding and dismissed a suggestion by CAB counsel Lee Hydeman that Continental should discretely raise the possibility of a lawsuit against the board of the Exchange.

The TI strategists sensed that their opportunity lay in cultivating the support of the staff which was understandably concerned with the consistent administration of Exchange rules. Phil Bakes says that they spent "a good deal of time with the staff," expecting that it would be "a little more loyal to the rules that they wrote." TI cited numerous public statements of Continental executives and CEA leaders to the effect that the ESOP would give control to employees; but realizing the elusive and widely shared nature of this control, it advanced an alternative argument: the ESOP would take control away from

TI. A CEA lawyer noted on his copy of the TI brief, "The CAB will love this!" The argument seemed to imply that the CAB had violated its statutory duty. Regulatory legislation forbid an airline from obtaining control of another without a formal CAB order. In approving TI's voting trust, the agency purported to confer powers that fell somewhat short of control.

On Friday, June 19, Rod Hills received news from a trusted source on the Exchange that seemed to vindicate his long-expressed optimism: the Exchange was favorably disposed to the application, and it would in all likelihood issue a letter Monday morning permitting Continental to list the ESOP stock. Confident of this report, Hills advised Continental to act immediately to arrange a closing for the ESOP on Tuesday, June 23. A feeling of relief and elation spread through management. Mike Conway remembers celebrating that Friday evening with Jack Sage at a Manhattan Beach restaurant. He says, "It looked like the end of seven-day-a-week work, and the culmination of a lot of hard work."

On the eve of victory, Feldman could best express his appreciation for his colleagues with a gesture. He was too private a person to communicate his feelings directly. If he confided in another person—as he had once with John Huber and Lee Hydeman—he would maintain a distance afterwards as if he had committed an indiscretion. To express his thanks for those who had fought the right with him, he invited a number of executives and professional advisors, together with spouses, to a dinner at Chasen's, the famous Beverly Hills restaurant, on the Saturday evening after the scheduled closing, and he ordered an enlarged bronze reproduction of the pro-ESOP button, saying "Continental the Airline Pride Built (and Bought)," be mounted on wooden plaques and awarded to each member of the CEA board.

The Exchange did not issue the letter on Monday, but Hills was told that a committee was considering the application and would have a decision "promptly." He believed that Continental's application was still on course and promised to place a call to Los Angeles the next morning at the scheduled closing to confirm the listing of the stock. The banks participating in the ESOP transferred $171 million, representing the market value of the stock, to Security Pacific National Bank for the stock purchase. The closing was set for 7:00 AM provided Hill's call was received. Between 5:30 and 6:00 AM, the bankers and attorneys began to arrive at a large conference room in the office of O'Melveny and Myers, the banks' counsel. A pile of documents about two feet high was placed in front of every seating position on a table roughly twenty feet long. All of the elaborate documentation was executed and needed only to be exchanged. The Union Bank representative, Robins Bogue, recalls that by 7:00 AM about twenty-five people "were all sitting around the conference table waiting for the phone call." An hour later, Latham & Watkins lawyers began trying to reach Hills. About 9:30 AM they were informed that there was a problem.

Hills flew out to Los Angeles that evening to confer with Feldman, and he was in the executive office, trying to prepare him for an unexpected decision, when a hand-delivered letter from the president of the New York Stock Exchange arrived. The letter informed Feldman that the Exchange would require shareholder approval for the issuance of stock to the ESOP; it relied heavily on an assurance, received from Lorenzo the same day, that TI would vote its shares proportionately to other shares in the shareholder vote. TI had fought in the CAB proceeding to secure permission to vote its shares in a block against the ESOP; at the last moment, it had surrendered this right to obtain the desired New York Stock Exchange decision. To a lawyer, the concession was a veiled threat of a lawsuit; Lorenzo was positioning himself to sue the Exchange if it permitted the issuance of stock to the ESOP. In a very brief letter to the Exchange, Lorenzo said simply:

> This will confirm our commitment to vote our shares of Continental Air Lines common stock in proportion to the manner in which all other such shares are voted in the event that the Exchange requires a vote of stockholders to approve Continental's proposed Employee Stock Ownership Plan.

Vandeman regards the Exchange's decision as a "good faith determination" based on its concern to maintain "the integrity of its rules." The ESOP would indeed effect a certain change in the locus of control even though it did not involve the sort of transfer of a control block that would fall squarely within the pertinent rule. Nevertheless, the decision was a close and difficult one. Like other observers, Vandeman thinks that TI's last-minute concession of voting rights may have been "enough to tip the scale."

When the issue of TI's voting rights had been debated before the CAB in late April, a shareholder vote on the ESOP was a realistic option, but two months later the time required to conduct a shareholders' vote presented a formidable array of problems. In normal course, it takes forty-five to ninety days to complete the steps required for a shareholders' vote—drafting of proxy materials, obtaining SEC clearance, printing and mailing proxy materials, and soliciting shareholder support— and TI would have a good chance of delaying the vote further by challenging the proxy materials before the SEC and in court. Vandeman was very pessimistic that the banks would keep the ESOP credits available in the face of a prolonged proxy battle, particularly in view of Continental's poor financial performance in the preceding weeks. He says flatly, "There was no way that this large and delicate transaction could be held together for this time."

To keep the option of a shareholders' vote open, Feldman asked Latham and Watkins to work on preliminary drafts of proxy materials, and he directed Georgeson and Company to plan for a proxy solicitation campaign. The proxy solicitors pursued their preparations even to the point of hiring a detective agency to check on the telephone numbers and personal whereabouts of shareholders. They did not foresee any problem in gaining shareholder approval. The independent shareholders, who had rejected the tender offer, were generally loyal to management. If necessary, the employees would assist in shareholder solicitation. "We could have persuaded the ordinary shareholder," says Georgeson executive Peter Harkins. But with every week that Feldman deferred a decision to authorize the shareholder vote, it became an increasingly impractical alternative.

The Continental management now saw a negotiated buyout —an opportunity spurned a week earlier—as a very attractive option. Finally authorized to negotiate, Vandeman hastened to call Bakes. There was general jubilation when Bakes replied that Lorenzo would fly out to Los Angeles that very weekend for discussions. "I was surprised that they were willing to deal," Vandeman recalls. Bakes explains that they remained concerned about the financial condition of Continental and the possible success of the ESOP. "We saw about fifty PAC men heading toward us all the time," he says.

As the Continental executives awaited Lorenzo's visit, they assumed that the buyout could be accomplished by use of a scaled-down ESOP. Any other form of financing would be unacceptable to employees and very difficult to secure. But the ESOP buyout could invite shareholder litigation charging the board of directors with fiduciary liability. Continental's stock was now trading more than $3 per share below the tender offer price. Even if TI made no profit on the buyout, Continental would undoubtedly have to pay a large premium over current market value—a practice resembling what would later be called "greenmail." Hoping to lay a solid basis for the transaction, Feldman accepted Vandeman's conservative advice to conduct a shareholders vote to approve the ESOP buyout. In this context, Continental was less concerned about the delay required for shareholder approval since TI would not engage in a proxy battle.

The Saturday night dinner at Chasen's, if not the victory celebration Feldman had planned, turned out to be a festive occasion. A negotiated buyout seemed imminent; Lorenzo and Bakes had arrived in Los Angeles, bringing their families with them for a long visit. The chairman of Continental's special committee of the board, Joe Kilgore, had flown in from Texas to be on hand. The next morning George Vandeman, accompanied by several Continental executives, began serious discussions with Bakes and a team of TI lawyers. He soon found that TI was still weighing the pros and cons of a buyout. John

Phillips, a financial analyst who participated in the discussions, remembers arguing that "it was an opportunity for TI to get out without being burnt." The employee uprising, the poor business results in May, and the inevitable prospect of collateralizing the fleet meant that TI might come out a loser. After a few hours, Bakes apparently acceded to the arguments and offered to sell TI's shares in Continental for its cost of $93 million. The negotiators quickly reached what Bakes describes as "the verbal outline of a handshake deal."

Feldman was elated to receive the news as he sat waiting in a nearby room. Standing up with a broad smile, he said, "We got a deal!" Kilgore called Six and obtained his approval as chairman of the board. A half hour later, Feldman met Lorenzo to ratify the understanding. Meeting each other for the fourth time since the tender offer, the two men exchanged congratulations and shook hands on the deal.

Lorenzo and Feldman soon left to allow their negotiators to put the agreement into a written document. "Within minutes," remembers Vandeman, "it became apparent that the parties had reached agreement based on a serious misunderstanding." The Continental negotiators had not made clear that they intended to finance the buyout with an ESOP subject to shareholder approval. "A little thing like that!" remarks Bakes incredulously. TI was under pressure from Manufacturers Hanover Trust for a rapid settlement, and it wanted a definite and immediate commitment that could be closed within days or at most a week. The proposed use of a scaled-down ESOP, they objected, not only deferred the buyout but made it highly uncertain. They doubted that the transaction could be closed even within the sixty-day period that the Continental negotiators projected. Fully convinced of their criticisms of the ESOP, they maintained that IRS disapproval, a class action lawsuit, or even the shareholder vote was likely to upset the plan.

Throughout the night, the negotiators searched for a mutually agreeable formula, caucusing separately in the law offices of Latham & Watkins and Hughes Hubbard & Reed, located in neighboring office towers in downtown Los Angeles, and then meeting in one office or the other to discuss new ideas. Both sides struggled to break the impasse. By 5:00 AM, a group of about ten exhausted lawyers and executives could be seen in the lobby of Latham and Watkins trying to come up with new creative suggestions, but Vandeman recalls, "We were unable to bridge the gap." Vandeman called Feldman and woke him out of a deep sleep to inform him of the impasse. Feldman gave a sigh and said, "I'll see you at the office." Later that morning, Vandeman confirmed that the proposed deal could not be salvaged.

With the collapse of negotiations, Continental still retained the option of voluntarily delisting its stock from the New York Stock Exchange in order to close the ESOP without a shareholders' vote. The delisting was not in itself a matter of great consequence. In recent years, the over-the-counter market has been aided by computerized reporting that has made it somewhat competitive with the national exchanges. Lehman Brothers was prepared to offer an opinion that the listing of the stock on the over-the-counter market would cause shareholders "no material loss in the marketability or liquidity of their investment."

The option of voluntarily delisting Continental stock from the New York Stock Exchange presented a strategic dilemma only because it would deprive the company of an exemption from California securities regulation and put it potentially in conflict with the California Corporations Commissioner. The Continental strategists did not have a fallback plan to deal with the California agency's hostile assertion of jurisdiction. This obstacle was not perceived until May when optimism about the New York Stock Exchange application ran high. They now faced the choice of defying the state agency by claiming an exemption from state regulation or seeking a state permit to issue stock to the ESOP. The ESOP specialists of Kelso and Company urged a strategy of defiance. In the previous six years, numerous leveraged ESOPs had been closed in reliance on the stock bonus plan exemption of California securities law.

Let the Corporations Commissioner try to attack the ESOP, they advised. With past practice on Continental's side, a court would be unlikely to order rescission of the transaction. Jack Curtis, a Kelso and Company attorney, regards the company's failure to claim the exemption as "*the* strategic error of the battle."

Latham & Watkins had a different perspective: its reputation in financial circles depended on its giving sound, conservative advice. The Department of Corporations' interpretation of the stock bonus plan exemption was not unreasonable and had been publicly expressed in 1978 through an advisory opinion of Willie Barnes, then Corporations Commissioner. The exemption applied to "any transaction whereby an issuer . . . *contributes* any security . . . to a pension, profit sharing or stock bonus plan." Strictly speaking, a leveraged ESOP does not involve a "contribution" of stock but a sale. The securities expert at Latham & Watkins, Randy Bassett, though personally a strong partisan of the ESOP, concluded that he could not offer the sort of opinion affirming the availability of the exemption that the banks would require.

A lawyer remembers Feldman listening impassively after the New York Stock Exchange decision as Wachtell, Lipton lawyer Bernard Nussbaum urged him to fight to save the ESOP. Among other things, Nussbaum thought that Continental should consider a lawsuit against the Exchange. Although Nussbaum won the praise of colleagues for his contribution to the battle ("A real fighter" and "a wonderful human being," says CAB counsel, Lee Hydeman), his combative ideas sometimes clashed with Feldman's sense of propriety. Feldman feared leading the takeover defense into a path that would cast discredit on his management. Just as he refused to challenge the New York Stock Exchange for a good faith decision, he recoiled from the notion of avoiding the California Corporations Commissioner because of an early indication of hostility. To put the transaction beyond challenge, he thought it best to seek clearance from the state agency. On June 30, Continental applied to the Commissioner for a permit to issue stock to the ESOP.

Feldman was visibly disheartened in the days after the New York Stock Exchange decision. When the CEA secretary, Patrice Boyd, saw him in the hall, she tried to cheer him up. "Don't take it so hard. We're going to win!" she said. "Gee, I really hope so," he replied. Erica Steinberger recalls, "All of us knew he was extremely depressed. He had this enormous sense of responsibility. He couldn't see it as the tactics in a game." Nevertheless, Feldman clearly hoped that the application to the Corporations Commissioner would be successful. He always expected others to accept what he regarded as rational arguments; he had even hoped to persuade Lorenzo of the benefit of the Western merger after the tender offer. Would not the Commissioner recognize the benefit of a transaction that had passed the scrutiny of Lehman Brothers, Bear Stearns, and the federal court? Mike Conway observes, "Logic can be your worst enemy. If you really believe that this is the best thing for shareholders, employees and the corporation and good reason has to prevail, a lot of times you set yourself up for disappointment." It soon became apparent that, having been placed at the mercy of the Corporations Commissioner, the ESOP was in trouble.

The California Corporations Commissioner, Geraldine Green, was an unusual political commodity when she was appointed in 1980 by Governor Jerry Brown—a black woman and a Democrat with a long association with big business. She had worked in the corporate law department of IBM and then of ARCO for eleven years before entering public life. She says she first learned of "the Continental ESOP problem" from Steven Gourley, her chief deputy commissioner, during a semi-annual trip in May to talk with New York investment bankers and officials of the American and New York Stock Exchanges. The Continental ESOP was on a list of enforcement problems that Gourley wished to discuss with the New York Stock Exchange. Green easily accepted her deputy's criticisms of the transaction. The decision of the New York Stock Exchange not to list the stock clinched the case. Green argues, "State standards shouldn't be lower than those of a quasi-regulatory agency like the New York Stock Exchange. It lost a customer."

Gourley concedes that Green told her staff, even before the Continental application was filed, that she would not approve the issuance of stock to the Continental ESOP without a shareholder vote, but this decision was not conveyed "in so many words" to Continental lawyers while the Department was processing their application.

Continental found its first opportunity to present the ESOP to Green in a large, tape-recorded meeting in a state office building on June 26, two days after the New York Stock Exchange decision. She appeared well versed on TI's objections to the plan, questioning Continental attorneys about dilution in book value and the price of the stock; and she searched for new flaws in the plan. Among other things, she criticized a provision giving Continental the right to amend or terminate the plan. The provision is universally included in all varieties of employee benefit plans, and a lawyer's failure to include it might be grounds for legal malpractice. "When you heard issues like that raised," says Kelso and Company attorney Roland Attenborough, "you knew she had made up her mind."

The California Corporations Code gives the Commissioner power to enjoin any "sale of a security that is not fair, just and equitable," but this broad grant of discretionary power is coupled with only a very limited procedural safeguard: after the Commissioner issues an order, the applicants have a right to request a hearing to reconsider it. Green acknowledges that the Department's procedure in reviewing applications is "informal." "We listen to anyone who has anything to say," she says. Any person can interject an objection to an application who cares to write a letter or succeeds in getting the ear of a staff member. Applicants have a chance to discover what their adversaries say only by requesting copies of written communications under the state Freedom of Information Act. The Continental lawyers received only fragmentary information, long after the fact, about the communications of TI attorney Willie Barnes that laid the basis for the staff's analysis.

After the initial meeting with Green, Feldman began to consider for the first time a political strategy. The best hope seemed to be to persuade Governor Brown to put political pressure on the Commissioner, and the company retained Jeremiah Hallissey, Brown's northern California campaign treasurer, to present its case. The employee leaders secured the cooperation of David Roberti, the president *pro tempore* of the Senate, who led a delegation of lawmakers to the governor's office, urging him to do something to influence Green. The employees' grass-roots political campaign now directed its guns at Sacramento. In response to CEA appeals, Continental employees let loose a flood of telephone calls, letters, and mailgrams directed at the governor and local legislators. Green remembers that she was barraged with calls from legislators, city councilmen, and county supervisors. "There wasn't anything that wasn't tried," she says.

Green's opposition to the ESOP had nothing to do with political considerations, but, in the face of political pressure, she wished to justify the anomaly of supporting the takeover of a California-based carrier by a Texas airline. She asked TI for an assurance that it would not curtail operations within the state. Lorenzo complied with a letter stating:

> This letter will confirm that Texas International has no plans to move the headquarters of Continental Air Lines out of the State of California. In fact, Texas International, should it acquire control of Continental Air Lines, plans to retain Continental's headquarters in Los Angeles. Further, Texas International has no plans to move any part of Continental's operations currently conducted in California to a location outside of California.

During a dinner conversation with Hallissey, Governor Brown professed to be sympathetic to the employees' cause, but he was subject to conflicting pressures. The partners of the Manatt law firm enjoyed political relationships and a record of fund raising that no politician could ignore. When Roberti and his colleagues later approached him, Brown, for whatever reason, had shifted ground. The lawmakers argued that the ESOP fit his image: it was an innovative new way of doing things. But Brown now protested that he had no legal authority to intervene in the case. The governor's neutrality ended any real hope of influencing Green's decision.

On July 13, Commissioner Green issued an order that fulfilled the employees' most pessimistic forebodings. In a six-point statement of issues, the Commissioner accepted all TI's arguments, finding among other things that the ESOP was a management entrenchment scheme. The order followed the New York Stock Exchange decision by requiring a shareholders' vote on the ESOP but it added two further requirements: the company would have to distribute a detailed prospectus to all employees and obtain employee approval of the ESOP in a second employee poll. No regulatory agency had ever required that employees be given a prospectus for an employee stock plan funded by their employer, and Continental's employee poll was itself without precedent in the field. To require a second poll with a prospectus was an astonishing innovation.

In a press conference, Green presented other arguments apparently overlooked in the formal order. To employee leaders who had been absorbed in the struggle for months, many of her remarks seemed not only illogical but misinformed. The tenor of the press conference is best suggested by an exerpt from the press release:

> Over half of the employees of Continental do not have union representation and did not get to vote on the plan except in the initial straw poll. The machinists who rejected the plan, represented 25% of the employees. The result therefore is that a majority of groups representing 75% of the employees have either voted against the ESOP or have not voted at all, except in an initial straw poll. Therefore, acceptance of the ESOP has been based solely on the acceptance of the plan by 25% of Continental's employees.

The conclusion that the ESOP had been accepted by only 25 percent of Continental's employees was reached by (a) misstating the actual size of the union groups (the IAM, ALPA, and UFA represented 19 percent, 12 percent, and 17 percent of the work force, respectively), (b) imputing to machinists the policy of the national IAM leadership and mistakenly claiming that they had voted against the ESOP, and (c) discounting entirely the employee poll.

The CEA issued a press release that declaimed, "Yesterday, July 13, 1981, a date which will live in infamy in the history of the American working man, the hopes and dreams of 11,000 employees of Continental Airlines were shattered by the California Corporations Commissioner." The sense of outrage was compounded by the nature of the proceeding—the undisclosed *ex parte* communications, the staff's wholesale acceptance of TI's arguments, the bizarre requirements of a prospectus and a second employee poll, and the poorly informed press conference—but three years later Green and Gourley wish to stress only one point: the ESOP would have cut the book value of the shares in half without a shareholders' vote. It was this argument—by no means a trivial one—that had the power of persuading Green and her staff.

Bernard Nussbaum had no doubt what should be done next. The ESOP might still be salvaged by appointing a trustee in Nevada, the state of Continental's incorporation, and closing the transaction in that state. "We really had a shot," he says, "if we would move fast and aggressively. Why not just pick up the goddamn ESOP and take it to Nevada? The ESOP was magic. No court would have enjoined it. No court ever did enjoin it." It was actually doubtful that the use of a Nevada trustee would avoid application of California law. The legal field of choice of law has tended to evolve from simple, mechanical rules to a more rational approach which weighs a transaction's contacts with a state. Since the ESOP had been negotiated in California, this approach would bar Continental from evading California law at the eleventh hour by switching trustees. But even if a court should apply California law, the use of a

Nevada trustee would allow Continental to litigate the stock bonus plan exemption in a favorable time and forum. A federal court would issue a preliminary injunction rescinding the ESOP only if TI could establish a "strong probability of success on the merits."

In a long and agitated debate in Feldman's office, Nussbaum fought hard for a Nevada trustee. He recalls that Feldman objected, "It's too flaky. It's too far out." Latham and Watkins would not countenance the strategy; it was plainly a gamble and the firm was accustomed to lending its prestige to tightly negotiated transactions. Feeling that Nussbaum was pressuring him too much, Feldman finally became angry. "I argued so hard for moving it to Nevada that Al stopped talking to me," Nussbaum remembers. "Oh! We had some business conversations. But we were such close friends for the two or three months before. I used to go to his apartment. He talked to me about his wife and daughter."

As a last resort, Nussbaum urged that Feldman authorize a suit in a California federal court to challenge the Commissioner's order. "It took a fight to get him to bring a lawsuit in California court. I had to almost pound the table," he recalls. Wachtell, Lipton pursued the lawsuit vigorously, arguing that the order "stands as an aberration in the history of state regulation," but any favorable court ruling was almost certain to come too late.

Judge Lydick, who was again assigned to the Continental litigation, was on vacation until July 27. Another four to six weeks would probably be needed to obtain a ruling on the motion for preliminary injunction. There was little possibility of keeping the banks on the line this long. Feldman seemed to be doing no more than playing out his hand. Nussbaum says he did not understand, until three weeks later, why Feldman refused to pursue a strategy that offered a better chance of success.

The ESOP both gained and lost ground on other fronts during July. The IRS routinely issued a determination letter affirming the tax qualification of the plan. A California state court denied a preliminary injunction in a class action lawsuit brought to challenge the ESOP. And in a defeat mixed with moral vindication, the CAB administrative law judge recommended approval of the acquisition but still adopted Continental's analysis of the ESOP and many of its criticisms of the takeover. Judge William Kane agreed that a merger of Continental and TI would result in an airline overburdened with debt. "TI's evidence that it will be able to pay such debts without significantly dismantling Continental Air Lines rests on some very tenuous assumptions," he found. He praised the ESOP as an alternative that "would benefit the Continental employees and . . . strengthen the corporation and enable it to become a more effective competitor." He continued:

> The ESOP is an exceptional opportunity for Continental to attract a new and highly beneficial form of equity capital. . . . The carrier will benefit immensely from the fact that Continental's employees will be paying the entire interest on the ESOP loan, thereby producing a substantial $24 million annual reduction in Continental's interest expense and a corresponding improvement in its cash flow and profitability.

> The claim by Continental and CEA that the direct involvement of the employees in the economic process resulting from the ESOP will lead to higher employee productivity, efficiency and innovation is adopted. Without putting a dollar sign or a percentage figure on the extent of the productivity increase . . . it is concluded that it will be substantial.

Judge Kane reasoned, however, that the public interest standard of the Airline Deregulation Act required the CAB to encourage "the free flow of capital." His analysis of the benefits of the ESOP had to be weighed against this ideologically tinged policy embodied in the statute. Faced with a choice between empirical analysis and ideology, Judge Kane believed he had no choice under the law but to choose ideology. He concluded:

Notwithstanding the foregoing strong advantages of the ESOP plan from the point of view of both Continental Air Lines and its employees, it is not considered that these benefits are such as to outweigh the greater interest in permitting the free market for capital to operate so as to allow Texas International to acquire Continental.

Though technically a defeat, the opinion was a kind of public relations victory: it gave official recognition of the validity of Continental's analysis.

In the final oral arguments before the CAB on July 29, the Board appeared interested only in the question whether it was compelled to refer its decision to the president for a further sixty-day review required of orders affecting foreign service. In the case of Continental, the question turned largely on the issue of Micronesian routes. The board was predisposed to end the proceedings quickly. The antitrust division of the CAB described a further sixty-day delay of the takeover as a "harsh result," and chairman Marvin Cohen was reluctant to allow technical legal considerations stand in the way of the free flow of capital. One of his questions gives an insight into his personal values:

> What would happen to the public interest . . . if a non-airline came in and did just what you are concerned with here; dismembered Continental to pay for buying it and made a profit? The airplanes would not then disappear nor would the employees, would they? They would all be recirculated in the society. . . .

Failing to see Continental as a human community, Cohen equated employees and machinery. Both should be "recirculated in society" as dictated by the free play of market forces.

A decision ordering presidential review became, however, politically inevitable when the departments of defense, interior, state, and transportation issued letters in the week following oral arguments that recommended the additional sixty-day review. The letters were largely the personal triumph of pilot Larry Schlang—the fruition of months of work. He could claim full credit for engineering the critical Department of Defense recommendation—delivered to the CAB minutes before closing time the day before the Board voted on the case—which was written in trenchant language and hinted at possible litigation if its advice were not followed, and he had helped lay the groundwork that enabled Continental's CAB lawyers to secure the cooperation of other executive agencies. The final CAB decision approved the takeover as expected, but gave a new sixty-day lease to the employee movement by ordering presidential review.

The employee leaders struggled to find alternatives as they watched the ESOP slip out of their grasp. A group of Denver pilots visited Royce Griffin, the Colorado Commissioner of Securities, who assured them that the ESOP would be welcome in his state. Eckel secured an opinion of the Powell Goldstein law firm that cautiously approved a method of using the pilots' defined benefit pension plan, the B-fund, to provide financial support for the ESOP. The company could convert the B-fund into two separate funds—a diversified investment fund and a fund devoted entirely to Continental stock—and pilots could elect to place their accounts in either fund. But the employees could take the initiative only in the field of political action. Shortly after Feldman decided to apply to the Corporations Commissioner, Eckel asked a well-regarded young assemblyman, Douglas Bosco, to introduce legislation that would clarify the stock bonus plan exemption by placing leveraged ESOPs clearly within its provisions. Bosco introduced the legislation on July 7 while Continental's application was still before the Commissioner. The bill would be considered by committee in mid-August after the legislature's summer recess.

Feldman placed little hope in the employees' bill. The legislation, he thought, would come too late, even if it could be enacted. Continental had no political presence in Sacramento. The company had never made campaign contributions or cultivated political relationships in the state. Over the years, it had paid a lobbyist, Donald Brown, a fee of one hundred dollars a month merely to keep it informed of legislation affecting the airline industry. Brown possessed considerable influence in Sacramento as the representative of the two largest agricultural enterprises in the state, but he offered discouraging advice. In his view, Continental had to make up for past inaction in state politics if it wanted the legislation to pass. He recommended that the company immediately set up a $100,000 political campaign fund. Feldman indignantly dismissed the suggestion.

Like other employees, Eckel found it difficult to understand Feldman's cautious strategy. "I was a 'damn it! do it! proponent," he says. His impatience turned to anger when a *Forbes* magazine reporter suggested that he was participating with Feldman in a management entrenchment scheme. "Anyone who thinks I'm out to save that bastard is wrong," he snapped in a rare outburst of profanity. Deeply humiliated to find his words in print, he wrote Feldman a letter of apology. Feldman replied with a handwritten note on executive stationery:

8 July

Dear Paul—
No apology is called for. We are in a tough battle and we both know that the press doesn't always pick things up the way they really are.

Even more important, I trust you and I believe in you. In the long run that's far more important than all the coordination in the world.

So relax about Forbes and relax about the state legislature. We are doing the best we know how to do and we are doing it to our own *ethical standards.*

Best regards,
Al

At the time of writing the note, Feldman was still hoping that the ESOP would succeed, but it had already suffered a setback more serious than either the New York Stock Exchange or Corporations Commissioner's decision. Discounted fares had spread in the first months of 1981 to the point that in May about 80 percent of Continental's passengers traveled at a discounted rate. On June 15, the financial projection for the year was changed from a $11.5 million profit to a $4.4 million loss on operating revenues of $1189.6 million. The marketing department still expected other carriers to cut back on discounts in the summer season, but the last weeks of June offered no relief, and financial results of the Fourth of July weekend—the first significant test of what the summer offers—gave cause for alarm. In this weekend, competitive discounts had increased, rather than abated, and revenues per passenger mile were very low. Feldman asked the financial planning department to prepare projections for the month of July and the entire year on the assumption that no relief would be forthcoming.

The crisis was quite general among the major carriers in the industry. The third quarter is historically the equivalent of the Christmas season for retailers—the period in which airlines hope to earn large profits to offset losses in other periods. But in 1981 the country was in a recession and traffic declined for all major airlines except Northwest. In a mutually destructive struggle to keep their planes full, the major carriers bid relentlessly for passengers with discounted fares. The third quarter at first promised narrow profits but later produced losses. As a group, the twelve major carriers suffered a loss of $53 million in this quarter, ordinarily the most profitable of the year. TI found itself in a market position similar to the smaller trunk carriers and also suffered a loss, no less than $6.6 million for the quarter.

Conceding after the Fourth of July weekend that discounts would continue, the market planning department provided a new estimate of the magnitude of Continental's losses for the year: while traffic would be as projected, revenues would be about $100 million below the original projection. The revised revenue projection, though still tentative, had to be disclosed to the banks. Continental customarily gave the banks periodic revenue projections, and it was expected to reveal immediately any unusual commitments or adverse occurences. Jack Woodlock remembers the date, July 16, when he called the lead banks to give them the appalling news. He recalls saying, "I guess that means the ESOP is a dead issue." The bankers agreed.

CHAPTER
ELEVEN

A PILOT
AMBUSH

By a cruel coincidence, the fortunes of Continental began to fall apart the day before the anniversary of the death of Feldman's wife, Rosemily. The ESOP bankers met on July 17, immediately after receiving the revised revenue projections. Sharing a concensus that the ESOP could no longer be implemented, they were most concerned now with obtaining collateral to secure their existing loans. Feldman could only ask them to wait a while before taking action. The next day, Feldman had invited his children to join him in La Jolla in a remembrance of their mother's burial. Though he had long avoided any kind of religious observance after breaking with his Jewish family by marrying Rosemily—a Roman Catholic —in a Unitarian church, he preserved a memory of the Jewish ritual of unveiling the tombstone a year after burial. The family journeyed together to visit the grave. Then, leaving his children, Feldman walked to the top of a small rise and stood alone facing the ocean. Rosemily had ordered a porch built on their seaside home so that she could spend her last days in the presence of the ocean, but the construction was not completed in time.

While still burdened with grief, Feldman decided to negotiate a surrender to TI. After the collapse of the buyout negotiations in June, Vandeman saw very little hope for the ESOP. The airline's financial reverses, the Corporations Commissioner's order, and the CAB proceedings appeared to end any real power of resistance; but there remained enough uncertainty that Continental might secure valuable concessions. Feldman had talked to Vandeman about finding a dignified way out. He should act now, Vandeman advised, while he still had some bargaining power, to negotiate a takeover agreement on terms favorable to shareholders that would offer a graceful end to the battle. Feldman knew that Vandeman had been right in the past, and he was resolved not to err again by rejecting his advice.

Feldman intended to discuss negotiation of a settlement at a board of directors' meeting on July 20, but, as a courtesy, he agreed to allow Eckel to speak first to the board about the CEA bill in the California legislature. Eckel appeared before the directors accompanied by most of the CEA board. He remembers that he tried to express the employees' "unflagging determination to fight." Visibly disturbed, Feldman criticized his plans, but other members of the board seemed receptive to the idea of continuing the fight in Sacramento. In fact, Audrey Meadows Six staged a spirited defense of the legislative alternative after the employees left, summoning up her considerable dramatic talent. When Robert Six tried to quiet her, she protested, "I'm an advisory director, and I'm going to advise." It was like a scene from "The Honeymooners," the television series that had won her fame. But Feldman's sober analysis carried the day. The board of directors authorized him to negotiate a settlement based on an exchange of securities with TI. The matter would be handled with great secrecy; it seemed premature to inform the employees until some actual understanding with TI had been reached. Besides, the threat of legislative action served as one of the company's last bargaining chips.

The decision cost Feldman deeply. A few days later, he tried to continue his custom of periodically eating with employees in the cafeteria, but he returned within a few minutes. "That was quick," said his secretary, Rita Salisbury. "I can't face them," he said, his voice breaking, as he turned into his office. The employees' faith in the ESOP had been so closely associated with confidence in Feldman that he had been placed, against his will, in something of the position of a messiah. He knew what he was now doing would be regarded as a betrayal. To prepare for this odious role, he directed that the accounting department discontinue the voluntary pay-roll deductions for CEA contributions, placing the CEA more clearly in a position of dependence on management. He also tried to reestablish a distance between himself and the employee leaders. Chuck Cheeld found that he was no longer welcome to bring ideas to his office. Apart from the pain of facing employees, the decision to negotiate a surrender wounded Feldman's sense of his own persona as an executive. He had always excelled and tended to judge others on their competence. Jack Sage notes, "To lose—and to lose so ignominiously to Lorenzo whom he disliked—was more than he could tolerate."

The patriarch of Continental, Robert Six, who was convalescing very successfully from heart surgery, had stayed away from the takeover battle partly out of preference. He didn't like the ESOP, which was inconsistent with his management style, but he was willing to support it as the only defense against Lorenzo. After signing a few pro-ESOP letters prepared for his signature, he left in May for an extended vacation in Europe. Joined to a June board meeting by conference telephone, he remarked, "I'm visiting all the cathedrals of Europe praying for you." In fact, Six was deeply concerned that Feldman was too preoccupied by the takeover battle to respond to other business challenges. Feldman had discussed with him the possibility of hiring a chief operating officer and mentioned as a good prospect George Warde, a man like Six with modest educational credentials and great practical ability. Warde had begun work in the industry as a mechanic and had risen to become president of American Airlines. After a dispute with the board chairman, he left to become a marketing vice-president of Airbus Industrie, the French-led aircraft manufacturing consortium. While attending the Paris air show in June, Six called Warde at the Airbus headquarters in Toulouse and asked him to come to Paris. Six then offered him the job. It was the first time that Six had intervened in management since Feldman's appointment.

Feldman not only acceded to Six's initiative but wished to offer Warde financial incentives to come to Continental as soon as possible. Warde agreed to begin employment on July 27. Journalists questioned why he would take the job in the middle of a takeover struggle. His employment contract provides the answer: extending over an ironclad five-year term, it entitled Warde to a salary rising to $275,000 with generous fringe benefits and lucrative provisions for consulting work after the five-year term. About the same time, Feldman hired a new executive vice-president of marketing, Michael Levine, a former CAB official then teaching at the University of Southern California. He seemed to be reacting to the airline's crisis by looking for other executives who might be able to deal with it.

While these plans were taking form, pilot Larry Schlang got an idea that had a chance of upsetting everyone's calculations. Could an amendment be attached to federal legislation nearing passage that would preempt the California Corporations Commissioner's ruling? After drafting language, Schlang called the pilots' lobbyist, Susan Williams, and found that she had already discussed the possibility with her partner, Terry Bracy. The Economic Recovery Act of 1981, President Reagan's tax bill, did indeed present an opportunity since it was scheduled for a Senate vote the next week. Williams and Bracy included the idea in a presentation to the Continental pilots' governing council. Being desperate to exploit every chance, the pilots told them to go ahead. On Friday, July 24, they revealed their plans to Feldman in a meeting in Los Angeles.

The meeting was attended by Feldman, Sage, Levine, and several of the pilots who bridged the gap between the CEA and the pilots' union, including Eckel, Cheeld, and Schlang. Feldman seemed taut and agitated. He listened silently for an hour as Williams and Bracy laid out various political strategies in a careful presentation that relied on a blackboard and charts. Then he responded with a kind of confused anger, mixed with hostility for Williams and Bracy. None of the ideas, he asserted, was worthy of serious consideration. He had only tolerated the Alcalde firm earlier; now he saw it as a serious obstacle to negotiations with TI. As Susan Williams remembers the scene, he seemed to be saying as he spoke to the pilots: "Don't you know what I've done for you?" When the idea of the federal tax amendment was mentioned, Feldman reacted with a rare outburst of irritation. "What stupid idiot thought of that idea?" he demanded. Schlang raised his hand, but Eckel rushed into the breach. "I take full responsibility. I approved the idea," he said. After the meeting, Eckel and his colleagues agreed not to tell management anything more about their plans.

The amendment had already been drafted by the Powell Goldstein law firm, and Senator Dennis DeConcini (D-Ariz) had agreed to act as its principal sponsor. The Senator professes enthusiasm for ESOPs ("I think they're great," he says), but he also had a personal commitment to Continental's side in the takeover fight. He first heard of the ESOP from his brother-in-law, a Continental pilot, and he actively interceded with the CAB on behalf of the employees during the spring. In the last two days before the Senate vote, Williams and Bracy sought to lay the groundwork for introducing the amendment without disclosing their plans to TI. They obtained appropriate clearances from the Senate majority leader, the Senate parliamentarian, the legislative liaison of the White House, the staff of the Internal Revenue Taxation Subcommittee, and the chairman of the Senate Labor and Banking committees. Four senators agreed to join DeConcini as co-sponsors—Armstrong (R-Colo), Matsunaga (D-Haw), Hayakawa (R-Cal), and Hart (D-Colo)—and Senators Alan Cranston (D-Cal) and Russell Long (D-La) offered to speak in favor of the amendment on the Senate floor.

The game plan of Williams and Bracy relied frankly on the element of surprise. The amendment would be introduced in the Senate during the dinner hour on Tuesday evening when only a few senators were on the floor. Assuming passage, it would be considered on Friday afternoon by the Senate-House conference committee which would have the power to include it in the tax bill. TI would have only two and a half days to rally opposition. When the time to introduce the amendment arrived, the pilots and the Alcalde firm stayed away so as not to alert friends of TI; only Larry Schlang sat in the Senate gallery in his civilian clothes. Senators DeConcini and Armstrong introduced the bill as a technical amendment to ESOP legislation without mentioning the name of Continental. Senator Russell Long, however, would not have anything to do with this tactic of legislative stealth. Speaking extemporaneously, he said, "I favor the amendment but at the same time I want everyone to know what is involved here." He told of the employee struggle to block the takeover and the support of the chairmen of the Labor Committee and Banking Committee. In conclusion, he observed,

> You cannot be on both sides of an issue like this. You cannot be for the people who run the airline, the employees, and also for the other company which wants to take the airline over against the wishes of the employees. . . . This Senator . . . feels he should take the side of the employees and the management, which would like to make the employees stockholders to a very major degree.

The amendment passed unanimously by a voice vote of the handful of senators present.

There was euphoria among the group of pilots who had carried out the coup. Acting against the advice of management, they seemed to be within one step of clearing the way for a closing of the ESOP the next week. Their exuberance was in fact justified. Lorenzo did not know of Continental's financial projections, and he could only infer that the ESOP was still alive. If the conference committee should adopt the amendment, he would be forced a third time to try to negotiate a buyout of his 48.5 percent interest.

TI learned of the amendment faster than anyone could have imagined. An associate of the Manatt firm, Tim Furlong, heard two people talking about it in the hall near the Senate chamber and quickly called Willie Barnes in Los Angeles who sent out an alert to the TI management and other members of his firm. "It really tied us in knots," recalls Phil Bakes. Indeed, the amendment's chance of enactment seemed to weigh rather evenly in the balance. It is true that the House has a tradition of rejecting most Senate provisions that have not gone through the hearing process. Stuart Eizenstat, a partner of the Powell Goldstein law firm, notes that this institutional resistance was "an enormous barrier to overcome." But with strong support in the Senate, the amendment might still be accepted by the conference committee. "A lot depended," Eizenstat observes, "on how much the Senate conferees wished to make an issue of it."

Lorenzo, accompanied by Bakes, flew to Washington the next morning. The Manatt firm had already organized a counterattack that clearly outgunned the Continental pilots. A Washington partner of the firm, Jim Corman, assumed responsibility for coordinating the lobbying effort. Corman was former chairman of the Democratic Congressional Campaign Committee and chairman of the Public Assistance Subcommittee of the House Ways and Means Committee. A genial and competent man, he was well liked by his colleagues and had been out of office for only a year and a half after suffering a very narrow election defeat in the Reagan landslide. TI also enlisted Akin Gump Straus Hauer & Feld, the firm of former Democratic National Committee chairman Robert Strauss, which had been expanding its Washington office as a reflection of Strauss's effectiveness on Capitol Hill. Strauss was known to be a friend and political ally of representative Daniel Rostenkowski (D-Ill), majority leader of the House Ways and Means Committee, who would chair the conference committee.

TI's most effective representative, however, was Lorenzo himself. With Phil Bakes at his side, he pursued appointment after appointment with the conferees or their staff. Jim Corman jokes that it was the only time he ever billed a client for a twenty-six hour day, but in this case the client was with him all twenty-six hours. In the period of intensive activity before the conference committee meeting, legislators and their staff work late. Terry Bracy saw Lorenzo in the halls of the House office building at 2:30 AM. Displaying a cool, matter-of-fact manner, Lorenzo made clear that he was fighting for his business survival. If the amendment passed, he said that he faced losses as high as $50 million. He explained the success of the tender offer and his plans for Continental. All that he had rightfully secured, he protested, Continental was trying to overturn by this devious legislative maneuver.

The lawyers from TI's political law firms also stalked the Capitol in search of conferees and key staff members. Attorney Warren Elliott went to the annual Democratic-Republican baseball game in Alexandria where, he says, he "ran into quite a few conferees." The lawyers argued that the amendment was procedurally unfair. Corman remarks that it was passed "almost in the dead of night with no legislative due process." He admits candidly, "I didn't know for sure all the merits. I hadn't heard Continental's side." Geraldine Green bolstered the argument by calling as many members of the conference committee as she could reach to assure them of the regularity of her agency's proceedings.

By the time the conference committee met, Lorenzo or his attorneys had talked to everyone they needed to see. Its association with the Akin Gump law firm seems to have paid an especially important dividend. In the pressure cooker atmosphere preceding the conference committee meeting, the chairman, Congressman Rostenkowski, was the focus of immense lobbying pressures. Veteran lobbyist Maurice Rosenblatt asserts that in the final hours before the meeting no more than four or five people in Washington could place a call to him. But TI received an opportunity to present its case. Corman acknowledges that "more than one person" talked to Rostenkowski on TI's behalf.

For their part, the Continental pilots retained a small army of lobbyists. A cartoon in a Washington newspaper, which now hangs framed in the office of Phil Bakes, showed lobbyists parachuting on the Capitol from a Continental airplane. All the partners and associates of the Alcalde firm deployed to contact the conferees and staff members that they knew best, and the firm associated nine other professional lobbyists believed to have contacts with particular conferees. A number of pilots were able to come to Washington in time to join the lobbying effort. The pilots and lobbyists had a good story to tell, but they were not always able to reach the legislators themselves. "Most of our contacts were with the staff," concedes pilot Gary Thomas. Significantly, the two lobbyists retained to contact Congressman Rostenkowski and the majority leader of the Senate Finance Committee, Senator Robert Dole (R-Kan), succeeded only in presenting their case to staff assistants.

The Washington office of the IAM dealt a damaging blow to the pilots' plans by issuing a letter opposing the amendment which TI's lobbyists distributed as widely as possible, contending that the employee movement was merely an interunion dispute between the pilots and the IAM. The IAM letter so obscured the nature of the employee struggle that liberal Democratic representatives, such as Charles Rangel (D-NY) and Fortney Stark (D-Cal), who might have been expected to support the employees' cause, emerged as outspoken opponents of the amendment. The pilots' credibility was further damaged when the Continental management refused to lend any support. The public relations department told reporters that it knew nothing of the amendment and board members, such as Joe Kilgore, who possessed political influence, kept at a distance. The legislators might well wonder if they should support a tactic that was apparently disavowed by the employees' own management.

The CEA office in Los Angeles appealed to all employees to send telegrams or make telephone calls to conferees to demonstrate the actual extent of employee support. Congressman Bill Archer of Houston (R-Tex) was besieged with so many telephone calls that he complained to the Alcalde firm that his staff could not conduct other business. But there were limited possibilities to exert effective grass-roots pressure since most uncommitted conferees represented areas outside the Continental system or with few Continental employees.

Nevertheless, when the conference committee met, the

Continental pilots still retained their best card, the deeply committed support of respected senators. Senator Russell Long, a key member of the committee, vowed that he "would fall on his sword" before yielding on the issue, and the pilots were confident of the strong support of several other Senate conferees. In a dramatic initiative, Senators DeConcini and Matsunaga requested and received permission to address the conference committee on the issue. The conference committee customarily meets in seclusion and infrequently receives non-members. By requesting to appear before the committee, De-Concini and Matsunaga put their personal prestige on the line.

The conference committee met in a small room in Rostenkowski's office. Jim Corman describes the deliberations of the committee as "a tremendous poker game." The conferees try to stay in session until they have reached agreement on all matters, a goal that can normally be achieved only by bargaining one issue for another. Members of both houses know that they must yield on matters of minor importance if they wish to prevail on major ones. The Economic Recovery Act of 1981 contained the tax cuts that were the center piece of Reagan's economic program and special interest provisions of great importance to the oil industry, farmers, and commodity dealers. The Continental amendment was by any economic measure a minor issue.

Outside the committee room, a group of pilots kept a vigil amid a diverse crowd of people so dense that it was physically difficult to approach the door. As the committee continued its deliberations into the early morning hours, Larry Schlang found an opportunity to introduce himself to Lorenzo who was also waiting outside. "I thought you'd like to know who did this to you," he said. "Wait until you see what I am going to do to you next week," replied Lorenzo poking his finger into Schlang's chest, in an apparent reference to the approaching CAB decision. Then, about 3:00 AM, the committee released the news that it would not adopt the Continental amendment.

CHAPTER
TWELVE

DEATH AT
CONTINENTAL
AIRLINES

The Sunday morning after the conference committee meeting a group of pilots met with lobbyists Susan Williams and Terry Bracy around a large table in the coffee shop of the Keybridge Marriott hotel in Washington. They had no thought of abandoning the fight, but what would they do next? The bill in the California legislature offered some hope, but it would take weeks to pass. The pilots foundered about in search of a quicker solution. Their brainstorming was reminiscent of the last days of the tender offer period when the employee movement was born. The next week the pilot MEC would again hold a marathon meeting looking for a way out. Some of the pilots' ideas would have invited trouble. It was asked, for example, why the company could not simply contribute a massive block of unissued stock to an ESOP—an action that would surely lead to shareholder litigation. But other ideas had a degree of practicality. Why not create a kind of mini-ESOP applying only to non-California employees? the pilots asked. Their ideas, however, did not have a chance of acceptance. Vandeman remarks, "Feldman set very stringent standards that had to be met before proceeding with anything." He would not sanction any last-ditch improvisations.

In March, Feldman had listened respectfully to less plausible ideas, but he had no patience now with the pilots' scheming. Back in Los Angeles, the pilots discovered that his mood had changed, and they stayed away from the executive office. Feldman was showing more signs of stress than at any time in the takeover battle. Though always a temperate drinker, he began to exceed his daily quota of one or two cocktails in the evening. He chain-smoked more heavily and complained to his secretary of insomnia. She saw him a second time turn his back while his voice cracked with emotion. But the takeover battle had been marked from the beginning by periods of intense stress; other Continental executives were also feeling tense and tired. Only Vandeman, the preacher's son, became concerned about him. He called Feldman's fishing pal, Rod Hills, in the Washington office of Latham & Watkins and asked him to come out to Los Angeles. "Al needs you," he said, "not as a lawyer but as a friend."

Feldman was concerned with a very different agenda than the employee leaders. Since late July, Vandeman had been pursuing conversations with TI for a takeover agreement that would provide a graceful end of the struggle. The federal tax amendment had temporarily interrupted the negotiations. Committed to the notion that there was no authentic employee movement, the TI executives refused to believe that the Continental management was not behind the amendment and imagined that director Joe Kilgore, as a former U.S. congressman, was the actual mastermind. Bakes still insists, "Kilgore's footprints were everywhere." Nevertheless, the conversations resumed shortly after the defeat of the amendment. On August 5, Bakes again came to the Latham and Watkins office in Los Angeles to talk with Vandeman. In the course of their conversation, a proposal emerged that offered additional protection to Continental shareholders. Feldman immediately referred the proposal to Lehman Brothers for an opinion regarding its fairness to shareholders. With Lehman Brothers' blessing, the way appeared to be clear for final negotiation of a peace treaty.

Exhausted and overwrought, Feldman was plainly looking for the end of the struggle. He again told Six that he was thinking of leaving the airline business when the battle was over. In a poolside conversation at Six's home, CAB counsel Lee Hydeman recalled that Feldman had always talked, almost obsessively, about doing things with dignity. "How is he going to get out of this with dignity?" Hydeman wondered. Other speculations began to circulate among top management when Feldman asked Continental's accounting firm, Peat Marwick Mitchell, to examine his children's trusts and his expense accounts. It was the sort of thing one would normally do in tax season. Jack Sage remembers, "We thought he was leaving for another top job."

On Thursday morning, after having kept employee leaders at a distance for over three weeks, Feldman unexpectedly called Chuck Cheeld to his office. "It was a much more reflective conversation than his normal business conversation," remembers Cheeld. In fact, Feldman did not seem to have any company business to discuss, but he talked about many things in a somewhat rambling manner for an hour or so. The conversation, Cheeld recalls, was a "definite downer. It was good to be back talking to him, but it wasn't the same—there was an emptiness there." Feldman looked and talked tired, and he seemed to assume that it was all over. "I don't see how the company is savable even if we do get it," he commented. "What are people thinking? Have I let them down?" The next day Feldman called another prime mover of the ESOP, Mike Conway, to his office and asked a very technical question about foreign exchange accounting. Their visit was cut short by a telephone call. "I've got to take this one," Feldman told him. As Conway left the executive office, he wondered if Feldman had any other reason to see him.

Continental's business losses presented Feldman with financial problems of immediate urgency: a looming cash shortage and new demands by the airline's banks. Contrary to all expectations, Continental suffered operating losses in June and July of $4.2 and $4.7 million, respectively. In the slow winter months, the company could expect further losses of a magnitude to strain cash resources. To avert or at least postpone a cash crisis, Continental plainly had to consider selling certain assets. One of the best prospects for temporary cash relief was the sale of cargo convertible DC-10s to Federal Express. After several months of negotiations, a sale appeared imminent. Robert Wyzenbeek, Continental's vice-president of aircraft sales, and Ron Anderson, his counterpart in Federal Express, finally reached a verbal agreement during the week of August 3 for the sale of one DC-10 at a price close to $20 million. The sale would help give the airline enough time to adopt a new business strategy.

A critical phase in bank negotiations was also approaching. Chase Manhattan, which had stayed aloof during the ESOP negotiations, now resumed its dominant role as Continental's lead bank. There had been no love lost between the airline's management and Chase's aerospace division since the bank had refused to participate in the ESOP. They wanted to collateralize Continental's fleet to secure existing loans, but he was prepared to wait a little longer. Chase and other banks formed a committee to closely monitor developments.

As summer progressed, Continental's financial situation deteriorated further. The airline remained in default, or marginally in compliance, on all its financial covenants. While the covenants provided increasingly stringent financial tests, Continental—like other airlines—faced a decline in traffic. Many passengers stayed away from air travel late in July because of fears of a nationwide air controllers' strike. Then on August 4, the airline's financial outlook suddenly became much worse: PATCO, the air controllers' union, finally called a walkout, provoking widespread disruption in service. In its first day, the strike grounded 107 of Continental's 353 daily flights. It ended any hope of a profitable third quarter, and Continental's banks lost no time in calling a meeting on Friday afternoon, August 7, to take action.

The meeting, attended by all of Continental's long-term lenders, was not an amicable occasion. The bankers and insurance company executives first caucused separately, and then a Chase banker, speaking in a brusk, staccato voice, announced the joint decision: the company would have to mortgage all of its fleet, spare parts and all; the details of the documentation would be worked out later in the month. Feldman tried to argue that some equipment, such as the cargo convertible DC-10s, might be left unencumbered, but he did not attempt to salvage the ESOP loan. The banks' demand for collateral obviously meant the end of the ESOP financing. It would be absurd to ask for new credits while the banks were demanding all the fleet as security for existing loans. The only thing that needed to be discussed was the manner of making a public announcement that the ESOP financing had been withdrawn. Feldman wanted to issue a press release on Sunday, August 9, after he had met with employee leaders. At this meeting, he might also break the news of the settlement negotiations with TI.

Despite some apparent successes, the week ended worse than it had begun. The good news of the sale of the DC-10 turned out to be premature. On Saturday, Feldman received a hand-delivered letter from Fred Smith, the chairman of Federal Express,which backed away from his earlier interest in purchasing the plane. The negotiations with TI also foundered on an unlikely obstacle. Feldman and Vandeman met with Lehman Brothers partner Ralph Hellmold on Saturday morning to hear the firm's verdit on the proposed settlement with TI. To their astonishment, Hellmold informed them that Lehman Brothers would not bless the settlement that had been negotiated: the firm had concluded that the terms were not fair to Continental's shareholders. Taken aback, Feldman vainly protested. It was the best prospect for a settlement that Continental had been able to secure. Now that the banks had withdrawn from the ESOP and taken the fleet as collateral it was not likely that Continental could negotiate better terms.

In the afternoon, Feldman approved an elaborate briefing paper containing a revised revenue projection, just completed by financial analyst John Phillips. It would be discussed by the board of directors in a meeting scheduled on Tuesday of the next week. The paper estimated that revenues would be $115 million below those that were originally projected. For a man who believed passionately in meeting commitments, it was an obscene discrepancy. The lower revenues might be offset somewhat by cost savings and the sale of assets; but, instead of a recovery, they clearly spelled disastrous year-end results. At Frontier, Feldman had turned the airline around within a year. At Continental, despite the most carefully conceived plans, he had presided over a downward spiral of losses.

Later in the day, Feldman dropped by Phillips's office to discuss the briefing paper. As he took his leave, Phillips remembers the formal way that he said good-bye. Feldman also found time to brief his top officers, who now included George Warde, on the day's misfortunes. After the tender offer, he had said it was the first time he had ever lost. Now everything he had touched had crumbled: he had even failed to negotiate his own surrender. The ESOP was dead, and the airline's financial affairs were in shambles, perhaps out of control.

The next day at 10:00 AM, a Sunday morning, Feldman met with employee leaders for the confrontation that he had accepted as inevitable since mid-July. About fifteen employees, including members of the CEA board and union leaders, arrived for the meeting. Eckel thought that Feldman was going to reveal some grand final strategy, possibly involving cash from the sale of the DC-10s. Instead, he announced that the banks had withdrawn their support for the ESOP. Reviewing the reasons to believe that the fight was lost, he used all his persuasive power to urge the employee leaders to give up. "Everything has its time," he said. "We've overshot the mark, and now it won't work." The CEA had arranged to take two large groups of employees to Sacramento that afternoon to lobby for the state legislation. The first hearings were scheduled in four days. Feldman appealed to Eckel to call off the trip. "If you succeed," he argued, "the money is no longer there to buy the stock." To reinforce his point, he told Eckel, "From this day forward, there will be not one penny of support for your effort. If you want to fight ahead, you're on your own, but I ask you not to fight." The employee leaders included some strong-minded individuals, not the least of whom was Eckel, but Feldman easily dominated the meeting. Eckel shook his hand and said he would cancel the trip to Sacramento. When Pearl Kelly saw Eckel shortly after the meeting, he told her that the battle was over.

Feldman had accomplished his task with apparent ease. He could not have suspected that the effect of his persuasion would be lost in a couple hours' time. Chuck Cheeld arrived at the corporate headquarters around noon to find four or five pilots gathered in the CEA office, still subdued by the confrontation with Feldman and debating their decision to call off the Sacramento trip. Cheeld protested vehemently. "If the company won't help, we'll do it ourselves," he urged. Eckel himself was never one to be discouraged by long odds. In his gritty Mormon tradition, giving up was never an option. He and his colleagues began to call other pilots who had contributed to the CEA in the past and to ask for another $250 contribution. When told what had happened, the pilots responded with almost unanimous support: sixty-five out of sixty-seven pilots agreed to make the contribution. This immediate display of support settled it; the pilots could fund the legislative battle on their own. Eckel never told the other employees how close he had come to canceling the Sacramento trip. The two flights of employees left for Sacramento as planned at 2:00 and 4:00 PM that afternoon.

Feldman had another business matter to take care of— the press release and employee bulletin announcing the banks' withdrawal from the ESOP. The documents would be read attentively by TI as well as by employees. Julian Levine had written brief, page-and-a-half statements, but Feldman wanted Sage and Vandeman to review them. The four men debated for a long time before agreeing on a text. As they walked out of their conference room, Feldman said he had left some cigarettes in his office. He soon returned carrying a briefcase, thanked the others for their trouble, and then shook each man's hand and said good-bye. Levine was surprised by his ceremonious manner and remarked, "That's pretty formal!" Feldman meant what he said.

Feldman went home to his condominium and then returned to his office in the late afternoon, carrying in his briefcase a small package that still contained a receipt of purchase fifteen days earlier. Seating himself at his desk, he wrote letters to Vandeman, his secretary, and his three children. The letters to Vandeman and his secretary were brief notes of appreciation; he called Vandeman a good friend and a good lawyer and tried to assure him that he had not failed Continental. The letter to his children spoke from his heart. With his accustomed discipline, he called the security office to tell them to turn off the lights in the executive offices. Then, dressed casually in a long-sleeved blue shirt, open at the neck, he stretched out on his office couch, put a pillow under his head and raised a newly purchased pistol to his head.

At 8:00 PM, about forty Continental employees from all employee groups were sitting in a small conference room in the Holiday Inn at Sacramento when a mechanic burst into the room. He had just called Los Angeles for an authorization. "Have you heard the news?" he asked. "Al Feldman is dead." As the crowd sat in shocked silence, Eckel bolted from the room and called Feldman's office. Another person answered the phone and confirmed the news. Ashen faced, Eckel returned to tell the employees that it was true. The shock of Feldman's death called up all the emotions that had united the company during the takeover fight. There was sorrow. "He just might be one of the finest men I ever met," says Mike Conway. But there was also anger. "I've never felt so devastated in my life," says Chuck Cheeld. "So let down. How could he give up?" Cheeld went to his room in the Holiday Inn and wept alone. He recalls, "Feldman was such a dynamically strong person you couldn't imagine that he was contemplating suicide." Nobody had seen the tragedy approaching. People now wished they had been able to do something. "I would have shaken him and said, 'Hey dude! you're not doing this!'" says Eckel. Other employees thought, "I would have talked to him and been his friend. I would have done anything for him."

Jack Sage called Continental executives that Sunday evening. "There was absolute shock and disbelief and then almost a hatred," remembers John Phillips, adding in explanation: "He was the leader and rallying point." Like most employees, Jack Riddle learned the news when he arrived at work on

Monday morning. "It was all over the place," he says. "Rumors were flying, and people were trying to piece it together. It took a while to register." Carole Mitchell describes the employees' sense of loss:

> There had been such a relationship over the past five months that we were losing a person we regarded as a friend. He came through when we needed him. He was helping protect something we cared desperately about, and he had stayed with us and fought with us when he didn't have to. Now, people asked,"How can he do this to us?"

Six received the news while vacationing in Hawaii and responded quickly to supply needed leadership. Taking the next flight back to Los Angeles, he arrived early at the corporate headquarters and called a staff meeting at 9:00 AM. Dramatically seating himself in the chair that he had relinquished to Feldman, he began to plan what needed to be done to get the airline back on course.

The board of directors meeting on Tuesday had been scheduled to consider plans for Continental's future and to elect Warde to the board. It turned out to be a long and somber meeting that lasted through the lunch hour. The board appointed Warde as chief executive officer, with an appropriate increase in salary, and gave Six a more active role in management as chairman of the executive committee. The directors held no hope for the ESOP but could not arrive at any alternative. Warde would say only that he was "committed to fighting our way out of these bad times."[1]

Later in the week, a Continental 727 made a special flight to San Diego, carrying Feldman's friends and associates. He would be buried beside his wife, Rosemily, in a cemetery located in rolling hills near La Jolla. The mourners reflected Feldman's long absorption in business; most were executives from Aerojet, Frontier, and Continental, but they also included relatives, a few executives' wives, and some of Rosemily's friends. Feldman's sons asked Father David Clark, a

Jesuit prominent in Denver civic affairs, to conduct the ceremony. A year earlier he had buried Rosemily. At the request of Feldman's brothers, both wearing the traditional Jewish yarmulke, a rabbi agreed to assist. The ceremony was held during midmorning, outdoors, on a beautiful sunny day. In his eulogy, Father Clark read from Feldman's letter to his children:

Things have not been good for me since Mom died last year. Somewhere along the line I lost part of the purpose in my life. What has been left has been very painful for me, especially the last six months. I have suffered defeat after defeat and feel that I have failed those I have fought so hard to protect. I know I have done the best I have been capable of—worked as hard as I have been able to—but it has never seemed enough. I am urged to continue on by forces I can no longer control, and for this battle I have already been consumed. I simply have no more to give.

Any death, but especially a suicide, evokes a search for meaning. Having given all he had to give, did Feldman succeed in closing things with dignity? It is hard to see beyond the tragedy. Still, Feldman left a legacy of hope. His death intensified the employees' desire to continue the fight. While she listened to the rabbi talk of Feldman, Pearl Kelly wrote out her thoughts on the back of a guest list:

I experienced the finality of death today, surrounded by God's evidence of life.

A brilliantly colored butterfly hovered over the rabbi as he reminded us of the love and attention Mr. Feldman had bestowed on us as employees, family and friends.

The smell of flowers permeated the air. A mourner held a new born baby.

A great humanitarian, a brilliant executive, a father, a wonderful man is at *Peace*.

He touched my life briefly but left behind a legacy of hope, inspiration and a determination to fight until every means of staying independent has been exhausted.

CHAPTER
THIRTEEN

A CRUSADE IN
SACRAMENTO

After Feldman's death, the employee leaders were resolved
to carry on the fight against all odds, but did they really have
a chance? When Eckel returned from Feldman's funeral, he
found "about twenty messages" from self-styled financiers
offering access to Arab oil money. One of the financiers appeared to be credible: he was recommended by a former
chairman of the CAB, and unlike the others, he did not ask
for a prepaid fee. He assured Eckel that he could get financing
in forty-five days. Eckel also contacted Continental's lead
banks to ask if they would reconsider the transaction if the
California legislation were passed. John Eckman of Security
Pacific replied, "Come and talk to us." Eckel interpreted this
courteous response as an expression of continued interest. On
August 23, he held a press conference to announce that
financing for the ESOP could still be obtained. Other employees did not question his optimism. Kelso & Company
attorney Roland Attenborough shared the employees' belief
that the ESOP had a fighting chance; he thought the passage
of the bill would be a moral victory of such magnitude that it
might generate new and unpredictable opportunities. "At the
time we believed it," he recalls. "We felt that if we could get
the legislation, one way or another we could put it together."

The employee crusade in Sacramento during the next four
weeks became an emotional struggle that remains deeply
etched in the memory of many employees. The bill was first
considered in a hearing of the Finance, Insurance and Com-

merce Committee of the Assembly on August 12, three days after Feldman's death. The sponsor of the bill, Assemblyman Douglas Bosco, opened his presentation by saying, "Gentlemen, this is probably one of the most heavily lobbied bills the legislature has ever seen."[1] It proved to be an understatement. By the time of the Assembly vote on August 24, many observers would call it without qualification the most intensely lobbied bill in California history.

The employees who flocked to the legislature presented an unprecedented spectacle that was well captured by a Los Angeles reporter:

> They, the employees, are a vocal, emotion-charged and noticeably attractive group. One cannot help notice the large number of good-looking men and women —many dressed in pilot and stewardess uniforms— who attend, reportedly at their own expense, every meeting concerning the takeover attempt.

> They are led by CEA president Paul Eckel, a 43 year-old El Segundo pilot who looks and talks like he came straight from central casting—ramrod straight, tall, dark, handsome and articulate. But Eckel is for real.[2]

The bill's sponsor, Assemblyman Bosco, saw it as an example of democracy in action. "It was like a breath of fresh air," he says. But perceptions of the employees varied. "It was like a circus," says Corporations Commissioner Geraldine Green, referring to the parade of uniformed employees in the capitol building. The employees generally found legislators and staff to be friendly. "They were so, so supportive and so interested," remembers flight attendant Pearl Kelly. But toward the end of August, employees began to encounter some resistance from legislators who felt harassed by the constant employee pressure. A TI lobbyist, Dennis Carpenter, calls it "a badly over-lobbied bill."

The CEA leaders originally envisioned a systematic lobbying effort conducted by teams composed of a pilot, flight attendant, mechanic, and nonunion employee, but they soon changed their strategy and issued an open invitation for all employees to join them in Sacramento. Scores of employees arrived in the capital every day, coming on their own time and expense but with the benefit of passes on other airlines. As many as two hundred employees could sometimes be found in the capitol building. Seeking to publicize their presence en masse, Eckel began to organize noontime rallies.

Pilots came in the greatest numbers, but the employees represented a cross section of the work force. Enough flight attendants, wearing their Continental uniforms, attended committee hearings and the Assembly vote to form a conspicuous contingent in the public galleries. Among the core group of committed employees who worked for weeks at a time, mechanics were better represented than any group except pilots. Ticket agent Bill Miles had the impossible task of coordinating the lobbying efforts. He set up appointments for the lobbying teams to visit legislators and staff and tried to direct the flow of other employees to appropriate offices. As he briefed newly arriving employees, he found many were a little "goosey" about visiting the state lawmakers. He would tell them, "Remember, they are your representatives."

Flight attendant supervisor John Bailey was typical of many employees who became most deeply committed to the cause of the ESOP at this late date. He visited district offices of the legislators representing his city of Torrance, California, and persuaded the mayor of Torrance to write a letter to their assemblyman. During his vacation time, he spent a week in Sacramento at his own expense. Learning that Ernest Konnyu, an assemblyman from the San Jose area, was opposed to the legislation, Bailey called friends in the area to urge them to contact their representative. Konnyu later voted for the bill. While back on the job, Bailey wrote long, carefully composed letters addressed to the peculiar concerns of wavering legislators.

The movement continued to bring recognition to employees of unsuspected abilities. Houston flight attendant Sheri

Pennington proved to be the premier employee lobbyist. She so distinguished herself that she received two job offers from Sacramento lobbying firms. "We didn't get much sleep in Sacramento," she recalls. "We were up at 6:00 AM to attend early briefing sessions and to receive assignments. We worked during the day and went to debriefing sessions in the early evening. Later on, we would continue lobbying in two or three restaurants next to the capitol that were always filled with politicians and other lobbyists." Attractive, articulate, and poised, she gained an excellent command of the issues. Her abilities caught the attention of Willie Brown, the brilliant black leader of the California Assembly, who staged a confrontation, pitting her against Governor Jerry Brown. While dining with the governor in one of the capital's political restaurants, Willie Brown invited Pennington to come to his table. "Miss Pennington is involved in the Continental ESOP," he told the governor. When Governor Brown began to expound the reasons for his neutrality, Pennington responded with well-prepared answers. Willie Brown could be seen leaning back with a broad smile on his face as he watched the debate develop between the governor and the flight attendant.

The intense lobbying caused many legislators to conclude that the company was underwriting the effort. "It's fun to watch the heavy weights of the world," one assemblyman mistakenly inferred.[3] In fact, the pilot MEC, which had recently made a $350,000 assessment of union members, paid the expenses that were not covered by the employees themselves or by the meager resources of the CEA. The company did no more than grant a certain number of leaves and rent a few rooms—always filled to overflowing—in the Sacramento Holiday Inn. The pilot dues collector, Hal Provo, had no trouble collecting. Once, he recalls, the employees needed $10,000 in three days to pay a bill, and he was able to get commitments for the money "in three or four hours."

The pilots developed a grass-roots political organization that acted in tandem with the CEA. Pilots' wives did much of the work. In Orange County, Judy Brown met with local legislators and organized a telephone network that relied largely on other wives to convey messages and to respond to appeals for telephone calls, telegrams, and letters to legislators. The pilots could quickly launch a blitz of telephone calls to legislators. Hal Provo remarks that the system worked almost too well. A few hours after issuing an alert, the pilots would get calls from lawmakers saying, "Enough is enough. We've got the message."

Letters on file with the legislature leave a vivid record of employee emotion. Harold Mitchell wrote:

> I have worked very hard my entire life to prepare myself for my career. Flying is what I wanted to do since I can remember. Now I am confronted with a situation wherein I may lose my employment and my career as the result of the hostile takeover of my airline. As a Californian, I am asking my California elected representatives to come to my aid.

The most common theme of the letters was the employees' desire to control their own destiny. Steven Sewell wrote:

> I am an employee of Continental Airline. Please support AB 2271. Please help save my job, and the jobs of 5500 other Californians. We, the employees of Continental, are acutely aware of the problems facing our company and the airline industry in general, but we are ready to do whatever is necessary to keep our company viable, competitive and productive. We do not want ourselves and our families to become pawns in Mr. Lorenzo's monopoly game.

A pilot's wife, Patti Weikert, made a similar appeal:

> I would like for you to support the bill AB 2271 that is now in Banking and Financing Committee. It's very important to my family. As my husband's job and future as a Pilot is in grave danger. Our home and

family would like to continue living here in California. We don't need Mr. Frank Lorenzo and Texas Air to manipulate us for the rest of our lives.

A quantity of letters came from the general public that had followed the struggle in the press. An Eastern Airlines employee, Marie Johnson, wrote a particularly incisive letter:

> I have been very distressed with the news concerning Continental Airlines Employee Stock Option Plan, running into so much trouble with our State Offices.
>
> I understand that there is a bill before the Assembly, AB 2271, supporting the ESOP program. I strongly urge you to support this very worthwhile program. As far as I can see, this is a very American way for 'free enterprise' to go. Who has more interest in their company than the employees? And who has more to lose than the employees in the event of failure?

With no previous experience in politics, the employees were an ingenuous group which expected the legislature to function in an ideal manner that might be described in a high school civic book. As pilot lobbyist Clay Jackson observed, they thought of the legislature as "their government," but soon discovered that it was in reality a large and underfunded professional organization. Most employees active in lobbying tell stories of being asked for campaign contributions. Mechanic Doug Schoen remembers being told by a legislative staff member in an elevator that the employees would have to push more money around to win. The CEA leaders began to receive invitations to fund-raising events. The CEA received, for example, an invitation from the Friends of Chet Wray to attend a reception in a Sacramento restaurant—reservations were five hundred dollars a person. Once, Eckel says, he "flat stomped out of the capitol building" rather than attend a meeting that he perceived as a play for money. But both the CEA and ALPA did try to play the game. The CEA formed a political action committee that received about ten thousand dollars in employee contributions.

Despite its preoccupation with campaign finances, the legislature responded to the CEA bill in a way that partially vindicated the employees' faith in the democratic process. After two hearings, the Finance, Insurance and Commerce Committee sent the bill to the Assembly by an 11 to 4 vote. One of the TI lobbyists, William Bagley, interprets the committee vote as a personal victory for the bill's sponsor, Assemblyman Doug Bosco, who was himself a member of the committee. "Bosco fell in love with the bill," he says. "If an author has clout and if he says personally this is one I need, you throw him a vote." During two terms in the Assembly, Bosco had been something of a workhorse for the Speaker, Willie Brown, carrying legislation that Brown supported but didn't have time for. In recognition of his effectiveness, he had won valuable committee assignments and the position of chairman of the majority caucus. Before Eckel approached him about the CEA bill, he had read press accounts of the ESOP and viewed it as "a very interesting concept, especially in airlines, a labor intensive industry." Soon he began to give the bill top priority, lobbying actively for support and spending evening after evening with large gatherings of employees in debriefing and strategy sessions.

Knowing his own reputation as a liberal, Bosco says his greatest fear was that the bill might provoke a united Republican opposition. As emergency legislation, AB 2271 needed a two-thirds majority to pass. But the bill actually began to pick up support equally from Democrats and Republicans. Some of the credit goes to an ESOP consultant, Dickson C. Buxton, with excellent connections in Republican politics. During the summer, Buxton had left Kelso and Company to found his own firm, Private Capital Corporation. When the Continental management terminated his retainer shortly before Feldman's death, he continued to work for the CEA without compensation. Eckel was also helpful in bringing the employees' case to conservatives. A conservative Republican himself, he had always advocated employee stock ownership as the path to a democratic capitalism that could prosper free of government interference. In a memo circulated among legislators, he elaborated on this theme:

> As for the employees of Continental Airlines, we are not so naive as to harbor the illusion that our acts alone will reverse the nation's drift in the direction of ever-increasing government redistribution. However, in our own small way and to the extent we are able to gain control of our own economic future we intend to rely on the fruits of our own labor and the benefits of ownership of our own capital to secure the future for ourselves and our families. We implore our government to help by simply permitting the free enterprise system to work for everyone.

While the bill clearly demonstrated the nonpartisan appeal of employee stock ownership, the support in the Assembly seems to have been mostly the result of constituent pressure, applied equally to Democratic and Republican legislators. "It was universally regarded as special interest legislation," says Charlene Mathias, staff consultant to the Finance, Insurance and Commerce Committee. The issues of employee stock ownership took a second place to personalities and politics. Assemblyman Bosco notes that many legislators saw it as a "bag bill," legislation likely to elicit campaign contributions. The employees had an apparent advantage in this special interest fight: they accounted for fifty-five hundred California residents who earned a total annual payroll of $150 million. As a Texas raider, TI possessed no natural counterbalance to their political presence in the state.

With no California constituence, TI counted on the influence of retained lobbyists and the Manatt law firm. The masterminds of TI strategy were two Manatt partners, Mickey Kantor, who was Governor Jerry Brown's chief fund-raiser in his 1976 campaign for president, and Pete Kelly, who would soon become California State Democratic Chairman. Lorenzo did not feel sufficiently threatened by the legislation to come to California, but Phil Bakes worked against the bill throughout August, staying in the same Holiday Inn as the employees. As lobbyists, TI retained two prominent former assemblymen, William Bagley and John Knox, who, in the words of a Sacramento reporter, were still "part of the club" and could trade on their personal familiarity with assemblymen.

The TI spokesmen construed the fight as simply a contest for control of a corporation in which the existing management had used an improper tactic. "It was a fairly complicated corporate maneuver," says John Knox. The Corporations Commissioner, Geraldine Green, emotionally upheld their arguments. "It's the most obvious management entrenchment scheme I've ever seen," she said, referring to the ESOP.[4] TI vigorously denied charges that it would dismantle the airline or move the corporate headquarters to Houston. In a letter sent to all legislators and key staff members, Lorenzo stated:

> Contrary to what has been speculated, Texas International has no plans to move the headquarters of Continental out of the State of California. In fact, should we acquire control, we plan to retain Continental's headquarters in Los Angeles. We plan to retain in California all Continental operating units presently headquartered in California.

TI's best arguments had enough merit to persuade one of the Assembly's most intellectually detached members. Assemblyman Byron Sher, a Stanford law professor, says he was torn by sympathy for the employees but still voted against the bill because he saw it as a legislative end run around the Corporations Commissioner's decision. He thought that the proposed dilution of book value per share without a shareholder vote presented a legitimate issue that should be resolved by normal legal processes.

The IAM proved to be TI's most potent ally. The chairman of the local legislative committee, Milt Burdick, explains, "We were afraid to spend funds to oppose the bill because the membership favored it. So we got local 1781 to work on opposing the bill." Local 1781 represented a large group of United Airlines mechanics in northern California. Burdick also asked for the help of James Quillan, the state Secretary Treasurer of the IAM, who sent an official, John Pina, to Sacramento with the specific assignment of lobbying full time against the bill. Mechanic Doug Schoen found an opportunity to confront Pina in a hallway. "You may represent the union but you don't represent the people," he told him. The IAM officers at Continental did not wish to incur personal unpopularity by appearing at Sacramento, but they contacted legislators by telephone and issued a joint letter opposing the bill which was widely circulated by TI's lobbyists. Their opposition allowed TI to interpret the ESOP as merely the project of an elite category of employee, the pilots. Those Democrats, who opposed the bill, invariably cited the opposition of labor as justification.

When the bill came before the Assembly at 10:00 AM on August 20, the employees had the support of most leaders in both parties. Counterbalancing Bosco's liberal image, a conservative Republican, Donald Sebastiani, the wealthy scion of a wine-producing company, gave an eloquent speech in support of the bill before departing for a meeting with President Reagan. The Democratic whip, Maxine Waters, led the floor fight against the measure, arguing that the Continental management was "fooling the employees."[5] Tensions rose when the roll call vote fell short of a two-thirds majority, and Bosco moved for a call of the Assembly. Under this procedure, Bosco had an opportunity to seek votes from absent or abstaining legislators and to ask opponents to change their vote. During an hour of frenetic activity, Bosco and Waters buttonholed assemblymen on the floor, professional lobbyists passed notes asking to talk to assemblymen or actually hung over the railings to intercede, and both sides searched out absent lawmakers in their offices. Slowly the vote in favor began to approach the two-thirds majority. At a decisive moment, Speaker Willie Brown dramatically came down from his office to cast an aye vote. Shortly thereafter, the fifty-fourth vote was recorded, and the Continental employees filling the legislative galleries burst into applause. Ticket agent Bill Miles remembers, "When it passed, we couldn't help but shout."[6] The final vote was 56 to 20 in favor of the bill. The formal passage, however, was delayed four days when Assembly-woman Waters introduced a motion to reconsider the vote. (She let her motion lapse on August 24.)

The employee leaders had been on an emotional roller coaster for five months. Once again it appeared victory was near. "We have won another one! We've got a roll going. Keep up the good work," the CEA telexed to all stations. The employees had found more support in the Senate than in the Assembly; now, the only apparent obstacle to passage of the bill was the pressure of legislative deadlines. The legislature would adjourn on September 15, and it was too late to assign the bill to the last scheduled hearing of the Banking and Commerce Committee, the only committee with apparent jurisdiction. But legislative deadlines for committee hearings —as well as the legal requirement of holding hearings—are waived wholesale at the end of every legislative session. To bring the bill before the Senate, the employees really needed only the cooperation of Senator David Roberti, the chairman of the Rules Committee and president *pro tempore* of the Senate. He was one of the employees' strongest allies in their early campaign for public support, and he continued to answer employee letters by saying he was "extremely sympathetic" to the ESOP. "We had no reason to believe that Roberti would oppose the bill," recalls Assemblyman Bosco.

Phil Bakes believes that TI lost the vote because it refused to descend to the ethical level of the California Assembly. "It was a pit!" he exclaims. "I have never seen any place as blatant as that in terms of talk about money and contributions. That's the reason we lost in the Assembly. We wouldn't play the game." Indeed, the record of reported campaign contributions indicates that TI dispursed only $7200 among seven of the twenty assemblymen who opposed the bill. Maxine Waters got the largest contribution of $2500.

The TI strategists turned their attention quickly to Senator

Roberti and the Senate Rules Committee. Within hours after the Assembly vote, a group of TI representatives, headed by Phil Bakes, visited Roberti's office. Four days later, TI retained a lobbyist, Hedy Govenar, who was thought to have influence with the staff of the Rules Committee. Govenar was a former business associate of Jerry Zanelli, the executive officer of the committee, and maintained a close and public friendship with him. A longtime aide of Senator Roberti, Zanelli normally proposed the agenda for Rules Committee meetings and controlled staff recommendations. An article in *California Magazine* notes, "In Sacramento it pays to be nice to Jerry Zanelli."[7] The fate of bills could turn on his cooperation.

The employees expected that the Rules Committee would assign the bill to the Banking and Commerce Committee in its meeting on August 26, two days after the bill's formal passage from the Assembly, but, to their surprise, they learned that the committee had taken no action on the bill. When Assemblyman Bosco asked for an explanation, Jerry Zanelli replied that there was a controversy over committee assignment. "That's the first time we figured out we were in trouble," says a member of Bosco's staff.[8] Why did the committee fail to consider the bill? Zanelli angrily refused the author an interview. ("There's no reason I should talk to you!") Rick Rollins, the legislative aide who writes staff recommendations on committee assignments, explains that the bill was "clearly within the jurisdiction of the Banking and Commerce Committee" but two other committee chairmen had requested the assignment. The bill reached his desk after he had already completed writing a report for the August 26 meeting, and he then handled it "like any other." Senator Roberti acknowledges that it was "pretty clearly a Banking and Commerce bill," but he points out that the Rules Committee merely followed normal procedures in waiting another week for a staff report.

As the lobbying campaign entered another week, Assemblyman Bosco was briefed every night by employees and lobbyists on conversations with senators. He says he was "confident" that they had the support of a two-thirds majority "with a small margin." The majority and minority leaders of the Senate and the caucus chairmen of both parties appeared to be probable supporters. Throughout the week, the employees pursued the political game they had so recently learned. The CEA hosted a fund-raising reception for assemblymen who had voted for the bill. A number of senators, identified as "responsive to pressure," were deluged with calls, telegrams, letters, and employee visits. But with the week's delay in committee assignment, the bill would have to compete with hundreds of other bills for passage in the last days of the legislative session. The support of Senator Roberti was critical if the bill were to survive this legislative congestion, and Roberti now seemed to have shifted away from his early support. On September 2, he said he was uncommitted but would soon make a decision. Employees could only cling to the hope that he would maintain his earlier support. A pilot leader, Felix Tomlinson, optimistically told the press, "It's looking very good."[9]

TI had a very different perception of the bill's prospects. Hours before it was finally assigned to the Banking and Commerce Committee, employees found the TI executives standing in the lobby of the Holiday Inn, their bags packed, ready to leave. Two days later, the employees learned the reason for their early departure: on September 4, Senator Roberti announced that there would be no more committee hearings in the Senate prior to adjournment. Roberti denies that his decision was directed at the Continental bill. The president *pro tempore* calls an end to further hearings at some point near the end of every session. But Roberti now spoke publicly against the bill, calling it a "special interest" measure "opposed by organized labor." "The only group to support it," he claimed, "was a 'sweetheart organization' set up by management."[10] He acknowledged that previously supported the ESOP, but he says that after the decision of the Corporations Commissioner, "the issue was a horse of a different color." His explanation reflects a curious change of heart. In July he had interceded with Governor Brown to put political pressure on the Commissioner for a decision favorable to the employees.

Roberti's announcement effectively killed the bill. A few senators, including majority leader John Garamendi remonstrated him, but they were unwilling to lead a floor fight to overrule his decision. Bosco himself believed he had no chance to get a two-thirds majority with the opposition of the president *pro tempore*. The chairwoman of the Banking and commerce Committee, Rose Ann Vuich, a conservative representative of agribusiness, took no interest in the bill. In a few days the employee leaders were persuaded that Roberti would make his decision stick.

The employees had believed in the ESOP with an idealism that sometimes carried an implicit condemnation of their opponents. They now found it impossible to believe that TI had not used improper means to defeat their bill. The TI spokesmen vehemently denied the charges. "Not one penny was promised anybody," says Texas Air vice-president John Carlson.[11] "I want to state flatly . . . that my associates and I have neither promised nor given any campaign contributions,"[12] stated TI lobbyist John Knox. But back in Houston, Phil Bakes found himself facing the accusing eyes of Continental employees who had worked in Sacramento. He sought out flight attendant Sheri Pennington at the airport. "You got to believe me," he said. "There were no bribes paid in Sacramento."

For Eckel, who had led the employees into the legislative campaign and promised success, it was a time of personal anguish. Against the advice of the CEA lobbyists, he delivered a press release on the capitol steps to vent his emotion:

> The employees of Continental Airlines came to the California State Legislature with high hopes. We leave in near despair—despair over the rampant abuse of power by public officials and the corruption which is widespread in Sacramento.

We came here with a compelling case: a group of California citizens attempting through our own efforts to save a California company; to prevent an "asset raid" by a Texas wheeler dealer; to save 5,500 jobs; and to prevent the effective removal of Continental Airlines' headquarters to Texas. We believe we are doing something that is good for our company, our employees, our stockholders, our state and our country.

In Sacramento, the merits didn't matter. We struggled and fought and through the diligent efforts of Assemblyman Doug Bosco, won a two-thirds vote in the Assembly. Despite the fact we were constantly queried about possible contributions to legislators, we stuck to the facts and fought our fight on the basis of issues. We did not enter "the bidding war" which was widely reported in the press. Maybe that was our downfall, because we learned today that despite the merits of our issues, and the urgency of our cause, we will not get a hearing or a vote in the Senate. And we have been refused due process, not by the entire Senate, but by a single man—President Pro Tem David Roberti. While claiming to be a supporter, Senator Roberti has used the power of his office to prevent a vote, and thus turn over control of our company to Texas International. . . .

In spite of the outcome here, we will not rest until we have won. We will take our case directly to President Reagan who has the power to block the Texas International takeover—and what has happened in California will make our case even better. . . . We will not rest until those who have so poisoned the people's government have been exposed.

The Continental lobbyist, Donald K. Brown, circulated a letter to state senators disassociating himself from Eckel's press release. Roberti simply says, "It got pretty mean."

If the TI executives returning to Houston thought the battle was over, they soon received another surprise. A deputy secretary of defense, Frank Carlucci, had written a letter to the White House advising that the takeover presented national security issues in Micronesia. The advice unquestionably drew on staff recommendations carefully cultivated by pilot Larry Schlang. But TI had no difficulty repelling this last counter-offensive. The airline had recently gained a business justification for continuing air service in Micronesia: a surge of Japanese tourism had caused the Saipan-Tokyo service to become highly profitable. The theory that the takeover threatened Micronesian air service had always been implausible. ("We made something out of nothing," says a Schlang colleague, pilot Gary Brown.) It was now a patently untenable notion. The directors of Texas Air adopted a resolution committing the airline to continued air service in the region, and TI asked the Texas senator John Tower to intercede on its behalf. Phil Bakes recalls saying, "We think something crazy is happening." Tower soon secured an opinion of the general counsel of the Department of Defense stating that the takeover involved no defense considerations meriting further review. The employees' last real chance was that a favorable Department of Defense recommendation would go unchallenged. The chance was now gone. On October 12, President Reagan approved the CAB order that would sanction the takeover.

In the months after Feldman's death, the management of Continental continued to act independently. Jack Sage describes the general attitude toward the employees' legislative campaign as being, "I hope they can do it, but I don't think they have a chance." During September and early October, Continental successfully opposed a TI lawsuit to force a special shareholders' meeting. The slim chance of a favorable Department of Defense recommendation was enough to cause the Continental board to keep up the fight for independence. But a few days after the presidential decision, George Vandeman led a delegation of executives to Houston to negotiate a peace treaty. An agreement signed November 25 contained only one significant concession: the outside directors would remain in office until the next shareholders' meeting scheduled in March. The cost of Continental's defense of the takeover, including large fees of Lehman Brothers, Latham & Watkins, and Wachtell, Lipton, now totaled about $11 million. The Continental pilots had spent another $600,000, and the CEA about $100,000.

Most employee leaders tried to put the struggle behind them, hoping that their fears about the takeover had been groundless. They could take some solace in having fought well. Flight attendant Pearl Kelly remembers, "I felt disappointed to have lost but proud to have fought such a good fight that came so close to success." Like other CEA leaders, she was required to sign a release promising to take no action harmful to the new management, but she wished to make a personal pledge to Lorenzo. With well-pondered words, she told him, "We fought hard to stay independent, and we failed, but I offer to you the same dedication that I have to the old company."

Ticket agent Bill Miles helped Eckel to close the CEA office the day after the presidential decision. It is never easy to accept defeat when one has believed deeply in a cause and expected to win, but on October 12, Eckel summoned up the resolve to make a last statement to employees. It struck a very different note from his angry parting salvo in Sacramento:

> Today the White House made public their decision to approve TI's takeover of Continental. The concerted effort of the past six months by the 11,000 employees of Continental Airlines to control our own destiny has demonstrated our enormous desire—and drive—to share an ownership interest in our company.
>
> We are extremely disappointed that this desire and the effort by so many individuals at all levels—mechanics, flight attendants, reservations agents, pilots, office personnel, and management has not, as yet, succeeded. We continue to believe strongly in the concept of the

221

employee stock ownership plan and feel that it, in some form, is a wave of the future for America's workers.

You have been magnificent—don't change a thing! We must do whatever is necessary to be profitable no matter who the majority owner of the airline is. Let's unite behind Mr. Warde's leadership and get Continental's current loss situation turned around.

We've done well; even in losing, and we will be heard from again!

EPILOGUE
PART ONE

CHAPTER 11:
THE MOST
EFFECTIVE STICK

A year and a half after the takeover, Dick Adams, senior vice-president of operations, was the only former Continental executive remaining in the top echelons of management. George Warde had been exiled to Air Micronesia; all other top officers had retired or resigned. The corporate head-quarters had been moved to Houston, displacing hundreds of Los Angeles workers, but Dick Adams commuted weekly from California. He had only one year until retirement and had found a position of trust within the inner circle of the Lorenzo management team.

A personal idiosyncrasy brought Dick Adams into the center of controversy: he was in the habit of taking volumi-nous notes of business conversations on small white pads of memo paper. When the company fell into litigation with its employees later in the year, other executives displayed de-plorably vague memories, but Dick Adams's notes were sub-poenaed, and he was required in lengthy questioning to explain all relevant details. One memo dated June 14, 1983, partic-ularly drew the attention of his interlocutors. It contained Adams' reflections on how the company might best secure labor concessions. "I don't believe we can get these conces-sions on a voluntary persuasive basis. . . . We must get awfully big stick," said the note. "The most effective stick may be Ch. 11."

Three months later, the airline would in fact use Chapter 11 bankruptcy as a stick against employees. In an unprecedented bankruptcy proceeding, the company succeeded in abrogating union contracts, eliminating pensions and work rules, and slashing the pay of noncontract employees by 30–40 percent. Phil Bakes, who is currently the president of Continental, insists that the bankruptcy "was foisted upon us,"[1] but the truth appears to be more complex. After experiencing certain limited successes in the first year after the takeover, the company faced huge operating losses in the first three quarters of 1983 as a result both of industry conditions and failed marketing strategies. Management responded by staging a series of three labor confrontations—first with the flight attendants, then with the IAM, and then with all employee groups. In each instance, it demanded not simple economic relief but ambitious, long-term productivity gains in a form peculiarly unpalatable to employees. The labor confrontations failed to achieve their purpose and aggravated marketing problems, sending the airline into a financial tailspin. As the crisis deepened, management came by degrees to view Chapter 11 bankruptcy as a desired objective. When the petition was filed, it was clearly the product of management decisions. It fully justified the employees' fear of the takeover.

Continental and TI were now both wholly owned by a new holding company, Continental Airlines Corporation, which was in turn controlled by Texas Air. TI was the weaker partner in the combination; in 1982, it incurred a larger net loss than Continental on one-third the revenues. The union of the two airlines had failed, moreover, to produce any important marketing benefits. At the end of the first year of combined operations, Continental's operating revenues showed almost no increase. The new management coordinated the routes of the two carriers and repainted TI's fleet with the Continental logo, but these measures produced a disappointing increase in passenger business—Continental's traffic (excluding the effect of strikes) rose at about the national rate. This gain was achieved only by aggressively offering discount fares that caused the average fare to fall from 12.86¢ to 10.91¢ per passenger mile. Revenues consequently rose only $4 million (from $1,090 million to $1,094 million).

As the merger itself failed to generate new revenue, Lorenzo saw the reduction of labor costs as the path to the airline's survival. He had two advantages not enjoyed by the managements of other troubled airlines: a large nonunion work force representing 42 percent of the payroll and an unusually compliant pilot group. Soon after the takeover, the company furloughed fifteen hundred mostly nonunion employees, and it carried out a similar furlough the next year, but it refrained from taking the further step of ordering pay cuts for noncontract employees, even though many of these employees were clearly paid, as Phil Bakes observed, "an above market rate." Management seems to have been deterred by a fear of Teamster organization. The Teamsters represented several employee groups at TI that were unrepresented by any union at Continental. The company was apparently willing to maintain wages at an above market level to discourage the spread of Teamster influence to Continental.

Nine months after the takeover, the pilots gave the new management its most significant success by accepting a precedent-setting concessionary agreement. Management had demanded permanent concessions, primarily in the form of work rule changes leading to employee furloughs, and it had rejected a pilot proposal for a democratic employee stock ownership plan as a quid pro quo for concessions. But in August the company responded to an important pilot concern by offering a side letter from Texas Air pledging not to establish another nonunion subsidiary such as New York Air. With this nonmonetary issue resolved, the pilots accepted an agreement involving both the Continental and TI pilot groups that gave the company $91.4 million in concessions over a two and a half year period beginning in 1983. The settlement included work rule changes that would result in the furlough of about 10 percent of the pilot work force. For the year 1983, the agreement offered payroll savings of no less than $43 million —an amount equal to 30 percent of the scheduled pilot payroll—and it gave Continental flight crew costs below such major competitors as American Airlines, United Airlines, and Frontier Airlines.

The Continental pilots had led the industry in concessionary bargaining. It was the first time that a pilot group had agreed to productivity improvements leading to the furlough of a substantial part of the work force. Lorenzo acknowledged the significance of the agreement, calling it "a very far-sighted and crucial step," and asserted that it vindicated his negotiating strategy. At the end of the year, he remarked, "We could have gotten a huge boost on the P&L side by taking a temporary agreement much earlier, but our philosophy has always been long-term."[2]

The pilot concessions raised hopes that the airline might be on course for a business recovery. Following the employee furloughs in 1982, payroll costs had fallen sharply from $428 million to $377 million, and the airline's net operating loss had consequently declined to $26 million from $43 million a year earlier. The pilot agreement offered the prospect of a further substantial reduction in labor costs for the year 1983. But a fateful and unnecessary confrontation with flight attendants proved to be the first of several events that precipitated the airline into a deeper crisis.

Management approached flight attendant negotiations with the conviction not only that payroll costs were too high but that flight attendants had escaped from effective management controls as a result of the contractual protections against perceived sex discrimination. The vice-president of personnel, John Adams (not to be confused with Dick Adams), bluntly told the union president, Darenda Hardy that he was "tired of hearing how the flight attendants felt and what the flight attendants wanted." They would have to realize, he said, "they were not a group of independent contractors but a work force which was going to be managed."

Shortly after the takeover, the new management presented the flight attendants with a demand for $19 million annual concessions in a singularly unwelcome form: $12.4 million would be achieved by work rule changes, and $6.8 million by permanent wage concessions. It was not the economic demand, however, that aroused emotional opposition among flight attendants. Management also proposed to reinstate controls on weight, hairstyle, makeup, and nail polish. The union bulletin scarcely mentioned the economic demand but inveighed at length against the attempt to revive outmoded and sexist standards:

> Some of us are overweight, some are too thin, some are in-between and some are 'just right'; just like the pilots, the secretaries, the machinists and the PUBLIC. Apparently, since we are a predominantly female group, someone in the Company thinks we should be required to look like the perfect 'Barbie' doll. The only person we know who might agree is Hugh Hefner, and we all know what he is selling. Is THAT what the Company thinks THEY need to sell for 'Prosperity'? If it is, then we all better cash in our chips.

After the pilot agreement, the flight attendants decided, in the words of negotiator Claudia Lampe, "to bite the bullet." In September they dropped many of their demands for a quid pro quo and offered $21 million in wage concessions over a twenty-five-month period. Four months later they substantially improved this offer, but the company wanted more; it would not settle for anything other than permanent concessions involving sweeping work rule changes. Lorenzo had recently appointed a Pan Am executive, Stephen Wolf, as president and chief operating officer of Continental. During an informal conversation in his office, union president Darenda Hardy asked Wolf why they weren't able to make progress toward an agreement. Wolf replied, "You won't come up with permanent productivity concessions. If you don't do it, we are going to do something bizarre." It was not an empty threat.

On February 2, the flight attendants for the first time made a concessionary offer approaching the level of concessions management and pilots had negotiated five months earlier: it entailed $35 million in concessions over a twenty-one-month period—a reduction in scheduled flight attendant payroll expense of over 20 percent. The offer is reproduced in Appendix 1. Four items, valued at $9.5 million, were in the form of permanent work rule changes that would lead to flight attendant furloughs. The flight attendants said they would reverse the order and make these four items temporary and all the others permanent. They intended to meet the company halfway on this issue.

The next day, the flight attendants learned the significance of Wolf's threat. Vice-president of personnel John Adams commented that they had made a "valiant effort" but it was "not enough." He then handed the negotiating committee a letter that served notice on the union that the company would "reopen" every section of the contract for negotiation. The company claimed this right under a clause giving it the power to "reopen" particular provisions for negotiation, within the contract term, in the event "new equipment" or "deregulation" should change the factual assumptions on which the provisions were based.

In an internal memo, Phil Bakes described the reopening notice as an "ambitious proposal." Under the Railway Labor Act, management and labor must negotiate after the contract term until they reach an impasse. Either party can then petition the National Mediation Board for a thirty-day cooling off period. After this period, management is permitted to amend unilaterally the contract, and labor is free to call a strike to press its own demands. By invoking the reopening clause, the Continental management aimed to confront the flight attendants before the end of the contract term with the threat of unilateral amendment of the contract and thereby to accelerate the progress of negotiation. It was willing to force such a crisis involving the clear risk of a strike not for the sake of immediate financial relief—that had already been offered—but to get concessions in the form it wanted.

Lorenzo has gained the reputation of a gutsy speculator with a penchant for long shots, but few of his business gambles have been as audacious as the reopening notice to flight attendants. The flight attendants had made an offer of concessions that gave the airline a reasonable chance of financial survival. The $35 million was in itself a big step toward profitability, and it would ease the way for securing concessions from other employee groups. By rejecting the offer, Lorenzo stood a chance of getting the sort of concessions that would bring the airline into the ranks of the low-cost carriers, but he raised the risk of a general labor relations crisis. He was taking the risk, moreover, at a time when the airline faced financial problems that would have inspired caution in other executives.

The first quarter of 1983 brought ruinous losses to the industry. Continental Airlines Corporation suffered an operating loss of $51 million on revenues of $318 million. The eleven major airlines as a group suffered similar operating losses amounting to $567 million. The unprecedented losses were due to what *Aviation Daily* described as the industry's "most costly example of self-inflicted wounds."[3] Although revenue passenger miles actually increased 18.2 percent, the industry fell into a price war touched off by Pan Am's offer of an unrestricted $99 fare. Continental responded aggressively by offering its own $99 fare in fifty-eight markets and emerged from the battle as one of the most deeply scarred airlines. In the second quarter, it suffered a further operating loss of $14 million.

By ordinary odds, Continental's huge losses should have precipitated a cash crisis in the early months of 1983. Instead, Lorenzo raised $131 million in four transactions during the period of January through April 1983. Twenty-one million dollars came from the sale of aircraft. The remainder represented a triumph of Lorenzo's personal prestige in financial circles. In January, Continental obtained a new $32 million revolving credit agreement from a consortium of banks led by Chase Manhattan. The credit was secured by a large collection of miscellaneous assets that remained unencumbered, such as accounts receivable, stock in a Micronesian hotel corporation, a Honolulu cargo facility, all ground equipment of any value, and the airline's gates at ten airports. The agreement was followed by the sale of $40 million in notes to American General Corporation, the large Houston-based insurance company. For the lender, the transaction had a two-fold attraction: Lorenzo offered warrants and options to 25 percent of the stock in Continental and agreed to move the airline's corporate offices to a forty-story office building that American General was then building. The insurance company needed to obtain a major tenant for the building as the rapid growth of Houston had leveled off in 1983.

Further financial support came from the investing public. Through Kidder, Peabody and Company and Smith Barney, Harris Upham and Company, Continental Airlines Corporation made a public offering of two million stock units consisting of a share of common stock and a share of a convertible preferred stock. The prospectus makes interesting reading today in light of the company's bankruptcy five months later. Management surely cannot be accused of misrepresentation. The prospectus contains a litany of financial woes and offers no concrete hope. The cover page warns, "The units offered hereby involve a high degree of risk." A later section advises, "Many of Continental's competitors have advantages of size, greater financial and other resources . . . lower cost structures and superior established routes." The only attraction of the investment was Lorenzo's reputation as a financial wizard; it proved to be enough to market the stock for $37.5 million. According to Continental treasurer Mickey Foret, the company used the funds to pay overdue vendor invoices.

Despite operating losses of $65 million in the first half of 1983, the cash and temporary cash investments of Continental Airlines Corporation rose from $37 million to $89 million. Lorenzo himself says, "It was a fluke of financial history that Continental had been able to raise capital." He warned that the feat could not be repeated. Continental was now mortgaged to the hilt. With a long-term debt of $579.9 million and shareholders' equity of $24.4 million, it stood at the brink of insolvency, protected only by an extraordinary reserve of cash.

In this precarious position, Lorenzo was contemplating another labor relations confrontation. The IAM contract had expired on December 31, 1981, but the company and the union were still far from agreement on a new contract. In late April, the union notified its membership that it might ask for the thirty-day cooling off period legally required as a prelude for a strike. The next day management formed a Corporate

Coordinating Committee, chaired by vice-president of operations Dick Adams, to prepare contingency plans for an IAM strike.

Management intended to take a hard line in IAM negotiations. In March, Eastern Airlines had agreed, five hours before an IAM strike deadline, to a contract offering a 32.3 percent pay raise over three years with no major productivity concessions. Dick Adams explains, "We knew by April 25th that we could not afford it [a settlement like that of Eastern Airlines] . . . and we knew that the past history of the IAM was that they would not accept anything less, and it would take us to a strike." Under his direction, the Corporate Coordinating Committee devoted three weeks of effort to producing a thick package of materials entitled "Continental Airlines Strike Plan, May 18, 1983." The Continental management understood the implications of this strategy. A note of Dick Adams, written a few days later, contains the first mention of bankruptcy. "Creditors want $ now if see Chapt 11 coming," the note observes. And under the heading "impact on employees," it contained the cryptic jottings:

> carrot—Cont super attractiveness
> stick—bk is pb-imposed.

As a crisis with the IAM approached, the company made no progress in its dealings with pilots and flight attendants. Management twice presented the pilots with demands for further concessions, but the MEC refused to negotiate. The senior director of flying, Bill Laughlin, explains, "The problem was that no other group had given concessions. It irked the pilots that the flight attendants had given nothing." Management's strategy of pressuring the flight attendants by reopening their contract had also run into a snag. On May 16 a federal court ruled that the reopening notice created a dispute subject to arbitration. An arbitration hearing was set for mid-October 1983. The ruling curiously did not prompt the parties to renew the negotiations that had taken such a promising turn in February. The company, in fact, made no overture to the union until July 29—almost six months after the reopening

231

notice—and it then dropped the negotiations after a few meetings. A note of Dick Adams concerning a conversation with president Stephen Wolf gives a clue to management's thinking. Adams observed, "Flight attendants in our control, but timing is not soon enough. We can do what we want at appropriate time." Management was still waiting for a showdown with the union as soon as the contract could be unilaterally amended. Meanwhile, it paid the flight attendants a scheduled pay increase on June 1, 1983.

The crisis with the IAM had been slow in brewing. The parties had negotiated until the end of 1982 before petitioning the National Mediation Board for a mediator. The bargaining centered on productivity issues, such as contracting out the fueling work, new flight kitchen rules, and a scope clause giving management a freer rein in closing maintenance stations. The IAM was willing to make some concessions in each of these areas, but the union refused to depart from its traditional policy of seeking improved wages and working conditions. It would seek accommodation on individual issues only as part of a package that represented a general improvement over the preceding agreement. The national leadership of the IAM made no exception for any of the financially weak carriers.

On July 8, management advanced a new and unconventional proposal: it offered a base rate of $16 per hour that would actually place Continental above the level of pay of United, TWA, American, Pan Am, Northwest, and Eastern. In exchange for the new base rate, the company demanded major concessions, entailing large employee furloughs, on all productivity issues. The offer caught the IAM by surprise. There had been little discussion of wage rates in the negotiations. The company now combined an offer of a good base rate with a tough stand on all other issues. To an outside observer, it might seem to be a generous offer: it would actually increase the IAM payroll costs $18.6 million over a fifty-three-month period. At a time when the company was refusing to accept the flight attendants' offer of substantial concessions, it was prepared to give the IAM a modest increase in total compensation. But to a professional union negotiator, the offer seemed to be a bid to turn back the clock, to wipe out hard won gains in work rules. The IAM negotiator, King McCulloch, complains, "It went back to 1960 and '62, and they threw in the $16 an hour like a carrot."

The novel July 8 proposal had the effect of hastening the strike that management wished to delay until after the summer season. The IAM asked for the thirty-day cooling off period needed to call a strike. On July 13, the National Mediation Board ordered the thirty-day period to begin.

Dick Adams's notes again reveal the direction of management's thinking. In July, he quotes Lorenzo as saying that the airline needed "a quantum change in labor costs." The strike plan had evolved from a plan of business survival to an aggressive strategy intended to effect a major savings in labor costs. The strategy involved great risks; but if all went well, Continental would enter 1984 with the prospect of becoming a low-cost carrier, competitive with Southwest Airlines. There was a reason why management was prepared to take the risk of a strike: it now viewed Chapter 11 bankruptcy as a viable fallback strategy. Dick Adams insists, "We were looking at Chapter 11 as a final resort in case all of our other efforts failed." A memo of Phil Bakes, dated August 1, puts the matter in a somewhat more positive light:

> We probably will want to discuss the pros and cons of Chap 11 . . . but in the context of a possible risk, not a chosen strategy. The subject follows logically from the strike discussion.

Management now possessed carefully refined plans for the strike. Eight hundred IAM jobs, largely in the areas of flight kitchen, cabin service, and fueling, would be farmed out to independent contractors. "Try to eliminate as many people as possible," Dick Adams noted. To carry out maintenance work, the company hoped to lure some mechanics across the picket line with the offer of a $16 per hour wage, a substantial increase over the current wage of $13.45 per hour, and it planned to hire from a job contractor, C. Franklin Company, about 500 newly trained mechanics at a wage of $10 per hour. New work rules would enable a reduced staff to perform the essential maintenance work. Expecting the flight attendants (but not the pilots) to honor the IAM picket lines, the company enrolled 637 recruits into a flight attendant training school so that they would graduate in time to replace striking flight attendants at lower rates of pay. Despite the higher base wage for senior mechanics, the company hoped to achieve $49 million in annual labor cost savings by riding out the strike.

But how could the company, in its weakened financial condition, hope to survive the loss of revenue in the first weeks of the strike? The company's business plan for August calculated that service would be cut back only 15 percent while labor costs would be immediately and sharply reduced. The airline could take advantage of its unusual strength as a largely nonunion carrier by ordering a temporary 15 percent pay cut for noncontract employees. As a bottom line, the business plan actually projected a $8.6 million operating profit (later reduced to $2.2 million) for the month of August despite the effect of a strike.

When the Continental board of directors considered the strike plan on August 4, management had come to regard the strike not as a costly necessity but as a desirable business gamble, an opportunity to achieve a breakthrough in labor costs. With board approval, Lorenzo decided to take a step that would make the strike inevitable: he would withdraw the July 8 proposal and reduce the company's offer. Learning of the company's revised offer, IAM airline coordinator William Scheri flew to Houston and made a final personal appeal to Phil Bakes and John Adams shortly before the strike deadline. Bakes offered no hope of a settlement. Scheri says, "There was no movement through all my discussion with Mr. Bakes in what I call 'catch an opening,' in trying to get the spirit of negotiation going." Adams was equally firm in an hour-and-a-half conversation.

The IAM reported a 93 percent membership vote in favor of a strike—the union constitution required a two-thirds majority. The accuracy of the IAM's figure may ultimately be determined by the federal court; Continental has filed a $250 million lawsuit against the IAM alleging that the union stuffed ballots to secure an affirmative vote. The company's lawsuit relies on a deposition that a Denver negotiator, Gerry Smith, gave shortly before leaving the country for a job in Saudi Arabia. Smith explained that all ballots were sent to Los Angeles where they were counted by two officials. Later, in a Washington meeting, he saw a friend, C. K. (individuals will be identified here by fictitious initials), examining a tabulation of numbers. Smith continued:

A. Yes. We were sitting in the same room and I was sitting at one end of the table and A. Q. was next to me and C. K. was on the other side, and I observed C. K. looking at something that appeared to me to be a tally sheet, and he was using his calculator and doing some calculations. And I asked him what it was and he said it was the tally sheet for the strike vote and the company offer. And I asked him if I could see it when he was finished with it and he said sure. So he handed it to me in a few minutes and I read it and copied the figures down exactly as they were on that sheet onto my notes. (Mr. Smith's notes were later introduced in evidence as exhibit 16.)

Q. What percentage in favor of the strike does exhibit 16 reflect?

A. Sixty-five percent in favor of the strike. . . . But early in the week, I saw the bulletin where he [a Los Angeles union leader] had put out what he claimed the strike vote percentage was, and then to see the tally sheet that showed sixty-five percent, I was very disillusioned.

Q. Did A. Q. at any time during the period in which you were in Washington or at any time thereafter dispute the accuracy of the information contained on the tally sheet?

A. Not the accuracy of the information, no.

Q. Did he dispute anything else about the tally sheet?

A. Yes, he did. He made the comment that letting me see the tally sheet may have been the biggest mistake they ever made, which I didn't forget. I remember that comment very distinctly.

When the strike was called on August 13, the plans both of labor and management miscarried badly. At Houston, a member of the negotiating committee, John Showman, stood on the back of a pickup truck that was parked under floodlights near the maintenance shops and urged union members through a microphone to come to work. Sixty percent of the IAM membership chose to cross the picket lines. The strike did have a temporary impact on maintenance work in Los Angeles. Only about 150 of 900 mechanics reported for work the first day of the strike. But the company hired 250 mechanics through C. Franklin Company and was able to reroute enough work to Houston to restore service quickly. The daily flight schedule reached 93 percent of the prestrike level within seven days. A month after the strike, 56 percent of the mechanics throughout the system had returned to the job, and outside contractors were performing flight kitchen, cabin cleaning, and fueling work. The strike clearly had been broken.

Ironically, the company's carefully laid strike plans miscarried in an equally dramatic way. Management had counted on the strike to reduce labor costs, but the large number of IAM mechanics returning to work at the new $16 per hour rate had the effect of raising labor costs in August $1.8 million above projections. Moreover, the IAM unexpectedly released the Union of Flight Attendants from its pledge to support the strike, and the company remained saddled with the same costly contract as before.

It was the airline's marketing performance, however, that decisively upset earlier calculations. The management strike plan actually began to crumble well before the strike occurred as Continental's passenger traffic sank to an acutely unprofitable level. In July, Continental's traffic fell 15.7 percent from the level a year earlier, and the airline experienced a disastrous net loss of $7.4 million. While the strike had only a modest impact on business, it did cause this unprofitable level of passenger traffic to decline somewhat further. Revenue passenger miles dropped another 8.3 percent in August, and load factors slipped .5 percent. By the end of the month, Continental had incurred an operating loss of $10.5 million rather than the forecasted profit of $8.7 million.

Continental's losses occurred at a time when market conditions were taking a sharp turn for the better. In the spring, American Airlines had announced a new and higher tariff schedule based on actual mileage flown, and the industry had followed its lead. The third quarter turned out to be hugely profitable for the industry. The ten major carriers (excluding Continental) reported operating profits of $548 million. Continental was the only major airline not to reap the benefit of the improved market conditions in the summer season. In July, when Continental's traffic fell 15.7 percent, the eleven major carriers as a group experienced a 5.5 percent increase in traffic over a year earlier, despite higher fares. Part of the decline in Continental's passenger traffic can be explained by a 6 percent reduction in capacity caused by the sale of aircraft. The threatened IAM strike no doubt also began to discourage patronage as early as July. But the full extent of Continental's problems can only be explained by serious failures in marketing policies.

Early in the year, management had reduced schedules 15 percent in an effort to cut losses, but it continued to add new cities to the route system—five more cities were added in the first half of 1983. As a result, the airline entered the third quarter with a route system that defied a basic fact known to any airline traveler: people tend to book reservations on airlines offering frequent daily service. Continental served seventy-eight cities but offered more than four flights a day to relatively few. Among major carriers, only Pan Am had a smaller market share on its domestic routes, and it had designed its route system for the distinct purpose of funneling traffic to its international flights. Two-thirds of Continental's revenue passenger miles were flown on routes in which it had less than 30 percent market share. In contrast, Delta flew only one-fourth of its revenue passenger miles on routes in which it had less than this share.

A novel pricing strategy in the vital markets shared by Southwest Airlines resulted in a further loss of business. Management knew it could not make a profit by offering fares competitive with Southwest. In July, it adopted a different tactic; it raised fares to a level, well above competition, that was potentially profitable if a 60 percent load factor could be achieved. Predictably, travelers shunned Continental flights in favor of the more economical service of Southwest Airlines and other competitors. Continental's financial results in the Southwest Airlines markets ran counter to the normal seasonal trend toward increased traffic and revenues. As compared to May and June, July traffic was down 14 percent and revenues declined 3 percent.

Continental's marketing problems were also affected by changes in public perception of the airline. Since the takeover, the marketing department had experienced frequent changes in executive leadership. Many old-time employees left, and executive responsibility to planning and pricing shifted hands repeatedly. One newly hired senior vice-president lasted a period of weeks; and another about six months. The result was a marketing program marked by frequent changes of direction and recurring problems of communication with the travel industry. Concurrently, Continental was beginning to lose its quality image. Vice-president of market planning Barrie Duggan insists that the new management tried to maintain quality service; it took steps to improve food service, renovated aircraft interiors, and acquired new gates at Denver and Houston. Still, Duggan acknowledges, "I heard at least one hundred times that Continental's standards were going to hell. People would say, 'Look, this is the sort of thing that is happening now that TI has taken over.' "

During 1983, problems in passenger service began to assume a more tangible form after the company carried out another employee furlough. Lines grew longer at ticket counters. Ticket agent Donna Shaffer remarks, "People didn't treat the public as they had been treated before. They didn't have the time to talk or smile." Bob McMillan, head of the baggage-tracing department, says his staff was "pretty well innundated with claims" for lost baggage during the summer. Continental had begun to project the image of a troubled airline.

A kind of indifference to the airline's mounting losses began to effect business decisions in August. The ill-conceived fares in the Southwest Airlines markets remained in effect. Management decided not to impose the 15 percent pay cut for nonunion employees that had been contemplated earlier, thus voluntarily foregoing a savings of $3.3 million in labor costs. And a curious transaction with Texas Air added to the drain on cash and reported losses for the month. Continental repurchased for $5.9 million certain flight simulators and related equipment that it had earlier sold to Texas Air. The facilities were then sold to a subsidiary of TI for $4.4 million, resulting in a reported loss of $1.5 million in airline operations. The transaction had in fact been planned for several months, but management showed a certain lack of concern for the airline's finances by closing it at this time.

The Continental management was now making plans that explicitly contemplated the possibility of bankruptcy. In late July, general counsel Barry Simon retained bankruptcy specialists from the law firm Weil, Gotshal & Manges; and two days before the IAM strike, the law department asked vice-president of finance Howard Swanson for a list of unsecured creditors. When the strike failed to achieve the anticipated labor savings, Lorenzo considered for a while the alternative of another confrontation with the pilots. The company actually requested an emergency meeting of the pilot MEC on August

24 and planned to present a demand for $45 million in concessions. But when the pilot leaders arrived in Houston, Lorenzo was formulating a more ambitious strategy. The pilots were told that management wanted to meet a week later.

In the last days of August, Lorenzo decided again to raise the stakes. At the risk of panicking travel agents and vendors, he decided to increase the demand for pilot concessions from $45 million to $60 million—an annual savings that would cut the $130 million pilot payroll almost in half—and to present other employee groups with similar demands totaling $90 million. A $20 million savings had already been secured from the IAM; the flight attendants would be asked to contribute $40 million and the nonunion employees $30 million. Management would require commitments for the full $150 million by September 14. Seeking to justify the two-week deadline, Dick Adams explains, "We were concerned that once we revealed our financial situation straight . . . it would very soon become public knowledge and we would be subject to the very severe danger of losing all of our business because the travel agencies would book away from us just as they did with Braniff and put Braniff in bankruptcy." He concedes that planning for Chapter 11 played a part in choosing the deadline. The company bankruptcy attorneys were already doing groundwork for a bankruptcy petition. Referring to the appropriate time for a bankruptcy filing, Adams says, "I believe that was the basis for a September 14 deadline."

The $60 million demand was presented to pilots at a well-staged MEC meeting on August 31, 1983. Lorenzo appeared flanked by fifteen other executives. After offering apologies for use of a prepared script and a tape recorder, he announced, "My time is limited. I have a 45 minute presentation, and there will be 45 minutes for questions." When MEC chairman Larry Baxter objected to the tape recorder, Lorenzo turned it off and proceeded to read his script.

The prepared statement made a very persuasive case for management's demand, arguing that the $150 million of labor concessions was the minimum necessary to provide "a cost structure competitive with our low-cost competition and . . .

sufficient relief to give us the strength to finance our continuation, our growth and eventual profitability." The airline had lost $84 million in the first six months of 1984; management's demand would do no more than "bring us to a break-even" that would permit financing for growth. The script appealed to the pilots to face the reality of deregulation: "I am sure this will be the most difficult decision in your professional life," said Lorenzo. "The real choice is between the proposed cost reduction and breathing life into Continental in this new competitive era . . . or the loss of all pilot jobs. . . . We think it is in your own immediate economic self-interest to choose to accept our proposal." Three times the script alluded with carefully chosen words to the consequences of failing to meet the September 14 deadline for concessions. "We are not going to go out of business as Braniff did, that is, with no cash," Lorenzo stated. "Rather, we are firmly committed to take other steps to protect our remaining liquidity and our assets. . . . That leaves us with the two alternatives I began with—dramatic and immediate voluntary cost reduction or actions to protect our liquidity and other resources." When a pilot asked what he had in mind, Lorenzo said, "Something you may not like." Pressed further for an answer, Lorenzo would only say, "We're not prepared to divulge that at this time."

The script was an eloquent appeal to reason that would greatly strengthen management's hand in the ensuing legal and political struggles. Continental's Washington representative, Clark Onstad, later gave the script to all congressmen who would meet with him. But in the opinion of senior director of flying Bill Laughlin, who later resigned in protest against management policies, the apparent good faith of the presentation was belied by the actual proposal handed to the pilots. While the script was an artfully crafted document, the proposal itself was an extraordinary breach of negotiating protocol. It consisted of a two-page list of nineteen points that represented a complete departure from the existing pilot contract. The chairman of the pilot negotiating committee, Lou Colombo, says he was "absolutely shocked" to read it. "If you need economic relief, you get economic relief," he says. "Why would anybody take everything out of the contract. I'm telling you everything was changed." The nineteen points, moreover, lacked the level of detail normally found in negotiating proposals. Colombo protests, "A proposal is a comprehensive package you can agree upon. It's not a list of statements. There were days and days of work to do on it."

Senior director of flying Bill Laughlin declares that the proposal was "either the product of stupidity or a deliberate attempt to anger the pilots and assure unacceptability." Another executive, Bob Lemon, the director of flight training, shared his interpretation. As they chatted after the August 31 MEC meeting, Lemon remarked, "I bet the boys in the backroom are worried that this isn't bad enough, and the pilots will accept it." Laughlin points out that "the proposal had items that would set pilots off." The very first item—"no restriction in number of landings in duty period"—was on its face a dangerous idea; accidents occur when pilots are tired. Another item, allowing any qualified pilot to move into the captain's seat, was an attack on the pilots' most cherished institution—seniority. Other items verged on the ludicrous. Compensation for time spent in *ground* transportation between neighboring airports would be measured by *air* travel time between the airports. Thus, if a pilot had to drive from a flight in San Jose to begin a trip in San Francisco, he would be compensated for the (extremely brief) air travel time between the airports.

If the proposal was written in a form calculated to assure rejection, it accomplished its purpose. "The pilots threw it away," Laughlin recalls. "How could you respond to it?" Laughlin himself had not been consulted in preparing the proposal even though he was the second highest ranking executive in flight operations. In the following days, he undertook on his own initiative to revise the existing contract, the "Red Book," to achieve the desired $60 million in annual payroll savings. He thought this sort of revised contract might win pilot acceptance. But when he presented his boss, Donald Breeding, vice-president of flight operations, with a copy of the "Red Book," revised to achieve the $60 million in savings,

Breeding was not interested in finding common ground with the pilots. "I do not want anything that resembles the Red Book," Breeding told Laughlin. "I want something completely different and foreign to these pilots."

Defending the nineteen-point proposal, vice-president of personnel John Adams points out that management left the door open for a counterproposal. Lorenzo indeed stated, "[We] are more than happy to discuss with you alternative suggestions which result in the same savings." But, in a major tactical error, the pilots failed to prepare a counterproposal. Distrust of management ran so deep that the pilot membership would not accept, on short notice, a company demand for concessions that would so radically alter their careers. "If Lorenzo invited me out to dinner and said he was buying, I'd bring money," said pilot Dennis Higgins, reflecting the general sentiment.[4] Compounding other difficulties, the pilots were in the process of electing a new MEC chairman and could make no commitment for another week when the election results would be known. "We had no internal way of dealing with the company demand," says chief negotiator Lou Colombo.

Rather than accede to a scenario set by management—a politically and emotionally impossible course—the pilots decided to propose their own, more reasonable agenda. In a letter dated September 1, 1983, the MEC chairman, Larry Baxter (who was reelected a week later), rejected the company's nineteen-point demand and proposed a kind of summit meeting that would bring together all the key players—top management, each union, and the airline's lead bank, Chase Manhattan. Together they would assess the situation and decide what needed to be done to save the company. It was indeed a reasonable approach that would later be followed by other financially threatened airlines. But the pilots' assumption that they had the time and the bargaining power to impose their own agenda turned out to be a bad miscalculation.

Early in September, management began to prepare detailed plans for operation after a Chapter 11 filing. According to Dick Adams, the plans encompassed methods of reducing labor costs. When asked how the company intended to reduce labor costs through bankruptcy, Adams replied, "It was our expectation, based on counsel's advice. . . . We could change the contracts after a Chapter 11 filing." This advice of Continental's counsel was addressed to a disputed point of law on which there was conflicting authority, but in September 1983 a case was before the U.S. Supreme Court, *NLRB v. Bildisco*, that promised to resolve the question within a few months' time. In the *Bildisco* case, the Third Circuit Court of Appeals had held that a bankrupt company could unilaterally change wages and working conditions of union employees while applying to the bankruptcy court for an order formally rejecting the union contract. The bankruptcy court would have discretion to approve the company's action where "the balance of the equities . . . is found to favor the debtor." Among the factors that a court should consider in balancing the equities was "the good or bad faith" of management in dealing with the union.

The *Bildisco* decision, if it should be affirmed by the Supreme Court, called for a seemingly contradictory game plan. Management needed to pursue labor negotiations to establish its good faith in dealing with unions even if it did not hope (or want) the negotiations to succeed; but while the negotiations proceeded, management was free to plan new wages and work rules that it would unilaterally impose as soon as the company filed for bankruptcy. Dick Adams acknowledges that by mid-September management had developed a plan for labor savings under Chapter 11, known as "Plan B," that went well beyond the concessions then demanded of employees. The company was asking employees for $150 million in concessions. "Plan B" envisioned annual labor cost savings following bankruptcy of $250 million, a reduction by half of the airline's payroll.

After presenting the unions with the concessionary demands, management began to appeal directly to employees for support, bypassing the union leadership. Lorenzo gave presentations to large employee gatherings at the major bases; and president Stephen Wolf set up an "information hotline" to answer employee questions by telephone and sent a letter to all pilots and flight attendants asking them to send management telegrams in support of the requested concessions. On the day the letter was mailed, management took an action it had long resisted: it proposed a plan for employee stock ownership in Continental Airlines Corporation, the intermediate level holding company. The company offered to grant four million shares to employees as a bonus and make additional shares available under a stock option program. The plan offered employees almost 12 percent of the holding company's stock and an opportunity to acquire more through options, but it did not affect actual corporate control, which would remain securely in the hands of the parent company, Texas Air Corporation. The pilot leaders never received any documentation concerning the plan—they learned of it through the press release—but pilot negotiator Lou Colombo says he still thought the pilots "had a shot at putting a deal together" when it was announced. Employee stock ownership, he says, "was viewed by us as the key to making an agreement work."

By mid-September most employees knew that the airline was entering a crisis that could radically affect their careers. The nonunion employees, pilots, and flight attendants each responded differently to the crisis. The story of the nonunion employees is easiest to tell. Employee councils, formed a year earlier for each noncontract employee group, were asked to approve an immediate 15 percent pay cut, together with reduction in vacation time, holidays, sick leave, and insurance benefits. It was the first time nonunion employees had been asked to make a financial sacrifice to save their jobs, and they approved the concessions overwhelmingly.

Under the leadership of MEC chairman Larry Baxter the pilots were committed to the tactic of demanding their own negotiation forum and agenda. Management extended the deadline for concessions to Monday, September 19, but the pilots refused to meet with the company during the interim because management would not include the airline's lead bankers in the discussions. When the deadline arrived, Baxter was dismayed to learn that the president, Stephen Wolf, would not attend the negotiations. (Wolf would resign two days later.) Thinking that this climactic moment required direct conversations with the top executives, he informed the company that the pilots would not meet unless Wolf were present. Being unable to negotiate on their own terms, the pilot MEC passed a resolution that conveyed an ambiguous but genuine commitment:

> Whereas the Continental Airlines pilots MEC has determined that it is in the best interest of all Continental Airlines pilots to participate in a further cost reduction program to allow Continental Airlines to compete profitably in today's market place . . . therefore be it resolved that . . . the chairman convey this commitment to company officials.

Management let the deadline pass, and the pilots met twice with management negotiators later in the week, insisting on appropriate ground rules for negotiation. Friday, the eve of the bankruptcy, was the occasion of a confrontation between Baxter and Lorenzo. Bill Laughlin remembers the dialogue clearly:

> "We will do whatever it takes," Baxter assured Lorenzo.
> "Does this mean $60 million?"
> "It means $45, 60 or 100 million. Whatever it takes."
> "That's not enough. I have to have it in writing," countered Lorenzo.

When the bankruptcy petition was filed the next day, the pilots knew they had been merely going through the motions of negotiating.

The flight attendants responded to the crisis in a manner that in other circumstances might have led to a breakthrough. In a confrontation less dramatically staged than the pilot MEC meeting, management presented the Union of Flight Attendants with a briefly written proposal calling for $40 million in annual concessions. The proposal had the effect of completely recasting the existing Continental and TI contracts, and it contained no protections on the emotional issues of hairstyle, weight, scheduling, and verification of illness. But the flight attendants enjoyed unusually sophisticated leadership.

Union president Darenda Hardy recognized the clear threat of bankruptcy. She was prepared to meet the company's demand for $40 million in concessions even though it would mean a reduction of roughly 40 percent in the scheduled union payroll. In the days before management's deadline, the union leaders modified the concessionary proposal that had been on the table since February so as to offer permanent annual payroll concessions of $40 million.

When she presented the proposal on Monday morning, Darenda Hardy says that the management negotiators appeared "annoyed." They asked for a recess, and the meeting did not reconvene for several hours. Management then asserted that the proposal was actually worth substantially less than $40 million and demanded that the union immediately sign a commitment in principle for a full $40 million. Darenda Hardy refused to sign such a blank check, but she offered to meet the rest of the week with management in an effort to negotiate $40 million in concessions. If they couldn't reach agreement, the union would agree to defer payment of the end-of-the-month paycheck.

The union leaders knew that their costing was not above criticism. The proposal contained about $26 million in hard, verifiable concessions, but other items relating to productivity improvements were less easy to quantify. One of their experienced costing experts was unavailable on vacation and another, Carla Lawson, was on a trip to Sydney, Australia. Darenda Hardy asked that Lawson be recalled immediately. The union also requested an answer to a lengthy request for costing information that it had submitted a month earlier after negotiators encountered—for the first time!—serious costing disagreements with the new management. But management failed to respond to the request for information and waited two days before giving Carla Lawson a space-available ticket to the

U.S. on Qantas. Calling the Qantas ticket office, Lawson found that she would be bumped in Tahiti and decided to return on her regularly scheduled flight arriving in Los Angeles on Saturday.

The impasse continued throughout the week—management insisting that the union had rejected its offer and the union demanding a suitable opportunity to discuss the costing issue. After the Monday meeting, the parties did not meet again until several days after the bankruptcy filing.

The labor negotiations were played out against the background of an accelerating financial deterioration. The company's demand for extraordinary labor concessions had exactly the effect on the travel agent community that management had feared. Continental's treasurer, Mickey Foret, explains that his financial projections "began to change most precipitously for the month of September shortly after the beginning of the month and after the rumors of imminent Chapter 11 filings that we talked about were apparently circulating the travel community and after the load factors began to fall very dramatically. . . ." For the first twenty-four days of the month, the average load factor was 46.7 percent, and on some days it slipped below 40 percent. The airline needed a load factor between 65 percent and 70 percent to break even. In these twenty-four days of September—a profitable month for most major carriers—Continental lost $38 million. By September 24, its net worth had sunk to a negative $52 million. The company owed $42 million in overdue vendor payments and faced a payment date in the next week for $20 million in principal and interest payments.

The company was still solvent in the sense that it could pay the bills needed for continued operations: it retained about $20 million in unrestricted cash. The pilots and flight attendants had always stood ready to make short-term payroll concessions, and bank creditors were actively considering a management proposal for financial restructuring. But by staging the labor confrontations in September, management had really passed a point of no return. Travel agents, fearing an interruption in service, had caused bookings to drop to a level that was generating losses that could only aggravate existing fears and further discourage bookings. The airline was caught in a downward spiral that seemed certain to end soon in actual insolvency.

On Saturday afternoon, September 24, Continental Airlines Corporation and its two subsidiaries, Continental and Texas International, filed for bankruptcy under Chapter 11. Texas Air, which had carefully safeguarded its financial resources, remained solvent. (See Appendix 2.) In a press release, management announced that service on the profitable (or potentially profitable) foreign routes would continue without interruption, but domestic service would be suspended for two days and cut back about 80 percent. Daily departures would be reduced from 585 to 182 throughout the system.

Continental employees all retain a vivid memory of the moment they learned of the bankruptcy. Eight thousand of the airline's twelve thousand employees were furloughed the day of the filing. Patti Dobert, a reservations agent for ten years, was at work in Los Angeles. "About 3 o'clock they came in and told us to pack up our belongings, turn in our ID badges and leave the premises immediately," she remembers.[5] Carole Mitchell had been sent to Honolulu on company business and learned of the bankruptcy from a hotel clerk. "You will have to pay cash. Your company filed for bankruptcy," the clerk informed her. When she returned home three days later, she was told to turn in her ID badge.

The next day, Lorenzo discussed the bankruptcy filing with a *Wall Street Journal* reporter. "It wasn't a problem of cash," he said. "Our sole problem was labor." In reality, Lorenzo underestimated the airline's financial crisis—it faced an inevitable cash shortage within a month—and he overlooked the role that marketing errors had played in precipitating the crisis. Continental had somehow failed to benefit from the dramatically improved market conditions which rescued other financial troubled airlines in the third quarter of 1983. His remark might be taken as an exercise in personal exculpation, putting the blame on unions, but he didn't sound like a man announcing a business failure. He implied that the bankruptcy actually represented a business breakthrough for the airline. "We will implement a strategic plan to make Continental the largest of the low-cost airlines," he announced.[6]

The principal feature of the strategic plan was "Plan B," management's scheme to achieve $250 million in annual labor savings through Chapter 11. There was no time to prepare elaborate documentation, but management had in hand memos outlining new rates of pay and benefit programs and summarizing new work rules for each employee group. In a letter sent to employees, Lorenzo bluntly stated, "The terms on which we will be offering employment will be vastly different from those in effect prior to filing of the bankruptcy petition."[7]

In the case of the pilots, the emergency work rules were mailed to the union office and posted on bulletin boards Saturday night. The pilot leaders, less well briefed than management on current trends in bankruptcy law, were completely unprepared for the idea that the company could unilaterally promulgate new terms of employment upon filing for bankruptcy. Chief negotiator Lou Colombo says, "I just couldn't believe it! In what country can you throw out union contracts like that?" The terms of employment cut salaries almost in half, slashing an average captains pay from $83,500 to $43,000, sharply reduced vacation and medical benefits, and terminated *all* pension programs. But it was the new work rules that most provoked a sense of outrage. They might allow pilots as little as five hours sleep or call for fourteen-and-a-half-hour work days. The pilots knew that accidents could happen when they work under stress and fatigue. Like the earlier management demands, the rules attacked the seniority system by eliminating the rank of second officer and providing for interchangeable duties for first officers and pilots. The language, moreover, was carefully worded to preserve management discretion. A final clause gave management the right to suspend any other provision under "extraordinary" circumstances (the term was undefined). Chief negotiator Colombo protests, "The language was so, so vague. It was not a contract. The employer had escape clauses throughout the whole agreement. There was nothing they were bound to do."

The company publicly compared the emergency work rules to the contract ALPA had recently negotiated with the New Braniff. In terms of costs, the two contracts were in fact very similar, but the Braniff agreement was tightly drafted to preserve employee rights. Colombo insists that despite comparable wage and benefit levels, the emergency work rules were "nowhere close to the Braniff agreement. The Braniff agreement is an *agreement*."

Among the rank and file, the emergency work rules provoked a violent reaction. Unschooled in recent bankruptcy decisions, the pilots thought that the company's unilateral action had to be illegal. The pilot MEC delivered a letter to management asserting that the "unilateral announcement and implementation of so-called emergency work rules violates the Railway Labor Act." The company responded by stating a well-advised legal position. Under the bankruptcy law, it was free to reject the old contract and to unilaterally impose new terms of employment, subject to later bankruptcy court approval. The labor laws required it only to continue to bargain in good faith with the union. In a series of letters and telegrams, the company urgently requested an opportunity to negotiate with the union. The emergency work rules, it contended, constituted a company proposal for a new agreement.

The Continental management was playing a sophisticated game in which the rules were not yet defined. If the U.S. Supreme Court should reverse the *Bildisco* decision, the emergency work rules would indeed be an unfair labor practice. But if the Supreme Court should affirm the decision, the company would be justified in implementing the work rules, subject only to an obligation to bargain in good faith with the union. The pilot leaders would learn the nature of the game after they had already lost. In the week after the bankruptcy, they refused to meet with management negotiators, thus strengthening the company's legal case; and they failed to consider the option of filing a grievance protesting the emergency work rules—a legally safe course of action that would have left future options open. Instead, the union instructed pilots to fly under protest while the MEC met to decide how to fight the company's action. On September 29 the MEC voted to strike. Whatever might be the best strategic considerations, they emotionally had no choice.

When the pilot negotiators met with the company the next day, management offered to withdraw several of the most offensive provisions of the emergency work rules, but the pilots were now committed to the strike, and they were receiving unprecedented support from the national ALPA organization. The ALPA executive board met in a special session in Houston a few hours after the strike vote and authorized monthly strike benefits of $3800 for captains and $2500 for first and second officers. Striking pilots would actually receive somewhat more in strike benefits than they would be paid by the company under the new terms of employment. The extraordinary benefits would be financed by a stiff monthly assessment of the entire ALPA membership, ranging from about $70 to over $300 per month.

On October 1, the pilots walked off the job to force the company to withdraw the emergency work rules. Lorenzo describes the strike as a refusal of the pilots to accept the economic realities of deregulation. "Their [ALPA's] whole thrust is in protecting $100,000 a year jobs at other airlines and using Continental pilots as pawns in the process," he declared.[8] But the pilots themselves generally discounted the importance of the new levels of wages and benefits. "The money is not the issue, says pilot Dick Smith. "The issue is employee rights. We are in a situation where this company is saying it can unilaterally break its agreements with us and leave us without any say over our jobs."[9]

The pilots also stressed the issue of safety. Pilot Cal Harmon did not decide to join the strike until the last moment. "Sure I was overpaid," he says. "And if I worked for Lorenzo now I'd be underpaid. But I'd do it if I trusted him. But I think his work rules are unsafe. And I don't want to be the one who gets in an airplane tired or sick because he took away my sick pay, and be responsible for killing people. I won't do it. I guess I'd rather pump gas." Recurring in most pilots' remarks is an element of simple anger directed at Lorenzo. "I

252

flew in Vietnam for two years," says one first officer, "and it's hard to hate the communists as much as I hate this guy. He wants to go back to sweat shops."[10]

Before the strike, pilot leader Gary Thomas confidently announced. "We're going to shut the airline down. We will have picket lines up."[11] But the pilots fell far short of this objective. The first day the airline was forced to cancel only 15 of 118 domestic flights. Nine days later, cancellations due to the strike had dropped to zero. About 120 pilots crossed the picket line the first day; by the end of the month, 250 had returned to work. Within days of the strike, management began to advertise job openings for pilots and to conduct interviews in eleven cities. The company offered new recruits a second pay scale representing the lowest salary levels found in the industry— captains began at $28,000 and pilot officers at $15,000—but it still succeeded in hiring 40 new pilots in October.

Senior director of flying Bill Laughlin believed the company was goading the pilots into a strategic folly, damaging both to their own careers and the airline's prospects for recovery. If the company would offer work rules comparable to those in the New Braniff agreement, he thought the pilots would soon abandon the strike. As a licensed pilot, he was assigned to flight duty for Air Micronesia in the first days of the strike. Returning to Houston, he again brought his proposed revision of the pilot contract to the vice-president of flight operations, Donald Breeding. All the company's economic objectives, he argued, could be achieved by modifying the existing contract. But Breeding liked the management discretion conferred by the emergency work rules. "Why would you do that?" he objected. "It [the emergency work rules] is like the emancipation proclamation." A few days later, as the company began to recruit strikebreaking pilots, Laughlin decided he had to resign. In his letter of resignation to Donald Breeding, he said:

> As the emergency work rules were prepared, you rejected my input to modify the "Red Book", stating that you wanted a totally different concept. I felt and still feel that the new concept is contrary to the needs of a

world wide airline. After returning from covering trips on Air Mike, I was astonished to find all your efforts were directed at replacing pilots rather than trying to retain those pilots that have built this airline and have the reputation of one of the world's finest pilot groups. It is obvious that my opinion is not desired and my philosophy of management is not compatible with yours. Therefore, I resign as Senior Director of Flying.

The flight attendants faced the same dilemmas as the pilots. The new terms of employment cut their wages in half, slashed benefits and terminated all pensions. The Continental flight attendants had earned an average of $37,500 in wages and benefits; the company now offered about $15,000—a pay cut of 60 percent! The emergency work rules went well beyond the Braniff agreement by subjecting seniority rights and duty limitations to a large measure of management discretion. Management again reserved the right to suspend the rules in undefined emergency situations. "There were really no work rules at all," says flight attendant negotiator Claudia Lampe.

While charging the company with an unfair labor practice, the flight attendant leaders adopted a more conciliatory stance than the pilots. Four days after the bankruptcy, they requested a meeting with management and suggested a time and place. But the pilots' decision to strike soon forced their hand. Union president Darenda Hardy thought that by joining the strike they might successfully oppose the new terms of employment. "If the company couldn't operate, they would have to work out an agreement," she says. The union was, however, in a weak position to challenge the company; it did not have the resources to pay strike benefits, and striking flight attendants could easily be replaced—the company could still call on the six hundred flight attendants it had recruited before the IAM strike.

The first day of the strike, the great majority of flight attendants stayed off the job. Scores of flight attendants picketed the major airports and spirits were high. But enough flight attendants still crossed the picket line to staff the reduced flight schedule; the strike had almost no effect in curtailing daily departures. Sensing a losing cause, flight attendants soon began to come to work in greater numbers, sometimes braving the resentment of their colleagues. A weeping flight attendant who crossed the picket line in Houston explained that she had to choose between her friendships and her job. "It was the toughest decision I have ever made in my life," she said.[12] Another flight attendant, Chris Miller, added, "Some of these people are my best friends, and they won't talk to me. That really hurts."[13]

The strike lost all strategic purpose as the company hired enough flight attendants to staff a steadily increasing flight schedule. For those who stayed off the job, it became a matter of principle to refuse to work under the existing conditions. The Continental management acted to restore the standards of personal appearance that the flight attendants had successfully fought in the seventies as a form of sexual discrimination. The "Procedures Manual" revised the hairstyle regulations, and the company instituted quarterly "appearance checks." Indignation at such action strengthened the resolve of some strikers, but, as Houston flight attendant Sheri Pennington concedes, "They discovered that they were not as well qualified for other things as they thought." Other airlines were reluctant to hire flight attendants on strike. Even with a 60 percent pay cut, the airline offered as much as they were able to earn in jobs in other industries. Six months after the strike, Pennington observed that "not many flight attendants had found permanent jobs" and "no one was getting a better job." They were still surviving on unemployment benefits and the support of their families.

The financial pressure on strikers had a telling effect. By May 1984, about half the flight attendants had returned to their jobs. The former ESOP leader, Pearl Kelly, came back to work in February. She had emotionally supported the strike. "Lorenzo is pulling us around like puppets!" she exclaimed.[14] But she saw no purpose in staying on strike any longer. "A protest had to be made," she says, "but I've been flying for so many years." Back on the job, she reports that those employees who have made the difficult decision to continue to work for Continental are pulling together in mutual support. "There's a great team spirit among agents, flight attendants and flight crews," she maintains.

Perhaps no employee group suffered more in the months after the bankruptcy than the nonunion employees. During the weekend when the petition was filed, supervisors drew up lists of an "A team" to be offered continued employment and a "B team" to be informed that they were no longer needed. The selection had little relation to seniority; a ticket agent, Kay Phillips, charges, "The chose those who would make the fewest waves." The employees who were offered jobs faced pay cuts as high as 40 percent. The hourly wage of ticket agents was reduced from $12.60 to $7.50. After several months on furlough, Carol Mitchell was offered a job paying $1300 a month, and she had to meet mortgage and car payments totaling $1100 a month.

The company's contingency plans included no program for communicating with displaced employees. Suddenly out of work, they needed to know their employment status and rights of compensation. Were they discharged or furloughed? When would they be paid for the last days of work? Would they be entitled to severance pay, vacation benefits, early retirement, or payment of medical claims? The employees remained in the dark for weeks or months. Hopelessly understaffed, the employee benefits department resolutely ignored a barrage of telephone calls, telegrams, and letters.

For many nonunion employees, Continental had been more than a job: it was a vocation, a cause, and a community. Now set adrift and ignored, they felt personally abused. Much of the employee resentment was directed at Lorenzo. A Los Angeles reservation agent, Jacki Breitman, complains, "Historically, we have supported the company all the way. Yet he turns around and cuts us off. I'm feeling bitter toward the man, and a little bit hurt."[15] A ticket agent, Joan Kepp, remarks, "The anger in people is what is so ugly. That's what is so devastating. You only hurt yourself by feeling the anger." Fifty-six years old, with over ten years of service with the company, she received no notice of her employment status after the bankruptcy, but when she applied for early retirement, she was told she had been terminated. Two years later, she still has not received her last three weeks' salary or vacation pay. "I'm still trying to get my life in order, trying to find a job and get early retirement," she says. "They say there's no age discrimination, but I've tried to get a job in the airline industry, and it is impossible."

Customer relations employee Jeannette Martin was bound to Continental by a wide circle of friendships and a deep feeling of loyalty. She had been distressed by the high management turnover following the takeover. "There were days when it was hard to go to work because it was so depressing. Every day there was news that somebody we knew had left," she remembers. She was deeply resentful to find herself without a job or retirement benefits. "While there may have been a need for some very definitive action to save the company, we non-contract employees felt we were stripped of dignity by the method that was chosen," she says. Together with a few friends, she organized an association called CLEG, the Continental Lost Employees Group, to demand answers to employee questions and to represent nonunion employees in the bankruptcy proceedings. Over four hundred people attended their first meeting in a high school auditorium near the Los Angeles airport, and the association soon gained five hundred dues-paying members. For more than six months after the bankruptcy, she dedicated all her time to the association, postponing her search for another job.

Yet many nonunion employees rallied to the company and struggled to make the bankruptcy a success. Former ESOP leader Bill Miles describes the dedication of his colleagues, working long hours under pressure, as an example of a community's "will to survive." Houston ticket agent Carol McDougall worked sixteen-hour days in the week after the bankruptcy. Her counter was understaffed and mobbed by bargain-seeking travelers who asked about the airline and the industry. Exhausted but determined, she protested the unfavorable publicity of the bankruptcy. "We've had so many bad things written about us," she said. "I'm sick of it. We're gonna make it. I know we are.

I've worked here 17 years, and it's like old times again right now. There's a feeling of unity. We're a family again. It's been a long time. I love this airline. And we're gonna make it. Just watch."[16]

Within a few weeks of the bankruptcy, it became clear that the airline was indeed making it. Cash from foreign operations enabled the airline to reestablish its position in domestic routes. Continental's service to the South Pacific, Mexico, and Venezuela had accounted for about 15 percent of its operations before the bankruptcy. When domestic service was cut by 80 percent, the foreign routes represented about half of Continental's business. The bankruptcy had not interfered much with passenger traffic on these routes; most bookings had been made well in advance. Some of the routes, such as those in the South Pacific, had earned a profit throughout the year. With the abrupt reduction of labor costs, all the foreign routes suddenly became extremely profitable and provided cash to fund startling bargains on domestic operations.

For the first four days after the bankruptcy, Continental offered an unrestricted one-stop fare of forty-nine dollars on all domestic routes. The newspaper coverage of the bankruptcy widely publicized the new fares, and passengers were soon packing the Continental planes. The airline then offered a similar bargain fare of seventy-five dollars during the period of October 1 through 22. Long lines of passengers formed between the ticket counters and the picket lines of striking pilots. A more complex fare schedule introduced in the last week of October remained well below that of competition. The average October load factor on domestic flights was around 70 percent; the load factor throughout the system was 65.3 percent—the highest of any major carrier.

Although accurate financial figures remain confidential, Continental's cash position reportedly slipped somewhat in the first week of the bankruptcy and then began to improve. At the beginning of November, Lorenzo publicly stated, "Continental's cash position in total is not materially different than it was when we filed."[17] Later in the year, Continental secured bankruptcy court orders releasing $40 million in cash reserves for airline operations.

Enjoying high load factors and an adequate cash position, Continental began to rebuild its domestic route system. In the two weeks after the pilot and flight attendant strikes, it increased total capacity to 39 percent of the prebankruptcy level; in December capacity reached 50 percent of the former level. Continental's load factors—66.8 percent in November and 62.9 percent in December—remained the highest of the major carriers.

In the first half of 1984, Continental began to exceed its own optimistic goals for recovery. Management had planned to restore 90 percent of capacity by summer; it actually reached that level in early May. On July 1, the airline offered 107 percent of its capacity before the bankruptcy—3 percent more than it had ever offered. The airline's fleet was now fully utilized. Travel agent confidence gradually returned, and by the summer Continental was once again getting over 60 percent of its business from travel agents. Most important, Continental began to show a profit. After reporting a small operating profit and a net loss in the first quarter, it reported an operating profit of $27 million and a net profit of $10.4 million for the second quarter. With reason, *Business Week* wrote of its "astonishing" turnaround.[18]

An advertising campaign announcing "A New Tradition in Flying" reflected Continental's renewed marketing vigor and changed public image. Continental was offering fares competitive with new-entrant airlines and discount airlines, such as People Express, but it provided a range of passenger services comparable to the large old-line carriers. Bankruptcy had given it the best of both worlds. Management did not repeat the marketing blunder that had contributed to its plunge toward insolvency; it restricted service to fewer routes and offered more frequent flights on these routes. By mid-year it was carrying more passengers than before the bankruptcy but served only forty cities as compared to seventy-eight the previous year.

For vice-president of marketing Doug Birdsall this was an

exciting time. A former Eastern Airlines executive, he had struggled throughout much of his career to find a way to produce profits out of impossible cost equations. "Look, it's 9:00 PM and I'm not thinking of going home," he told the author. "You see how late people are working. They worked just as hard before the bankruptcy. They tried to figure out a formula that would work, but it wasn't there." Now Birdsall had a cost equation that was producing marketing successes. Under bankruptcy court protection, the cost per available seat mile had dropped to a little less than 6.5¢ by May 1984, and it was declining further as expansion reduced the burden of overhead. In domestic flights Continental could usually undercut major competitors by about 30 percent with fares producing 10¢ per revenue passenger mile. It needed a load factor somewhat less than 65 percent to break even and could make a profit with any additional traffic.

The pilots' union was not able to check the airline's surge toward recovery. About fifty striking pilots returned to work each month, and the company was able to hire enough other pilots to staff the expanding flight schedule. As the walkout failed to achieve its objective, the pilots turned to a public relations campaign, charging that Continental was unsafe to fly. There was undoubtedly some substance to the charge. In struggling to restore flight schedules, management relaxed past standards of hiring, training, and promoting pilots. The list of newly hired Continental pilots after the strike included a heroin smuggler, a pilot with a record of severe psychiatric problems, a pilot who crashed a private twin-engine plane, and several pilots who had been discharged from other airlines. New hires passed through brief interviews and a shortened program of classroom and flight simulator training. The testing program was simplified by dispensing, among other things, with psychological tests and a final oral examination by a review board. The company attracted new recruits despite its low pay schedule by offering the prospect of quick promotion to the rank of captain. More than sixty pilots who were second officers at the time of the bankruptcy assumed the responsibilities of captain the following May.

ALPA claimed to have verified sixty-six incidents of safety infractions in the first nine months after the bankruptcy. The list included a number of serious incidents, such as altitude violations and a hard landing that damaged the airplane's fuselage. Lorenzo himself flew on a flight to Denver that landed during a clear day on a taxiway rather than the runway. The taxiway was only half the width of the runway. A federal aviation administration operations evaluation report noted "system deficiencies and discrepancies . . . in three key program areas," but concluded that "overall Continental Airlines is providing for an adequate level of safety in their flight operations and aircraft maintenance programs."

It proved hard to arouse public concern about safety. In ALPA's greatest public relations coup, the TV program "60 Minutes" publicized the pilots' charges and vividly described two cases of altitude violations resulting in near misses. Two independent safety experts agreed that there was "a problem" while acknowledging that it might be temporary in nature. But the next week travel agents reported no change whatever in the bookings on Continental flights. The publicity had been completely ineffectual in discouraging passengers from flying on Continental.

The pilots suffered their most decisive defeat, however, at the hands of the U.S. Supreme Court five months after the strike. At the time of Continental's bankruptcy filing, relatively few of the thousands of companies that had gone through Chapter 11 had secured judicial orders abrogating union contracts. Only one large corporation, Wilson Foods of Oklahoma City, which had filed a year earlier, had unilaterally imposed new wages and working conditions in a manner similar to that of the Continental management. When Braniff filed for Chapter 11, president Howard Putnam was advised that the airline would have to adhere to union contracts unless it received a court order authorizing rejection. "We had a different interpretation than Lorenzo seems to be following," said Putnam, shortly after Continental's bankruptcy. "Any contract to be rejected would first have to go through a court hearing and win the judge's approval. That's the route we followed."[19] A leading bankruptcy lawyer, Victor Vilaplano, observed that the Continental executives were "betting the company on a new legal standard that still hasn't been established. It is a very risky tactic."[20]

On February 23, 1984, the Supreme Court delivered an opinion in the case of *NLRB v. Bildisco* that represented a stunning vindication of the legal advice the Continental management had followed. The court first gave the bankruptcy court wide discretion to reject union contracts, permitting rejection if a contract "burdens the estate" and "the equities balance in favor" of rejection, provided that the parties have first made "reasonable efforts to negotiate a voluntary modification" of the contract. Then, the Supreme Court held, by a narrow 5–4 majority, that a bankrupt company "is not guilty of an unfair labor practice by unilaterally breaking a collective-bargaining agreement before formal Bankruptcy Court action." The ruling turned the tables in the legal contest between the company and the unions. The pilots and flight attendants had regarded the unilateral imposition of emergency work rules as an unfair labor practice justifying an immediate strike. Now the company had established its right to impose the work rules, and the unions' action in calling a strike could itself be regarded as an unfair labor practice since the unions had not followed the strike procedures of the Railway Labor Act.

A year after the bankruptcy, Lorenzo had obtained the "quantum change" in labor costs that he desired. Labor costs had been slashed about 45 percent and represented only 20.7 percent of operating expenses, down from 35.8 percent before the bankruptcy. Continental was now the largest low-cost carrier in the industry with operating costs of only 6.3¢ per seat mile as compared to 8.5¢ a year earlier. With its entire fleet again flying, the airline offered damaging competition for other carriers that had pursued a more cooperative approach to labor relations. In September 1984, Eastern Airlines cut its daily flights out of Houston from forty-six to twenty. It had been doing good business with load factors in the 60–70 percent range, but it needed an average load factor around 80 percent to be profitable at fares competitive with those of Continental.

The financial results for the third quarter of 1984 exceeded management's most optimistic forecasts. The airline reported operating income of $43.8 million and net income of $30.3 million. Cash and temporary investments had risen to $126.8 million. In August Continental again achieved the highest load factor among the major air carriers, 69.4 percent, with revenue passenger miles up 40 percent over the same month a year earlier.

In the financial press, Lorenzo again enjoyed the image of a trend setter. A seven-page article in *Fortune* announced: "An Airline Boss Attacks Sky-high Wages."[22] *Business Week* proclaimed that under his leadership "Continental is coming out a winner."[23] An adulatory *New York Times* article described him as "a turnaround artist for an ailing airline."[24] The resilience of Lorenzo's reputation defies any simple explanation: it seems to flow from something deep within the American business ethos. Many commentators appeared to perceive him as a kind of Ayn Rand hero, achieving personal success by decisive action in the face of organized opposition. Whatever may be the explanation, Lorenzo knew how to capitalize on his restored reputation. In October 1984, Texas Air announced plans to sell $50 million in senior exchangeable variable-rate notes.

The former ESOP leaders have differing sentiments about Continental's extraordinary recovery. Reservation agent Karen Harvey, now promoted to area sales manager, feels only relief and gratitude that the airline has survived. After the bankruptcy filing, she feared that the company was going under. "It was chaotic the first months," she remembers. "I was excited to hear that we had carried the one millionth passenger in December. When we carried the three millionth passenger, I thought we would succeed." Harvey thinks it should be stressed that the airline's return to profitable operation "is due to extremely hard work of employees who remained dedicated to the company." It is a different company now, but she says that change was inevitable under deregulation. "I respect Lorenzo for having the courage to file for Chapter 11," she adds.

But the former Los Angeles team leader, Carol Mitchell,

left Continental when the recovery first seemed assured. She was recalled from furlough five months after the bankruptcy and then worked for only a few weeks before resigning. She explains,

It's hard to accept injustice as a *fait accompli*. People were not treated fairly—that's the reason they are on strike! I returned mainly to see if there was anything that could be done, anything to fight for. I had to see that there was no possibility to stay and fight.

She says that she found the employee community working under circumstances she could not accept:

There was still some camaraderie because of the mutuality of the devastation to our careers and economic circumstances. But I was working with people who were barely hanging on. They couldn't pay their bills. It affected our whole lives—our families, children and our self-esteem that was so much tied to pride in our company. I left because I couldn't continue apologizing for my product or follow the directions and policies of management. I had been so proud of my company, and I was now embarrassed. It's gone now—same name— different company. Everything is changed, and it is never going back the way it was before.

EPILOGUE
PART TWO

NEW
BEGINNINGS

Paul Eckel could not reconcile himself to the new working conditions at Continental, but he felt uncomfortable walking on the pilots' picket line. "I worked for Continental for so many years, I didn't like the idea of trying to tear it down," he explains. A few weeks after the strike, he conceived an idea as audacious as the ESOP itself: he would organize a new employee-owned airline, named "Pride Air," which would be staffed largely by former Continental employees. Former marketing vice-president Barrie Duggan agreed to join the venture as president and chief operating officer. Ticket agent Bill Miles and flight attendant Sheri Pennington were among the ESOP leaders who also joined the effort. Reflecting on the employees' defeat three years earlier, Pennington writes, "Perhaps it was meant to be because a higher power saw Pride Air in our future. I'm a firm believer in finding good in what appears to be totally devastating results of an event. I pray we will succeed in making Pride Air our dream come true."

On August 1, 1985, the dream briefly became a reality. Pride Air began flying eight 727s on a system of transcontinental routes centering on New Orleans. Employing over 650 people, the airline provided daily service at low fares from New Orleans to eight Western and seven Florida cities. The airline was financed largely by a $15.5 million sale of stock to its own employees, mainly former Continental pilots. Over 350 pilots made stock purchases ranging from $500 to $150,000. Some pilots drew on their accounts in a now-terminated pension plan, the B-fund; others took out second mortgages on their homes and tapped outside sources of income.

The airline's route system was designed to avoid any direct confrontation with Continental. "We're not Air Revenge," says Eckel. But in May 1985, when the airline's plans were well advanced, Continental announced that it would begin to develop a secondary hub in New Orleans, directly challenging five of the fledgling airline's routes. Once again, Eckel found himself leading a David and Goliath struggle against the financial power of Lorenzo. The odds were too great. Although it achieved unusually high load factors for a start-up airline, Pride Air lacked the financial resources to withstand sustained losses in the first year of operation. When an underwriter canceled a $1 million public offering, it ran out of cash and was forced to suspend operations late in November. For Eckel and his colleagues, this second defeat was more painful than the first.

But most of the employees who followed Eckel in the ESOP campaign are eager to tell about their experiences. The employee movement stands out in their memories as an intensely hopeful and vital period. The CEA secretary, Patrice Boyd, typically says, "It was so exciting. I feel lucky to have been there in the middle of it." Dispatcher Ron Aramini says simply, "I liked all the people I met on the ESOP." Mike Roach, who later became president of America West Airlines, says that the ESOP movement "forever changed my view of employees." A corporate lawyer by training and the son of a business executive, Roach says he inherited "an unarticulated view of the worker as a tool, an inanimate object that you had to manipulate and deal with." While working on the ESOP, he says, "I got to see employees as human beings. I now understand that in a service industry the only way a company can be successful is through motivated, productive employees who believe in the company."

Chuck Cheeld is among the thousands of employees who are beginning new careers outside the company. He now owns and operates two dry cleaning businesses in West Hollywood. Despite the employees' defeat at Continental, he believes he did something "very important and monumental" in fighting for the ESOP, and he points out that the list of airlines with ESOPs has lengthened to include Eastern, Republic, Pan Am, Western, and several smaller carriers such as Pacific Southwest Airlines, Southwest, and America West. In fact, even the national leadership of the IAM now accepts the idea of democratic employee stock ownership. King McCulloch, who fought the Continental ESOP in 1981, today announces proudly, "We've got one of our men on the board of Eastern."

Ironically, the new Continental management now seeks to publicize its own employee stock ownership plan. All "founding employees" of the New Continental have been given grants of one million shares of stock in Continental Airlines Corporation and options to purchase another one million shares. "Founding employees" are defined as those who remained on the payroll a month after the bankruptcy. The stock plan does not, however, give the "founding employees" any power in the corporation. They will own no more than 4 to 9 percent of the stock (depending on the extent that employees retain the stock grants and exercise the options), and they have no right of representation on the board of directors or stock ownership in Texas Air where actual corporate power resides. Similarly, the Continental management has designed a profit sharing plan as a vehicle for employee ownership—the plan is chartered to invest primarily in Continental stock—but a management administrative committee controls the voting of the shares.

It is a double irony that the new employee stock ownership plans have been offered in lieu of a pension program. The former Continental executives refused to compromise the integrity of pension plans by adapting them to employee ownership. The new management, which terminated all pension programs in the bankruptcy, has indicated no intention of offering *any* pension program in the future. It evidently regards the new stock ownership plans, particularly the profit sharing plan, as a substitute for a pension program.

Far from sharing corporate control with employees, Lorenzo has tightened the reins of his personal power over the company. At the May 1985 shareholder meeting of Texas Air, he recommended as an "anti-takeover" measure that an issue of voting preferred stock exclusively held by Jet Capital Corporation, the holding company that he effectively controls, be exchanged for a new issue of "Class A" common stock having five times the voting power of other common stock. A shareholder prospectus explicitly discussed the many disadvantages of the plan, but the shareholders still docilely followed his recommendation by voting to approve it. Lorenzo now effectively controls 45.3 percent of the voting rights in Texas Air.

After being so long the object of criticism for its labor practices, the Lorenzo management today has adopted unusual personnel policies that it offers as a model to the industry. The company has virtually eliminated seniority; ticket agents now receive only a 30¢ per hour wage increase after ten years of service. Management seeks instead to reward productive workers with a number of "gain sharing" programs. For example, reservation agents get a commission that reflects their success in converting calls to sales, and pilots receive a bonus reflecting their success in fuel conservation. The programs have brought some immediate results; the percentage of sales on all calls to reservation agents rose one percent after the commission program was put in effect. But it remains to be seen whether the programs will in the long run generate enduring job satisfaction.

Almost eight thousand old-time employees have returned to Continental to work under the changed job conditions. Will the new competitive work environment, coupled with low pay, no seniority or pension benefits, and the near abolition of work rules, allow for the feeling of community that existed in the old Continental? and will the company's employee stock ownership plans, poor as they may be at present, ever be enlarged to satisfy the employees' dream of controlling their own destiny? Lorenzo has sought permanent productivity improvements with singular determination. Is it possible that he will find ways of building the sort of strong employee community on which high levels of productivity can be most securely based?

Some employees have glimpsed an unsuspected side to Lorenzo's character behind the ugly images produced by the takeover fight and management's policy of confrontation with labor. Before the bankruptcy, Lorenzo sometimes sought to establish rapport with pilots by entering the cockpit for small talk. On one such occasion, pilot Dick Engle noted, with some wonder, how Lorenzo's face lighted up when his small children were mentioned. In another flight to Houston carrying Lorenzo's wife and daughter, Engle saw Lorenzo waiting at the gate. As his daughter dashed from the plane, he hoisted her into his arms in an affectionate hug. Engle struggles to reconcile the conflicting images in his mind. "Here's this ogre," he says, "and he seemed like any other happy father."

Lorenzo himself tells of experiencing profound emotion when he christened a DC-10, "Employee Owner Ship I," as part of an effort to publicize the new employee stock ownership program. A crowd of workers wildly applauded as he smashed a bottle of champagne on the plane. "It really hit me," he remembers. "I walked away in tears."[25] Could it be that he felt through his tears the common human desire for community? Later in the year Lorenzo expanded a system of employee councils, which offer employees an opportunity to make suggestions to management, and instituted a program of quarterly "CEO forums" in which he meets with leaders from the various employee councils. Before leaving to work for Pride Air, ticket agent Bill Miles helped organize the employee councils, believing that they offer part of what the employees fought for in the ESOP campaign.

One may still hope that the future will bring a rebirth of the vision—so passionately held in 1981—of employees working together in community to shape their own destiny. But whatever the future may hold, the Continental employees will have to deal with a harshly competitive environment exerting relentless pressure on working conditions and safety standards. The airline has a cost advantage now, thanks to the bankruptcy court, but other air carriers are catching up by holding the line on wages and hiring new employees at lower pay scales. More and more airline companies will be cutting back on wages, benefits, and job rights. As the advertisements say, it's "a new tradition in flying."

APPENDIX
ONE

Recovery Plan:

Union Proposal
February 2, 1983

Effective for 21 months (March 2, 1983-November 30, 1984) except as noted:

	1. Wage Cut/Fringes June 1, 1982 rates in effect through May 30, 1984. June 1, 1984—December 1, 1982 rates become effective.	$13,805,970
	2. Suspend Night Pay	251,045
	3. Suspend Holiday Pay	348,000
	4. Suspend COLA	1,721,917
	5. Reduce Domestic Trip Rig—1:4 (4-1-83)	1,295,636
PERMANENT	6. Requirement to Adjust to 75 Hours (4-1-83)	
PERMANENT	7. New Reserve Work Rules (4-1-83)	9,351,112
PERMANENT	8. Trades with Open Time (4-1-83)	
	9. Requirement to Deadhead if "Outbound" Cancels (4-1-83)	174,700
PERMANENT	10. 3 Personal Drops per Month (4-1-83)	168,995
	11. No Pay for Recurrent Training (1983 and 1984)	398,000
	12. No Pay for Training on New Equipment (one day)	190,000
	13. Par Diem Cut to 4-1-81 Rates	1,715,275
	14. Short Crew and Par Diem Paid on a Minute Basis	318,990
	15. Crew Meals for 8 Hours On-duty (4-1-83)	600,000
	16. Uniform Replacements on Need	204,540
	17. Suspend Uniform Cleaning Allowance	634,942

18. Reduce Retirement Contributions to 1%
    (Mar., Apr., & May 1983)   1,040,000
19. Disability for Pregnancy Only When
    Actually Disabled (4-1-83)   1,833,340
20. Flight Attendants Lifting Tickets at
    Jetway Entrance (4-1-83)   1,750,000

    TOTAL   35,802,462

Additional Items:

    Flag Waivers (10-81 to 12-1-84)   811,000
    1982 Recurrent Training   166,160
    Hotel Changes to Date   176,322

    TOTAL $36,955,944

Continental's Balance Sheet

	Debt			Equity				Debt/ Equity
	Cont.	ESOP	Total	Retained Earnings	Stock & Paid in capital	ESOP	Total	
At December 31, 1980	369	—	369	102	89	—	191	66/34
At April 1, 1981								
Sale of stock to ESOP	(185)	185		—	185	(185)		
Guaranty of ESOP loan	—	3		—	—	(3)		
ESOP contrib. by Cont.	—	—		—	—	—		
Other borrowings (payments)	31	—		—	—	—		
Net earnings	—	—		25	—	—		
At December 31, 1981	215	188	403	127	274	(188)	213	65/35
ESOP contrib. by Cont.	—	(9)		—	—	9		
Other borrowings (payments)	(78)	—		—	—	—		
Net earnings	—	—		40	—	—		
At December 31, 1982	137	179	316	167	274	(179)	262	55/45
ESOP contrib. by Cont.	—	(32)		—	—	32		
Other borrowings (payments)	(2)	—		—	—	—		
Net earnings	—	—		40	—	—		
At December 31, 1983	135	147	282	207	274	(147)	334	46/54

| | Debt | | | Equity | | | | Debt/ |
	Cont.	ESOP	Total	Retained Earnings	Stock & Paid in capital	ESOP	Total	Equity
ESOP contrib. by Cont.	—	(52)		—	—	52		
Other borrowings (payments)	6	—		—	—	—		
Net earnings	—	—		34	—	—		
At December 31, 1984	141	95	236	241	274	(95)	420	36/64
ESOP contrib. by Cont.	—	(61)		—	—	61		
Other borrowings (payments)	(1)	—		—	—	—		
Net earnings	—	—		38	—	—		
At December 31, 1985	140	34	174	279	274	(34)	519	25/75
ESOP contrib. by Cont.	—	(34)		—	—	34		
Other borrowings (payments)	36	—		—	—	—		
Net earnings	—	—		42	—	—		
At December 31, 1986	176	0	176	321	274	0	595	23/77

APPENDIX TWO

During the year before the bankruptcy, Texas Air experienced a success in the public financial forum paralleling that of Continental. In November 1982 it raised $44 million in an offering of common stock that was oversubscribed. In February 1983 it made a second $40 million offering of convertible junior preferred stock. But did the company's replenished cash reserve benefit Continental? Lorenzo asserts that Texas poured $83 million into Continental and TI after the takeover but it was not enough to overcome the disadvantage of high labor costs. In contrast, some ALPA spokesmen still adhere to the asset raid theory—Texas Air sucked its subsidiaries dry. In fact, Texas Air received little in dividends (Continental Airlines Corporation paid $1.3 million in dividends in 1983), and invested $83.3 million in Continental, TI, and Continental Airlines Corporation from June 1981 through May 1983, it usually got valuable assets in exchange. The following are the major transactions:

Sept 1981	$10.0	Series A Preferred stock in TI.
Dec 1981	25.5	Purchase of TI gates at Houston, three DC-9 aircraft, and other TI facilities and property.
Feb 1982	0.8	Purchase of modifications on one DC-9.
Mar 1982	3.3	Purchase of Jet Capital Corporation note receivable held by TI.

Dec 1983	10.0	Series B preferred stock in Continental Airlines Corporation.
Jan 1983	7.8	Purchase of unmarketable Houston revenue bond used to finance Houston terminal.
Mar 1983	9.0	Advance for purchase of Denver gates.
Mar 1983	15.0	Purchase of Continental Computer Services.
Apr 1983	1.9	Purchase of interest in delivery of two used DC-9s).

During 1981 and 1982, TI was directly extended $39.6 million as a partial return of funds that TI had earlier contributed to Texas Air. Fifteen million dollars involved the purchase of a very lucrative business, Continental Computer Services, that might well have been sold to a third party for a similar or better price. The remaining transactions, valued at $28.7 million, did involve significant cash infusions into Continental, but they were not enough to offset the additional debt burden that the airline incurred in the takeover.

NOTES

Chapter 1

1. *Fortune*, February 1963.
2. *Nation's Business*, September 1976.
3. *Wall Street Journal*, September 18, 1979.
4. *Texas Business*, February 1980.
5. *Houston Business Journal*, July 13, 1981.
6. *Air Line Pilot*, February 1981.

Chapter 2

1. CAB Order 77-12-115 at p 3; order 78-4-121 at p 31.
2. *Wall Street Journal*, September 18, 1979.
3. The last three quotations are taken from the *Los Angeles Times*, March 10, 1981.

Chapter 3

1. General Accounting Office, *Employee Stock Ownership Plans: Who Benefits Most in Closely Held Companies*, June 20, 1980.
2. Senate Select Committee on Small Business, *Role of the Federal Government in Employee Ownership of Business*, March 1979. Ninety-sixth Congress, first session.

Chapter 4

1. *Daily Breeze*, April 9, 1981.
2. *Los Angeles Herald Examiner*, April 9, 1981.
3. *Los Angeles Times*, April 9, 1981.
4. *Los Angeles Herald Examiner*, April 9, 1981.
5. *The Midland Reporter-Telegram*, April 15, 1981.

Chapter 5

1. *Wall Street Journal*, June 1, 1981.
2. *Aviation Daily*, April 27, 1981.
3. *Chicago Tribune*, June 11, 1981.

Chapter 6

1. *Daily News* (Los Angeles) June 25, 1981.
2. *Business Journal* (Casper, Wy.), May 13, 1981.
3. Ibid.
4. *Rocky Mountain News* (Denver), April 27, 1981.
5. *The Desert Sun* (Palm Springs, Ca.), May 1, 1981.
6. *New York Times*, April 13, 1981.
7. *Los Angeles Herald Examiner*, June 23, 1981.
8. *San Francisco Chronicle*, May 17, 1981.
9. *Washington Post*, April 17, 1981.
10. *Washington Post*, April 19, 1981.

Chapter 7

1. *Los Angeles Times*, May 20, 1981.
2. *New York Times*, April 25, 1981.
3. *Washington Post*, May 7, 1981.
4. Speech to Aviation & Space Writer's Association, April 13, 1981.
5. *Forbes*, July 20, 1981.

Chapter 8

1. *The Argonaut* (Marina del Rey, Ca.), May 7, 1981.

Chapter 9

1. *Chicago Tribune*, June 11, 1981.
2. *Business Week*, May 11, 1981.
3. *Chicago Tribune*, June 11, 1981.
4. *The Desert Sun* (Palm Springs, Ca.), May 1, 1981.
5. *Los Angeles Herald Examiner*, June 23, 1981.
6. *Star-Bulletin* (Honolulu, Hawaii), June 18, 1981.
7. *Daily Commercial News* (San Francisco), June 16, 1981.
8. *Los Angeles Herald Examiner*, June 23, 1981.

Chapter 10

1. *Forbes*, July 20, 1981.

Chapter 12

1. *Wall Street Journal*, August 12, 1981.

Chapter 13

1. *Los Angeles Herald Examiner*, August 19, 1981.
2. Ibid.
3. *Los Angeles Times*, July 7, 1981.
4. *Los Angeles Herald Examiner*, September 10, 1981.
5. *Sacramento Bee*, August 21, 1981.
6. *Houston Chronicle*, August 27, 1981.
7. *California Magazine*, November 1982.
8. *Sacramento Bee*, November 1, 1981.
9. *Daily Breeze*, September 3, 1981.
10. *Sacramento Bee*, November 10, 1981.
11. *Sacramento Bee*, November 1, 1981.
12. *Sacramento Union*, September 11, 1981.

Epilogue

1. *Aviation Daily*, April 5, 1982.
2. *Business Week*, November 15, 1982.
3. *Aviation Daily*, May 4, 1982.
4. *Wall Street Journal*, February 18, 1982.
5. *Daily Breeze*, October 5, 1983.
6. *New York Times*, September 26, 1983.
7. Ibid.
8. *New York Times*, November 8, 1983.
9. *Los Angeles Times*, September 30, 1983.
10. *Los Angeles Times*, October 10, 1983.
11. *Daily Breeze*, October 1, 1983.
12. *San Francisco Examiner*, October 2, 1983.
13. *Wall Street Journal*, October 9, 1983.
14. *Time*, October 10, 1983.
15. *Daily Breeze*, October 5, 1983.
16. *Los Angeles Times*, October 10, 1983.
17. *Business Week*, November 7, 1983.

18. *Business Week*, March 19, 1984.
19. *Los Angeles Times*, September 26, 1983.
20. Ibid.
21. *New York Times*, May 14, 1984.
22. *Fortune*, January 9, 1984.
23. *Business Week*, January 30, 1984.
24. *New York Times*, December 30, 1984.
25. *Wall Street Journal*, September 24, 1984.

INDEX

Adams, Dick, 223, 231, 232, 237, 240, 243–44
Adams, John, 226, 228, 234, 243
Adcox, Craig, 4, 20, 103, 139,
Air Micronesia, 105
Air Line Pilots' Association (ALPA), 5, 6, 19, 39–45, 53, 127, 128, 210, 251, 252, 261
Airline Deregulation Act, 23, 36, 107
Akin Gump Straus Hauer & Feld, 189
Alcalde, Henderson, O'Bannon, Bracy & Williams, 99–101
Alexander, Hal, 145, 147
ALPA. *See* Air Line Pilots' Association
American Airlines, 237
  DC-10 crash, 8
Anderson, Ron, 196
Appanaitis, Jan, 71
Aramini, Ron, 82, 129, 156, 266
Archer, Bill, 191
Armstrong, Senator, 187, 188
Attenborough, Roland, 85, 86, 172, 205

Bagley, William, 211, 213
Bailey, Elizabeth, 36, 37
Bailey, John, 72, 157, 207
Bakes, Phil, 23–24, 27, 45, 50, 51, 78, 94, 110, 111, 117, 119
  bankruptcy and, 224
  ESOP's apparent victory, 152, 159, 160, 161

as ESOP runs into trouble, 163, 167, 168
  Continental Airlines Corporation and, 225, 228, 233, 234
  crusade in Sacramento, 213, 215, 216, 220
  pilots' ambush, 189
Balance Sheet, 273–74
Bank of America, 87
Bank of Montreal, 118
Bankruptcy, 223–64
Barnes, Willie, 120–22, 170, 188–89
Barney, Harris Upham and Company, 230
Bassett, Randy, 120, 170
Batkin, Alan, 56, 152
Baxter, Larry, 146, 240, 243, 245, 246
Bear Stearns and Company, 126
Bedlake, John, 4, 38, 137, 157, 158
Benfield, Jim, 112
Bilbrey, Gary R., 70
Birdsall, Doug, 259–60
Bogue, Robins, 58, 165
Bosco, Douglas, 179, 205, 211, 212, 214, 215, 216–17
Boyd, Patrice, 139, 171, 266
Bracy, Terry, 99–100, 104, 186, 187, 190, 193
Bradley, Tom, 104
Braniff Airlines, 14, 16, 33
Braniff Airways, 73, 74, 251, 261
Breeding, Donald, 242–43, 253
Breitman, Jacki, 256
Brown, Donald K., 219

ABOUT
THE AUTHOR

Michael E. Murphy received a B.A. *cum laude* in government from Harvard College in 1964 and a J.D. from Stanford Law School in 1967. After clerking for the Oregon Supreme Court, he worked two years as an appellate lawyer for the Lane County District Attorney's office in Eugene, Oregon.

Mr. Murphy worked the next seven years as an attorney for C & H Sugar Company in San Francisco, where he specialized in personnel and employee benefits law. During this period he contributed a series of articles to such professional journals as the *California State Bar Journal, Personnel Journal, Arbitration Journal* and the *American Bar Association Journal.* While working as corporate counsel, he published a study in *Labor Law Journal* exploring the legal implications of employee representation on the board of directors.

In 1978, Mr. Murphy left the active practice of law to devote himself full time to scholarly interests. In 1983 he received a Ph.D. in historical geography from the University of California at Berkeley. His dissertation is slated for publication by Westview Press in a monograph series administered by Syracuse University.

A native of Roseburg, Oregon, Mr. Murphy is married to the former Mary Catherine Ragen. They have three young children—Gregory, age ten, Regan, age eight, and Paul, age six—and live in San Francisco at the edge of Golden Gate Park in a house built the year after the 1906 earthquake.